Media Travels

Media Travels

Toward an Atlas of Global Media

Edited by

Juan Llamas-Rodriguez

Amherst College Press

The complete manuscript of this work was subjected to a partly closed ("single-anonymous") review process. For more information, visit https://acpress.amherst.edu/peerreview/.

Published in the United States of America by
Amherst College Press
Manufactured in the United States of America
Library of Congress Control Number: 2024937527

DOI: https://doi.org/10.3998/mpub.14494542

ISBN 978-1-943208-92-0 (paperback)
ISBN 978-1-943208-93-7 (open access)
ISBN 978-1-943208-94-4 (hardcover)

Contents

Acknowledgments

This collection is the result of the dedicated labor and care of twelve scholars with novel insights into the questions that continue to drive the study of global media. I am foremost thankful to them for joining me in this endeavor and entrusting me to edit their work. I hope I have delivered on my promise to them to put together a project worth their talents and efforts.

The ideas for this collection began at the "Teaching 'the Global' in Media Studies" workshop during the 2021 annual conference of the Society for Cinema and Media Studies. My sincere thanks to the panelists of that workshop (Salomé Aguilera Skvirsky, Pamela Krayenbuhl, Weixian Pan, and Bhaskar Sarkar) and to those in attendance for offering critical and generous advice from their own experiences researching and teaching global media. Once I recruited all the contributors for this collection, we held a virtual symposium titled "An Atlas of Global Media" in February 2022. I am also indebted to those who attended that symposium and offered constructive feedback in early versions of the chapters. It was at that symposium that attendees first raised the question of the atlas as the structuring figure for the collection. I am grateful for those raising these questions early and I hope they find satisfying the final articulation of the project's stakes. This project would not have come together so smoothly without the tireless support and encouragement of Hannah Brooks-Motl at Amherst College Press. The three anonymous reviewers of the manuscript were careful, considerate, and thorough in their feedback, and the final version is much stronger thanks to them. My immense and enduring gratitude to Bhaskar Sarkar for first inciting me to approach my media studies scholarship through a global framework, and for actively participating in both the 2021 workshop and the 2022 symposium. For the many thoughtful conversations over the years about what constitutes the stakes of "the global" in media and communication studies, I also thank Michael Curtin, Hatim El-Hibri, Bishnupriya Ghosh, Wazhmah Osman, Aswin Punathambekar, Lia Wolock, and Eszter Zimanyi.

The three years it took to conceive, coordinate, and finalize this edited collection spanned my appointment at two different universities. I was only able to dedicate myself to this collection because of the access to time, resources, and staff support afforded by those institutions. At the University of Texas at Dallas, I thank Adrian Tapia and his communications staff for the promotion of the February 2022 symposium, my faculty colleagues in Critical Media Studies for attending and participating in the event, and Mohammed Rashid for his logistical support. At the University of Pennsylvania, I thank the staff at the Annenberg School Library for their help navigating the intricacies of fair use, the doctoral and postdoctoral fellows at the Center for Advanced Research in Global Communication for their inspiring work in the 2023 "Doing Global Media Studies" symposium, and Christiana Dillard for her support finalizing the manuscript.

Finally, an immense thank you to my husband Gabe for all the ways, big and small, he continues to support and cheer on my projects.

Introduction: What Is an Atlas of Global Media?

Juan Llamas-Rodriguez

Ten minutes into the documentary *Cameraperson* (Kirsten Johnson, 2016), there is a montage of people walking. Johnson's camera follows a variety of people of different ages and skin colors across busy markets, dirt roads, cemeteries, damp caves, soccer fields, and office corridors. Though the film overall does not have a connective voiceover narration, it does indicate with title cards the various locations where the footage was originally recorded, most of them unused scenes from Johnson's work as a cinematographer in other documentarians' films. The walking montage does away with the title cards momentarily to swiftly stitch together eleven different scenes in under two minutes. Some of the people walking we see later during the documentary; others we never see again. French philosopher Jacques Derrida, whose scene crossing the street kickstarts the montage, is the only person explicitly identified on screen. Through the use of quick editing and in the absence of contextual clues, the resulting montage is a snapshot of the peoples of the world in movement and of one person desperately trying to capture them all.

Cameraperson is one of the three key texts that I often assign at the beginning of my Global Media Studies course. Building on her extensive career as a documentary cinematographer, Johnson edits together scenes from her previous works along with footage of her own family spending time in Wyoming to create a reflexive portrait of a woman who has spent decades looking at the world through the lens of her camera. Her documentary excels at forcing viewers to make sense of the connections across seemingly disparate locations and between vastly different types of scenarios. Students tend to read the film's vignette structure as either a synchronic snapshot (a reminder that these scenes could be happening all over the world at once) or as a diachronic travelog (an example of how one person's travels around the world over the years get stitched together in their mind). I encourage them to explore the implications of both of those readings of the film: the impossibility of seeing it all at once and the immensity of trying to make sense of such vastness across time. The walking montage, then, serves as a reminder that, try as we might, the world remains elusive and in constant movement, and no single media production will ever be able to capture that elusiveness.

Teaching a course on global media often feels like the project Johnson takes on in *Cameraperson*: bringing together examples from different parts of the world and organizing them in a way that allows students to make connections and ask questions simultaneously. However many weeks there are in an academic term always seem insufficient to broach the historical, geographic, and mediatic diversity encompassed in the idea of *global media*. The process is likewise a humbling intellectual experience for the instructor who must admit the limits of their own expertise while also stretching beyond them. The idea for *Media Travels: Toward an Atlas of Global Media* began in spring 2021 at a workshop about precisely this problem held during the annual conference of the Society for Cinema and Media Studies. In the workshop discussions, faculty teaching at different types of academic institutions—from community colleges to small liberal arts schools to major public research universities—identified a key stumbling block to globalizing the media studies curriculum: the relative scarcity of resources offering an entry-level perspective into media outside the US-Anglo canon. Participants agreed that *in theory* there is a need to expand our pedagogical texts and perspectives beyond this traditional canon. Yet we also agreed that *in practice* such commitment runs up against material stumbling blocks, including faculty overwork, withering institutional support, and lack of translation opportunities.

While one edited collection cannot claim to be able to address all of these stumbling blocks, this collection's foremost goal is to begin to take on the task of mapping emergent itineraries in contemporary global media studies in a way that is accessible to the widest possible set of audiences. Instructors for introductory media studies courses wishing to expand the offerings in their curricula will find in these essays new ways of approaching foundational concepts and issues in the field.[1] For instance, how are thrills and formal strategies of early slapstick comedy remixed by current Russian roofing YouTube videos? Or, how do questions about sound aesthetics gain new resonance when understood through Indigenous collaborative practices? Scholars wishing to expand their research into specific media forms or representational issues can also turn to these case studies for approaches from beyond the traditional US focus. For example, what does games studies look like when considered from the perspective of South African industries? Or, how do the norms and practices of streamers' original productions shift within video-heavy industries like Nigeria? The authors included here have written their contributions in a way that does not assume readers have deep contextual knowledge of their medium or geographical context. Instead, the specificities of each case study allow readers to learn about the media texts and simultaneously discover more about the broader social and cultural networks within which these media exist.

At the same time, the articles in this collection invite scholars versed in particular socio-geographical areas who wish to explore different media convergences within that area. Those working in fields such as cultural studies, gender and sexuality studies, comparative ethnic studies, and disability studies will find that these essays offer critical perspectives on the key issues of those fields as understood through different media forms. By addressing multiple axes of identity and difference across and within media, these authors demonstrate the importance of intersectional analysis to global media studies: how ageism and ableism inflect the narrative of a true crime documentary from Mexico; how the fantasy genre shapes the gender politics of a South Korean TV series; how formal inventiveness allows for Indigenous perspectives to emerge within a state-sponsored educational campaign.

Finally, the writing and focus of these articles will make them appealing to those outside the field of media studies—and even to those outside academia—who are nonetheless interested in discovering more about media from around the world. The clear and accessible language of the written essays invite a curious reader regardless of academic background. The interactive elements of the collection facilitated by its publication in the Fulcrum platform offer *actual glimpses* at the media analyzed in these chapters, making such analyses both approachable and compelling.

Collecting eleven short chapters on different media forms from different parts of the world, *Media Travels: Toward an Atlas of Global Media* takes readers on an eclectic and variegated journey across locales in order to reexamine perennial issues in global studies, revealing how the "global" in global media is best understood as operating at multiple scales and temporalities, "nonlinear, unpredictable, and evolving."[2] Media globalization in the twenty-first century must look beyond the media capitals of Hollywood and Bollywood while still contending with their unparalleled reach and influence. The stakes of any project such as this one cannot lie in providing a definitive map of the state of media around the world. Much more important is highlighting the power differentials shaped by decades of economic, political, and cultural influence across localities. Why our understanding of "global media" remains tied to a handful of locations is a function not only of US and Eurocentric biases but also of material conditions that prevent access to, and deep engagement with, other locales and perspectives. To begin to contend with such disparities means expanding the points of reference from which we ask questions about media's role in the world. *Media Travels* is ultimately that: a guide across different media sites that, along the way, illustrates these sites as constantly mutating encounters between residual, dominant, and emergent global forces.

On the Impossibility of Mapping Global Media on a Scale of 1 to 1

The map is one of the oldest and most basic forms of global media. It is a symbolic representation of a part of the world that simultaneously tells a story about that part of the world. Maps make claims about a specific place—claims about how to make sense of that place, about its relative importance (or lack thereof), and about their reader's relationship to that place. Like other media, maps are always partial, yet they often give shape and power to totalizing ideas about how to perceive the world.[3]

The second key text I assign students at the beginning of a Global Media Studies course is Enrique Chagoya's color print *Illegal Alien's Guide to Somewhere Over the Rainbow* (2010) (see Figure 1). This print depicts a caricatured version of the traditional Mercator projection of the world, one where none of the countries' sizes are proportional to their real-life scale: while the entire continents of Africa and South America are miniscule, the countries of Russia, China, and the United States occupy almost a third of the entire map. Atop each of these latter countries are figures embodying national stereotypes: a brown bear with a surveillance camera for a head; a torso reminiscent of Mao Zedong with a mid-twentieth-century BMW luxury car for a head; a Superman-like body with a gun for a head, respectively. Everywhere over the map are several smaller repeated icons: sharks attacking cargo ships across different oceans; stencil-like oil rigs on every continent and on some oceans; small rectangular symbols signaling air pollution or nuclear waste. It soon becomes evident that Chagoya's map is not meant as an illustrated representation of the planet as it is geographically, but as an argument about the disproportionate effects of modern industrial practices on the planet's environment.

Through its extensive and ostentatious iconography, *Illegal Alien's Guide to Somewhere Over the Rainbow* neatly demonstrates how maps are media that shape perceptions about the world. Within a discussion of global media, Chagoya's print also opens up discussions about any such media's partial perspectives and multiple meanings. The map's insert on the lower left corner parodies the types of inserts in European colonial maps that used figures of white men greeted by the natives to weave tales of colonizers' saviorism. Yet here there is no redemption, only an overheated

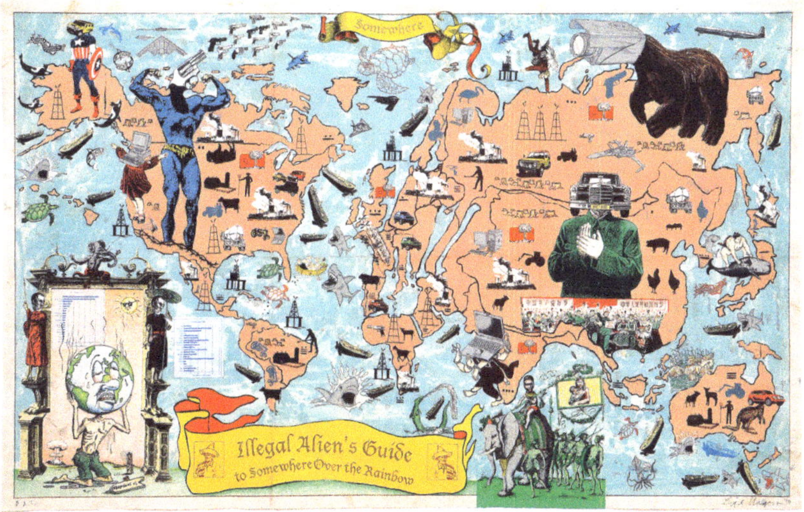

Figure 01. Enrique Chagoya's *Illegal Alien's Guide to Somewhere Over the Rainbow* (2010) depicts a caricatured version of the traditional Mercator projection of the world.

anthropomorphized Earth kneeling between two Death-like figures. Given this hopelessness, what is the "somewhere" in the title of the print and visually referenced within the insert and on the top of the map? Is this somewhere beyond the geophysical space of planet Earth or beyond the temporal framework of contemporary modern capitalist production—or both? Who is the titular "illegal alien" and how is this map supposed to serve as a guide? These sorts of questions and their lack of definite answers prompt us to reflect on how even a supposedly straightforward representation of the world—the map—contains within it a complexity of ideas.

Writers and scholars have long pondered the politics of the map and the creative ways of deploying this figure to re-imagine the world and its politics. In a paragraph-long short story about a guild of mapmakers trying to create a map of the empire in a 1-to-1 scale, Argentinian writer Jorge Luis Borges casts the impetus of empires to capture the entire world (through conquest *and* via representations) as a futile endeavor. Italian intellectual Umberto Eco pursued this question of the logistics of scalar representation to its logical conclusion in an essay titled "On the Impossibility of Drawing a Map of the Empire on a Scale of 1 to 1," where he deduced not only that a 1-to-1 scale of an empire would be untenable but also that a 1-to-1 map of an empire "decrees the end of the empire as such" since the representational qualities of the map are both practical and symbolic-mythical.[4] Any map of the world is partial and selective by its very design, and therein lies its power.

The atlas is, in its most straightforward sense, a collection of maps. Whether by collecting different thematic maps about one single location or by anthologizing a series of maps about several locations, the atlas operates as a holistic set of geographical texts with a distinct purpose. Two decades into the twenty-first century, the bound collection of printed pages is but a nostalgic figuration of the atlas. Yet its conceptual organization, as a collection of symbolic representations about different parts of the world, proves to be remarkably resilient as a form to organize disparate and often wide-ranging information about the vastness of the planet. The widely popular website (and subsequent book publication) *Atlas Obscura*, for instance, reports on "cool and unusual" locales for adventurous international travelers as part of its mission "to inspire wonder and curiosity about the incredible world we all share."[5]

For Eco, the fragmentary perspective of the atlas already disrupts the totalizing and colonizing goals of making maps on a 1-to-1 scale. The logistical impossibility of a 1-to-1 scale of the world in the figure of the atlas likewise presents a generative challenge for this edited collection focused on global media. Following Eco's conclusions, the "atlas" in the subtitle "*Toward An Atlas of Global Media*" already signals the need for breaking apart any sense of possibly addressing *the whole world all at once*. It would be disingenuous to assume that "global media" represents a unified totality, so the breadth of the areas and media covered in these chapters is certainly not meant to be exhaustive. Indeed, as postcolonial critics have long argued, a claim that any one project presents a totalizing view of the world—as in the idea of "world history" or "world cinema"—ends up replicating long-standing legacies of mapping as a colonizing tool.[6] Proposing to cover the world with one publication, or even with a number of publications, is futile: the global heterogeneity of media practices makes this an impossible task. At stake in this collection is, in fact, the opposite impulse: to embrace fragmentation and incompleteness as constitutive of our mediated understanding of the global.

Printed atlases emerged as European empires were expanding their control over parts of the world through colonization.[7] The purpose of these publications was not only to know other places and peoples but also, eventually, to bring them into the control of the empire. This colonizing legacy embedded in mapping and atlas-making is at odds with the interventions this collection pursues. Our goal, it must be clear, is not to make the world of global media known so as to make it manageable and controllable. Rather, the aim is instead to bring together careful close examinations of media objects and phenomena across different locales and, in doing so, propose the idea of "global media" as something that is multifaceted, complex, and always in flux.

By proposing an atlas as the organizing form to bring together different approaches to global media, the purpose of *Media Travels* is also to unravel the very idea that there is one such way to map—to see, to know, to make sense of—the multiplicity of global media formations. For that reason, this collection does not map global media in the sense of offering infographics, data visualizations, or other quantitative explorations of media titans and trends around the world.[8] The constant technological changes and industrial reconfigurations that characterize media in the twenty-first century, from corporate consolidations to subaltern resistances, would quickly render such an effort obsolete. Over twenty years ago, *The Global Media Atlas* edited by Mark Balnaves, James Donald, and Stephanie Donald offered an early attempt at this type of collection, featuring illustrated maps that sought to convey the state of new and emerging media around the world.[9] Despite its claims to include the "most up-to-date" information on such matters, the collection quickly became outdated. Nowadays, media studies instructors must update their teaching materials on "which corporation owns what media" at least every new school term.

The mapping enterprise of *Media Travels: Toward An Atlas of Global Media* is to illustrate what it looks like to ask critical questions about media and the world from specific localized contexts and through particular media examples. The goal is to *re-map* a field that has thus far been heavily US and Anglophone focused. Chapters in the collection focus on media such as film, television, online videos, music, and video games from places as varied as South Africa, Ukraine, India, Cuba, South Korea, Nigeria, and the Tohono O'odham Nation. Only one of these texts is exclusively in the English language and most of them address thematic issues that have long stood outside mainstream media. In tandem, the contributions in *Media Travels* not only demonstrate how vastly unexamined the field of global media studies remains but also engage with methods, research questions, and sources that can enable a richer exploration of this field.

Finding the World on Your Screen

The third key text I assign students at the beginning of a Global Media Studies course is *Transformers: The Premake* (2014), a video essay by Kevin B. Lee that takes the production of the 2014 Hollywood blockbuster *Transformers: Age of Extinction* as the starting point for an exploration into the dynamics of global media circulation. Using the format of the desktop documentary, Lee guides the viewer through a series of YouTube videos, Google Maps, and internet searches that, in tandem, demonstrate the always already globally networked aspects of contemporary media. The video essay consists of screen recordings of Lee's computer desktop, where he searches for the *Age of Extinction* trailer on YouTube then begins looking for user-generated videos capturing the filming of the movie in the streets of Chicago. Lee maps these videos by matching the urban locations depicted with their spots on Google Maps. At the same time, Lee overlays search results from scholarly sources, internet forums, and Wikipedia on the topic of "free" fan labor and co-optation. The video essay continues in this manner: finding and emplacing other user-generated videos of the *Age of Extinction* on-location shooting across the United States and around the world while juxtaposing news articles and snippets of critical analysis. Through these juxtapositions, the worldwide journey of the making of the fourth installment in the *Transformers* franchise becomes an opportunity to explore film tax breaks, the rising dominance of Chinese investment in Hollywood, state censorship, and cross-industry promotional tie-ins.

Transformers: The Premake illustrates the core takeaway of learning global media studies: the fact that we get to know most of the world through an increasingly complex network of media texts. By combining different types of media, from news segments to official industry releases to user-generated behind-the-scenes clips, the video essay demonstrates how media representations result from a series of historically varying technological, industrial, and aesthetic parameters and influences. At the same time, the video's form reveals the always partial and fragmentary nature of understanding the world through media, as the sources from multiple users provide a cacophony of voices on a single media event. The desktop documentary format literalizes the medium by which we most often come to (partially, fragmentarily) come to know the world: through our computers.

During its twenty-minute runtime, *Transformers: The Premake* allows its viewers to reflect on the intrinsically digital experience of learning about the world in the twenty-first century. Such intrinsically digital experience is also the reason why *Media Travels* is not only a physical book but also an open access multimodal online publication. The collection updates the atlas form in response to the ubiquitous digitization of everything by including multimedia excerpts within its chapters. As advocates of multimodal scholarship have convincingly argued, there is an added value to encountering scholarly research in the medium of its original object of study.[10] While the extended analysis of each media text in this collection is a written essay, each contribution also offers digital excerpts of its object of study and further online resources to explore. Authors engaging in textual analysis have included their analysis side-by-side to the relevant video clips so readers can explore these on their own. In some cases, the entire media under study is included in the chapter, particularly where these are short-length films, individual songs, or online videos. Though short, these essays offer a wealth of information surrounding their central media texts in an accessible and engaging manner, essentially functioning as hubs from which readers can then go off to explore and learn more about a variety of media and geographical regions. If the world is increasingly mediated through our computers, then we can learn much from studying media texts from around the world in a foremost interactive, digital environment.

Like the maps of yesteryear, contemporary interactive media raise questions about scale. In this collection, such questions lie not only in the selection of sample texts from around the world but also at the level of the analysis itself. From a global media studies perspective, what is the appropriate scale at which to study a specific media object? In their respective chapters, authors focus on a variety of scales, from specifics in form to transnational circulations, and often scale across and within media objects. As a whole, the collection also invites readers to make use of embedded links to move out of the different essays to other online sites and back. The embedded media's metadata also offer a distinct way of browsing through the collection's contents by focusing on time periods, medium specificity, or thematic concerns. These alternatives for traversing across an edited collection are intended to foster unconventional lines of thought. The digital format of the collection affords readers multiple and multifaceted opportunities to engage with the collection's broader questions about global media.

"Thinking Globally" for the Twenty-First Century

Media have always been global. Globalization itself is nothing new. The study of "global media" as such has likewise been around for a while. This book does not propose to be the first, nor the last, to call for the need to critically analyze media from around the world. But it does argue for the need to *think globally* when addressing media from any specific location. And it provides a blueprint for how to do it. As Michael Curtin explains, the topographies of today's media networks are ever "more plastic and complicated" as transnational media institutions scale their ambitions and operations in "an increasingly porous and dynamic environment."[11] With this in mind, our project seeks to probe basic questions about the role that specific media forms play in various places around the world. Each of the chapters turns its examination of a localized example into an opportunity to address broader "global issues": war and displacement, neo-imperialism, transcultural influence, to name a few. A chapter's case study serves as the launching point for a globalizing approach to the study of media and society. At the same time, some of these issues recur across different chapters, demonstrating the importance of thinking across spatial and temporal scales to make sense of planetary phenomena.

Several contributors, for instance, take up the age-old question of the variegated relationship between the global and the local and theorize its contemporary articulations. How do (increasingly more consolidated) global media corporations impact local media productions? How do purportedly national media adapt to imagine their publics beyond the borders of the state? As William Mazzarella argues, the "programmatic Formula of globalization studies" arose from scholars contending with the intransigence of binaries such as structure and agency, macro and micro, and political economy and culture; mediation, understood as a relation of simultaneous self-distancing and self-recognition, becomes a critical mode for understanding these changes.[12] The contributors of *Media Travels* demonstrate how this process of mediation continues to play out across media forms and at different scales, whether that is, for instance, tracing the influence of the global video game production norms in smaller markets like South Africa (Chapter 4) or detailing the aesthetics of "postsocialist" Cuban films for international export (Chapter 6).

While many of the case studies in the following chapters refer to media produced in the twenty-first century, the authors place these contemporary media examples into longer historical lineages, exploring how new media practices resonate with early-twentieth-century experimentations (Chapter 1) or how changes in the political economy of media during the late twentieth century contributed to the development of current production and distribution practices (Chapter 5). Some chapters explicitly focus on historical examples that offer critical insights into media practices still prevalent today, such as transnational circulation (Chapter 2) and transmedia remixes (Chapter 7). Taken in tandem, then, the temporal spread of the contributions point to the many ways that media have always been global and, simultaneously, illustrate how changes in technologies and institutions facilitate (or restrict) new global connections.

From unearthing hidden treasures in the international streaming platform Netflix to revisiting classic nationalistic educational programs, the authors in this collection foreground media texts that variously engage local, regional, and global publics. Several chapters also address more commonly studied areas with new approaches and through new media.

Authors explore video games about Palestine, online videos from Russia, documentaries in Mexico, television in South Korea. The practical purpose of bringing together such disparate approaches, from a variety of locations and perspectives, with the expressed intention of not being totalizing is the political project at the heart of *Media Travels*. Putting these different pieces into conversation will offer us insights into the gaps within existing media studies approaches and methodologies while, at the same time, introducing readers to new media texts they may be unfamiliar with. Ultimately, they will provincialize the US and Euro hegemony of global media by foregrounding how to study global media from any number of other coordinates.

Paths Ahead: Outline of an Atlas of Global Media

Although the chapters in *Media Travels* are self-contained and the open access nature of the book allows for readers to explore in any order, the organization of the chapters does stay true to the collection's atlas-inspired roots by offering readers a guide with which to engage with a series of central questions. The chapters in **Part I: Transnational Lineages and Flows** trace the circulation of media forms, texts, and genres across locations and historical moments. In Chapter 1, Maria Corrigan examines how the creative practices that make Russian roofing selfies and videos so popular nowadays draw on and remix the aesthetics of early-twentieth-century film. In Chapter 2, Sonia Robles illustrates how sheet music producers in Europe and early radio enthusiasts in the United States during the early twentieth century influenced what was considered "Mexican" about a piece of music by detailing the history of the creation, promotion, and circulation of a specific waltz. In Chapter 3, Benjamin M. Han considers the popularity of Korean dramas in Latin America to explore how conflicting tropes and trends within the genres of melodrama, the fantastical, and magic realism shape the narratives of these television series.

In **Part II: The Global Tensions in the Local**, authors return to the enduring global–local nexus through new perspectives, accounting for how rapidly shifting industrial configurations and newly muddied political definitions make the global–local traffic ever more complex and unstable. In Chapter 4, Rachel Lara van der Merwe analyzes how South African indie video game developers' ambitions to participate in an international market intersect with, and perhaps result in, their games' use of generic tropes about their nation's history of apartheid. In Chapter 5, Añulika Agina and Anthony Adah examine how a Netflix film about a man from Lagos sent to carry out his National Youth Service in Bauchi also serves as a political opportunity to recast the global image of Northern Nigeria. In Chapter 6, David Tenorio focuses on the recent political and economic changes to film production in Cuba and how these impact the development of a "postsocialist" sensibility.

Part III: Transmedia Figurations includes chapters that demonstrate how movement between media forms has long been and continues to be a productive area for understanding the complexity of media consumption and distribution practices. In Chapter 7, Kuhu Tanvir offers a historical instance of what has more recently been termed "transmedia" by tracing the history of how songs from Hindi films acquired new aesthetics and meanings as they moved through vinyl records, radio, and television. In Chapter 8, Angelica Marie Lawson analyzes how the creative decisions behind adapting Indigenous poetry to film can move beyond questions of fidelity or authenticity and instead respond to the long, troubled history of Indigenous representation in the medium.

Finally, in **Part IV: Intersectional Politics in Global Media**, authors consider how media forms attempt to articulate fraught issues ranging from the interpersonal to the geopolitical. In Chapter 9, Lilia Adriana Pérez Limón finds that tropes of pathology continue to shade the few instances where representations of disability and aging show up in Mexican documentaries. In Chapter 10, Meryem Kamil explores a video game about the institutional politics of Israel's occupation of Palestine and proposes alternative forms of play that respond to the game's ethical and representational failures. In Chapter 11, Anna Shah Hoque provides a decolonial feminist approach to revisit the legacy of Indigenous-themed shorts within the national heritage series Historica Canada.

Flows, tensions, figurations, and intersections. Across these types of mediatory encounters, the chapters' throughlines signal not a totality or a 1-to-1 reproduction of the world of media but rather the connections and disjunctures that characterize media in the current state of globalization. These are the "media travels" of the book's title.

In short, *Media Travels* is for anyone interested in further exploring and reflecting on how global interconnections affect the media we produce and consume and how such media, in turn, shape our perceptions of what it means to live in an increasingly global world. It is meant as a series of introductory openings into the richness of media from around the world. As a whole, these short entry analyses amount to a broader reevaluation of how different media can help us make sense of pressing social issues through a variety of lenses. The project's intellectual and political stakes lie in "re-mapping" what global media studies can do by introducing us not only to the texts that depict the world in innovative ways but also to the strategies by which to see the world anew.

Part One

Transnational Lineages and Flows

Chapter 1

The World's Most Dangerous Selfies: Post-Soviet Hijinks and the Attractions of New Media

Maria Corrigan

Roofing—also referred to as rooftopping or skywalking—has gained a large amount of attention over the last decade.[1] Captured in photos and videos that make one's insides lurch, roofing tends to reframe cities as playgrounds, sightseeing as a competitive sport, and world landmarks as props from which to dangle precariously. Like parkour, its predecessor in urban exploration, the activity seductively blurs the lines between sport, teenage misadventure, and art. A 2014 article in *Rolling Stone* defined roofers as a "loose-knit group of insanely non-acrophobic daredevils who scam and sneak their way to the tops of Russia's highest buildings [and] perform death-defying tricks—hanging by their fingertips, standing on one leg—that they capture in photos and videos that frequently go viral."[2] Roofing's virality—its circulation in the form of media objects—is precisely what has transformed the activity into a global phenomenon. Shared as photographs and videos via LiveJournal, YouTube, Facebook, Instagram, and TikTok, roofing has elevated the risky set of activities previously associated with teenage punks (breaking and entering, loitering on the roofs of city landmarks, hooliganism) to a professionalized and commercialized category of urban exploration, or UrbEx. And while there is a transnational community surrounding this form of exploration (you can find a wannabe roofer anywhere there's a high rise), the most famous roofers have generally been Russian or mistaken as Russian.

Roofing's rise to prominence has dovetailed neatly with a Western-facing tendency of social media to view Slavic people—post-Soviet identities inaccurately flattened to "Russian"—as foreign, inscrutable, and tending toward wild extremes. If, at any point before Russia's invasion of Ukraine on February 24, 2022, you entered the term "crazy Russian" into a Google search, you might have found yourself amused by the initial autofill, which would often supply a host of ridiculous and comic avenues of exploration: YouTube compilations of drivers, rappers, and, of course, roofers, to name but a few. Since then, the proliferation of Ukrainian wartime content on TikTok has resoundingly shifted the discourse on Russian vs. Ukrainian identity, but has in no way lessened the "extreme" qualities attributed to post-Soviet identities, qualities that have become an online commonplace, particularly in corners of Instagram or TikTok like @lookatthisrussian and @squattingslavs, accounts which, in their heyday, basked in the untranslatable ruggedness of your typical Slavic male, and his obsessions with alcohol, bears, cigarettes, Adidas, and Putin (referred to as Pooty).

In what follows, I highlight some of the ways these extremes—the "Russian" and the roofer—have collided, a clash that has generated uncommonly powerful media objects that provoke their viewer at the level of the body and the body politic. As an object of study, roofing can be almost infuriatingly rich, with high stakes for students of performance, affect, risk, and labor studies (not to mention the constant philosophical and political undercurrents attached to weighty concepts like ascent, the sublime, and victory). For the purposes of this short chapter, I will limit my scope to charting the ways that this recent phenomenon—so dependent on GoPro cameras, selfie-sticks, and social media platforms—is rooted in a much longer, unexpected, eccentric media history that is, at once, transnational, revolutionary, and comedic. To understand the full impact of roofing media, I argue that it is necessary to trace a longer history to the mediatized encounter between the human and the city, one that erupts in intense meaning at specific points of identity crisis spanning over a century. This is most powerfully demonstrated by one specific example of roofing—the 2014 prank that saw the star atop a Moscow skyscraper painted in Ukrainian colors and adorned with that country's flag. But even ninety years earlier, young filmmakers were also climbing cityscapes, deploying new technologies to capture the shocking thrills of a new Soviet urban life. In this chapter, I will demonstrate how specific instances of roofing from the 1920s and the 2010s present considerable challenges to our understanding of national identity, our global markers of difference, and, finally, the narratives of our media histories. Seen from this vantage point, these pranks defy gravity only momentarily. Once they are examined alongside the weighty history of the twentieth century and cinema's modernist attack on the senses, they invite the eye downward to explore the very real risks and stakes present in our global media.

Roofing and Its Iconography: Flags and Buildings

The practice of roofing began to garner attention in the early 2010s. While any description of the practice pales in comparison to the intense affective shock supplied by the photographs and videos themselves, I will begin this short history by recounting some of the big names and stunts that kicked off the social media trend. Some of the first prominent names associated with the budding sport are Kiev-born Vitaliy Raskalov, Tver's Evgeniy Romanov, and St. Petersburg's Ignat Chernyaev. From Moscow, Angela Nikolau and Ivan Beerkus have become leading figures, and their roofing—framed as a romance—has been captured in the 2024 documentary *Skywalkers: A Love Story*, directed by Jeff Zimbalist and Maria Bukhonina. Female roofers were consistently represented as part of bigger roofing crews but, with the turn to influencer culture, big names like Nikolau emerged, just as the focus on the athletic body standard in roofing media became more recognizably objectifying or commercial. Moscow's Kirill Vselensky rose to early fame; a scroll through his Instagram account (@kirbase) gives a clear sense of the rapid professionalization of the activity, specifically from 2013 to 2014, as his posts transition from hangouts with friends on rooftops (see Figure 1) to compositions that emphasize the stunning risks undertaken by the subjects (see Figure 2). Likewise, Raskalov's online following exploded in numbers as he moved from risky romps on Moscow's skyline, documented in detail alongside spectacular, heart-stopping photographs on his LiveJournal page, to global summits; the 2014 YouTube video of Raskalov and his partner Vadim Makhorov climbing the 128-story Shanghai Tower shot to the top of Russian YouTube within the first twenty-four hours and, as of the writing of this article, has over 1.2 million views.[3]

The year 2014 was pivotal for roofing, providing the most globally visible instance of the sport, when Pavel Ushivets, a Ukrainian fixture of the Russian roofing scene (who roofs under the aliases Grisha Mustang and

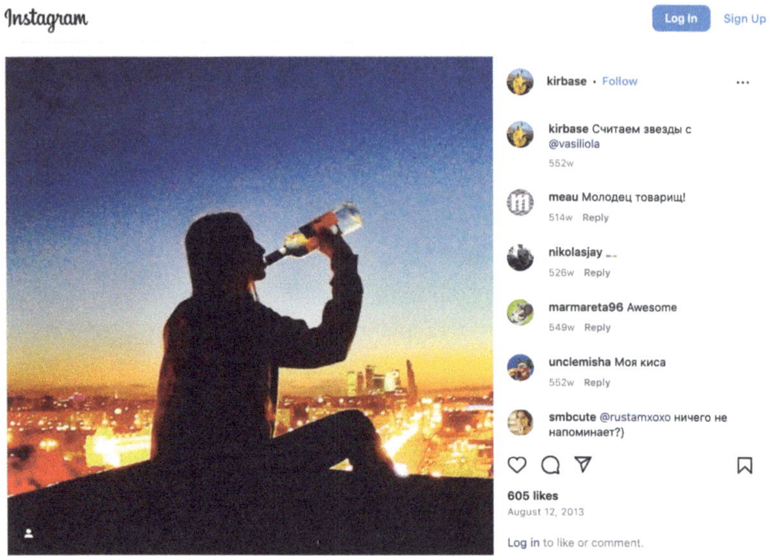

Figure 01. Kirill Vselensky's photograph of a woman named Vasilisa (@vasiliola) in silhouette against a darkening city skyline was posted on August 12, 2013. Vasilisa is centered in the frame, seated in profile drinking from a bottle of wine. She is perched on the edge of a roof, and the glow of the city below her combines with the sunset to create a halo of light around her and to illuminate the wine in the bottle. The photograph's composition is relatively conservative for roofing media, as the implied climb to a rooftop serves as a dynamic backdrop, rather than the source of shock or disorientation.

Mustang Wanted), climbed to the top of one of Moscow's Seven Sisters skyscrapers, hung a Ukrainian flag, and painted the star at the top of the building in Ukraine's colors. The gesture was no anomaly. Indeed, roofing was, from the very beginning, a political act with an obvious anti-authoritarian denotation. The presence of an outsider at the top of a building is already a violation, while the teamwork required to bypass the locks, guards, and police—referred to in the sport as infiltration—implies an informed and hidden collective of culprits working steadily behind the scenes. Russian officials have been actively engaged in curtailing the activities of roofers, with steady hikes in fines and initiatives like the Ministry

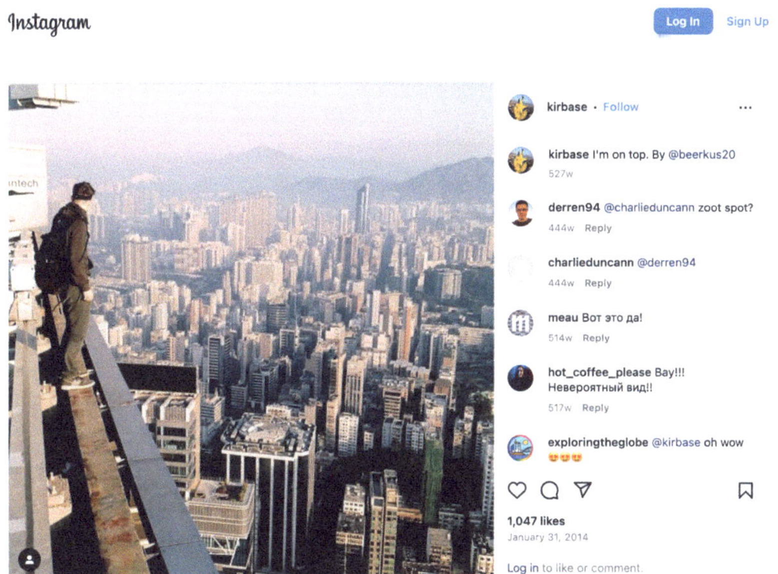

Figure 02. This photograph was posted to Kirill Vselensky's Instagram account on January 31, 2014. It features Vselensky, captured on the left hand of the frame, balanced along a high beam above a vast cityscape. He is dressed in muted dark colors and is wearing a backpack and some form of headgear. His face is turned away from the camera. He is empty-handed and notably without protective gear. He is photographed at a downward angle, as he looks out onto the view. In the distance beyond the city is a mountain range. The angle of composition emphasizes the staggering drop below Vselensky, and is exemplary of roofing media's ability to provide a fearful jolt or vicarious thrill to its audience. The photograph is captioned with the simple phrase, "I'm on top," and is accompanied by the credit @beerkus20.

of the Interior's "safe selfie" campaign. Beyond this, however, roofing carries with it a singularly rich challenge to authorities as well as an avenue for visible and powerful political protest, as when Romanov hoisted a rainbow flag on the top of Tver's administration building in 2012. Later in that same year, roofer Vasily Pupkin was photographed naked on a roof, flipping off the city's legislative assembly in solidarity with Pussy Riot members on trial (see Figure 3).

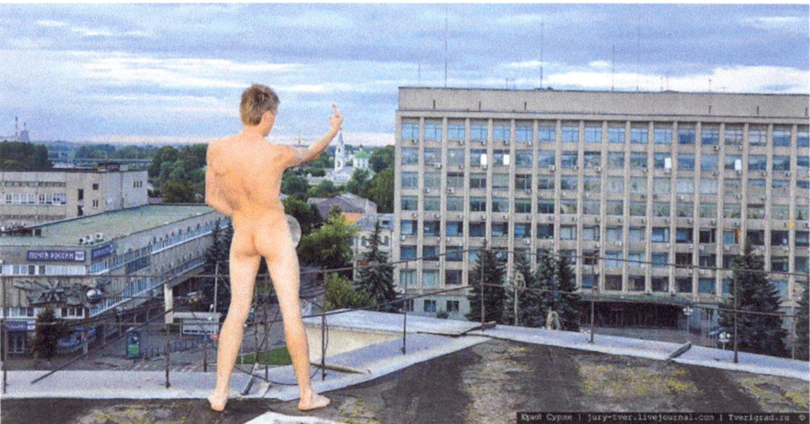

Figure 03. In this photograph, posted to @jury_tver's LiveJournal account on August 11, 2012, Vasily Pupkin (a roofer from Tver) is photographed from behind, naked and extending the middle finger of his right hand to the building across from him. Out of keeping with roofing media, the height of the building climbed by Pupkin is not impressive. Instead, the photograph is eye-catching for its display of Pupkin's naked body, just left of center, and his gesture of defiance to Tver's juridical government building. Part of the thrill of roofing media is the irrefutable evidence of the body in peril. While Pupkin is not in immediate danger from his climb, he is nevertheless relying on the danger implicit in the roofing genre to indicate the political risk taken by his vulnerable body.

While the so-called Seven Sisters were already a regular playground for roofers, Mustang Wanted's Ukrainian flag stunt was extraordinary for its political iconography, its real-life consequences, and for the semiotic challenge it presented to the very conception of Russian statehood and Soviet history. Performed in the wake of Ukraine's Euromaidan and during mounting Russian military aggression in Crimea, Mustang Wanted appropriated Moscow's own skyline and a particular Stalin-era skyscraper on the Kotelnicheskaya Embankment for the purposes of political resistance. The roofer posted a selfie (see Figure 4) to his social media, and the photograph provides a shocking perspective of the city from above—a common visceral effect of roofing media.

In the immediate chaotic aftermath, the Russian government levelled accusations of vandalism and hooliganism against a number of different types of urban explorers (base-jumpers and skydivers, who

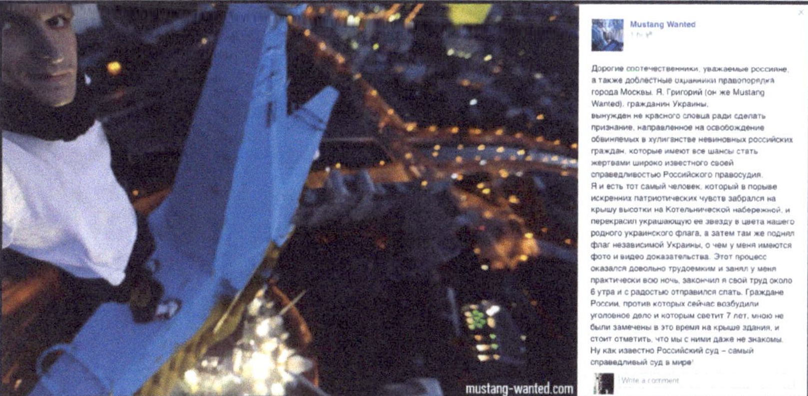

Figure 04. This screengrab was taken of Mustang Wanted's Facebook page, where he claimed the Kotelnicheskaya Embankment climb and flag stunt. The photograph is divided almost perfectly in two, capturing Mustang Wanted's perch on the star spire at the top of the skyscraper on the left side of the frame and the terrifying 176-meter drop down to the Moskva River and city below on the right. There is no evidence of any safety equipment. Squeezed in at the top left of the image, Mustang Wanted's face denotes a calm, steady presence that clashes productively with the visual drama of the rest of the frame. The roofer stands on top of the star, newly painted blue. The selfie crops out the Ukrainian flag, which has been secured to the top of the star with tape that has also been painted. The photograph is accompanied by a long caption in which the roofer describes the stunt, confesses that he has photo and video evidence thereof, and denies any knowledge of or acquaintance with the Russians who were detained for his crime. The caption ends with the following: "Well, as we know, the Russian court is the most just court in the world!" The photograph has been removed from Facebook in the decade since its posting.

were immediately arrested after an independent and ill-timed stunt at the same building). Mustang Wanted, already safe in Ukraine, claimed the stunt as his own in order to exonerate the accused, and offered to present himself before Russian authorities in exchange for the release of a Ukrainian political prisoner. No such exchange took place, and the five people accused were subsequently labeled by Memorial as "political prisoners," facing court proceedings in 2015. In the decade following the stunt, Mustang Wanted continued to post breathtaking photographs of precarious climbs but has limited his social media posts since Russia's invasion of Ukraine to brief updates from the Ukrainian front where he is currently serving.

The flag stunt—referred to by Mustang Wanted as an art performance—was particularly poised to garner international attention and seemed ready to continue the narratives set in place by the infamous Pussy Riot protest of 2012, which saw members of a punk band sentenced to hard labor for an anti-Putin performance in Moscow's Cathedral of Christ the Savior. Within this context, the seductive narrative of youth culture quashed by austere political retribution occupied the central role, while Russian authorities sought to brand Mustang Wanted as a Ukrainian right-wing extremist. Both Pussy Riot and Mustang Wanted aimed their protest at the heights of Russia's self-expression. A monumental problem materialized—roofing in this instance supplied a performative act that sees an individual body triumph over the political, national, localized icon of the Moscow skyscraper (and not just any skyscraper, but one of seven Stalinist buildings constructed after World War II and rumored to be built by German POWs). The concern in the aftermath was how the subversion of order accomplished in this feat could be put right again; the body victorious in one iconic moment might be then dwarfed in size by Moscow's judicial authority. The matter was settled in a surprising way: Mustang Wanted was arrested in absentia, but Ukraine refused extradition to Russia. Of the five Russians accused, four were fully exonerated, while the fifth pleaded "guilty in part" for aiding in the stunt's infiltration, and guiding Mustang Wanted through the building's security.

Such a resolution, though unexpectedly lenient, nevertheless demonstrated Russia's careful negotiation of the crimes committed. This lesser sentence solidified the bond between this roofing incident and Pussy Riot, particularly as the punishment in both cases reflected a greater concern over the iconography and visibility of protest rather than the criminal activities themselves, or as Masha Gessen views it, the concerns of a totalitarian state rather than a tyrannical one. The focus on the flag is highly telling, Gessen argues: "In a totalitarian state, climbing up to the roof of a building with someone who will plant the flag of a neighboring country can be a political crime punishable by hard labor—like dancing and singing in a church can be."[4] But the planting of the flag is not merely a crime to be punished from a legal purview; it is also quite clearly an attack on the sense of identity and national belonging triggered by the Ukrainian flag itself, which, having historically been used to delineate a border against Russian and Soviet territory/identity, evokes a host of concerns at the level of national identity and the military history of the twentieth century.

Subverting Victory: Soviet Iconography Meets Post-Soviet Iconoclasm

Mustang Wanted's performance, therefore, was crucial in bringing the tremendous affective potential of roofing to the unstable but potent iconography of post-Soviet national identity and memory. Unpacking this stunt is no mere semiotic exercise, as all its aspects seem overdetermined, oversaturated with meaning, from the highly symbolic field of the flag to the skyscraper and the shift of perspective supplied by the view from up top. For former Soviet subjects, this act conjures the highly symbolic terrain of Evgeny Khaldei's "The Victory Banner over Berlin," the famous photograph of a soldier brandishing the Soviet flag from on top of the Reichstag. While we now know it to have been carefully staged, the photograph became part of the "established symbolism" of the Soviet victory over Nazi Germany on German soil—a war referred to in Russian and Ukrainian as the Great Patriotic War.[5] The photograph accomplishes the tricky task of flattening geopolitical and military complexities into an easily digestible denotation of *victory*, one which has been central to postwar Soviet (and post-Soviet) identity and memorialization. Jeremy Hicks approaches the photograph using Murray Edelman's notion of "condensation symbol," "sum[ming] up attitudes toward the past."[6] Seen from this vantage point, the photograph serves official history, a dominant account that "underplays other facts, such as the specific fate of Soviet Jews, the Soviets' own alliance with Nazi Germany, and the invasion of their Polish and Baltic neighbors in 1939–1941," and which "denies outright the crimes committed during their own drive forward to Berlin."[7] While this history is a shared one—providing important memory markers for Russian *and* Ukrainian identity—Mustang Wanted's performance resonated powerfully with this "established symbolism" at precisely a moment where these shared meanings, already critiqued and demythologized after the fall of the Soviet Union, were disintegrating beyond repair. Though the Victory Banner—the hammer and sickle flag—was incorporated into both Soviet and post-Soviet memorialization via marches and parades, it was, by 2014, newly infused with specific pro-Russian sentiment in Ukraine.

But the impact of Mustang Wanted's performance was not limited to the sensation of the photograph itself circulated by the roofer in the aftermath of his climb. Indeed, the stunt continued its iconoclastic assault on the country's state-myth as it was particularly difficult to undo, and Moscow residents woke up to see a city landmark changed from their perch on the ground. Ilya Varlamov's photographs of the worker charged with removing the flag and repainting the star, widely circulated in Western coverage of the crime, are particularly evocative (see Figure 5). Unlike the roofer, the worker is equipped with safety equipment as he climbs the tower and begins repainting the spire. But like the roofer, the worker cannot help but photograph himself along this great height, capturing a view that has been inaccessible to Moscow residents since the building of the skyscrapers themselves. Varlamov's humorous photographs of the worker and his selfie put the stunt directly into conversation with another history hidden in plain sight: the postwar development of Moscow's skyline and the workers who built them, all of whom were the "first to see Moscow from the new vantage points created by the city's tall buildings."[8] Here, the word used for

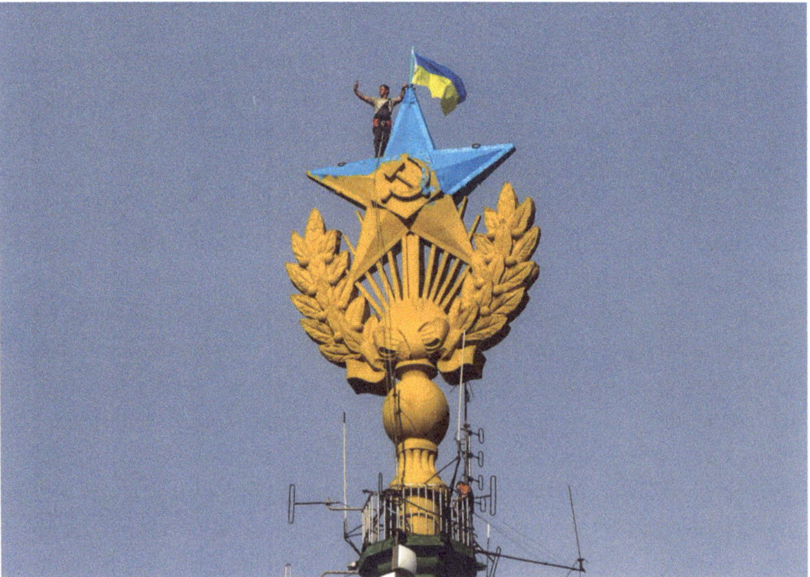

Figure 05. A Moscow worker takes a selfie while removing the traces of Mustang Wanted's Ukrainian flag and paint from the spire of a Moscow skyscraper.

the roofer—literally *rufer*, taken from English—has a linguistically Russian predecessor: *vysotnik*, from *vysota*, the word for height. According to Katherine Zubovich, the term *vysotnik* "applied to all construction workers engaged in building Moscow's skyscrapers [and] included in their ranks both skilled and unskilled laborers."[9] This was a class of worker that immediately became heavily mythologized and celebrated "in the mold of Soviet heroes before them," as "heroes of the sky—men and women who skillfully braved the elements in the pursuit of impossible heights."[10] In this sense, the workers were linguistically and mythologically connected to Soviet aviators who fascinated the popular imagination with daring flights in the 1930s. Such heroic stature certainly covered over the fact that Moscow's skyscrapers "were built in part by incarcerated laborers."[11]

But such iconic stature and myth are rarely tied to good memory and record keeping, and the same fate has followed the famous 1932 photograph *Lunch Atop a Skyscraper*, often mistakenly attributed to Lewis Hine and the building of the Empire State Building (the photographer is unknown and the building is the Rockefeller Center). Zubovich notes that New York City's "sky boys" and "poet builders" were similarly mythologized, though much earlier than was the case in postwar Moscow.[12] This spirit of transnational influence is noteworthy, not only for the iconography that becomes central to state-myth but also for the way these concepts travel across borders—particularly as the building of the skyscrapers themselves "signaled a shift in the way the Soviet Union positioned itself globally."[13] Zubovich specifically underscores "the newfound irony in transforming the icon of capitalist triumph, into a symbol of communism" and provides an in-depth history of the role these structures played "in the shifting dynamics of Soviet internationalism."[14]

In the North Atlantic context, however, the iconography of the skyscraper as capitalist triumph was not always as culturally settled and static as this comparison might lead one to believe. While skyscrapers had already become "tokens of urban modernity" prior to World War I and were occasionally represented in cinema as "creations of corporate capitalism" and "monument[s] to pure greed," Steven Jacobs points out the many complex ways people found themselves negotiating the new sensorial registers of the modern metropolis, an entity that he, following Georg Simmel, Siegfried Kracauer, and Walter Benjamin, characterizes as a "cultural constellation in which, through the confrontation with anonymous crowds and motorized traffic, 'shock experience has become the norm'."[15] Jacobs likens the skyscraper to the car, both of which offered new vectors—one horizontal, the other vertical—"of modern rationalized space…that defined the spatial logics of the urban environment."[16] In other words, people had to learn how to live among these new emblems of technological progress, and some of the most memorable—or shocking, to use the language given to us by these theorists—lessons of urban modernity emerged from cinema (another new technology).

An Embarrassment of Attractions: Architecture, Cinema, and Eccentrism

From this perspective, roofing has a decidedly long, rich, and unexpected prehistory. The performance of scaling buildings resounds strongly with the history of early-nineteenth- and twentieth-century "human flies"; Mustang Wanted calls to mind Harry Gardiner, who, between 1905 and 1933, "successfully climbed over 700 buildings in Europe and North America, usually wearing ordinary street clothes and using no special equipment."[17] In *The Thrill Makers: Celebrity, Masculinity, and Stunt Performance*, Jacob Smith charts the trajectory of human flies, which begins as a nineteenth-century female-oriented circus performance, and evolves into gut-churning spectacles of male heroics that can best be understood through their encounter with a rapidly evolving matrix of twentieth-century communication technologies: "This was a period when a new type of urban architecture, modern modes of advertising and publicity, the motion picture newsreel, and film stardom were all emerging, and all of these played a role in shaping how human flies were understood."[18] Ultimately, roofing as a type of media depends upon the jarring encounter of the human with modern technologies, with cinema providing these types of affective shocks in many different ways since its inception.

Within a genealogy of roofing, then, the skyscraper becomes far more than a monument to US capitalist industry or an urban structure offering new perspectives and vertical trajectories. We have already seen above how the skyscraper acted as a global provocation (which the Soviets accepted in the postwar context). To this, we can add what Jacobs refers to as an "architecture of attractions," arguing that the skyscraper corresponds precisely to the impulse for amusement and fragmentation that characterizes modernity's other great emblem, the cinema. Silent slapstick cinema, for instance, provides another pillar of roofing media history, as comedians such as Harold Lloyd and Buster Keaton incorporated skyscrapers into their comedies and used their stature as yet another monolithic structure against which the slapstick hero must prove himself. To quote Jacobs again, "it was precisely the confrontation of vulnerable bodies with the thrills of heights and the wonders of architectural progress that provided [slapstick comedy] with its most powerful images."[19] Soviet filmmakers also heeded this call, responding to the perilous thrills depicted in American films like Lloyd's iconic *Safety Last* by constructing their own sequences of comic exploits on Moscow and Leningrad roofs. Two films in particular stand out—Sergei Eisenstein's *Dnevnik Glumova* (*Glumov's Diary*, 1923) and Grigori Kozintsev and Leonid Trauberg's 1924 *Pokhozhdeniia Oktiabriny* (*The Adventures of Oktiabrina*). The short films share an extraordinary amount in common, though the former is considerably shorter (at roughly four minutes) than the latter (thirty-five minutes), and they were produced in different cities in the Soviet Union. Nevertheless, both films were their directors' first forays in cinema; both were conceived as a play on the American chase/detective genre; both staged these chases on the rooftops of their cities; and, curiously, both have been lost (though *Glumov* has been found and restored to the extent possible).[20] Even the films' fragments, however, demonstrate a fascination with new and exciting vectors for visualizing the world, though it is important to note that, in the case of *Oktiabrina*, rooftops are a realm not exclusive to male comedic acrobatics (see Figure 6).

Despite this transnational exchange of fascinations between the United States and the Soviet Union, however, the Soviet directors were working at something of a disadvantage, living as they were in imperial and baroque cities whose encounter with the twentieth century and with modernism was most forcefully staged through revolution and war. VGIK, the Soviet national film school, had to power through its early years with classes like Lev Kuleshov's "Film without Film," owing to a scarcity of equipment and film stock; in a similar way, filmmakers were forced to stage their daring rooftop chases without the skyscrapers. Indeed, one critic characterized *The Adventures of Oktiabrina* as "an unrestrained collection of all the stunts that directors starved of cinema fall greedily upon."[21] In a North Atlantic context, the slapstick hero is catapulted into a new and dizzying future by working through the gags and obstacles of the modern metropolis. By contrast, Soviet slapstick protagonists had no modern metropolis

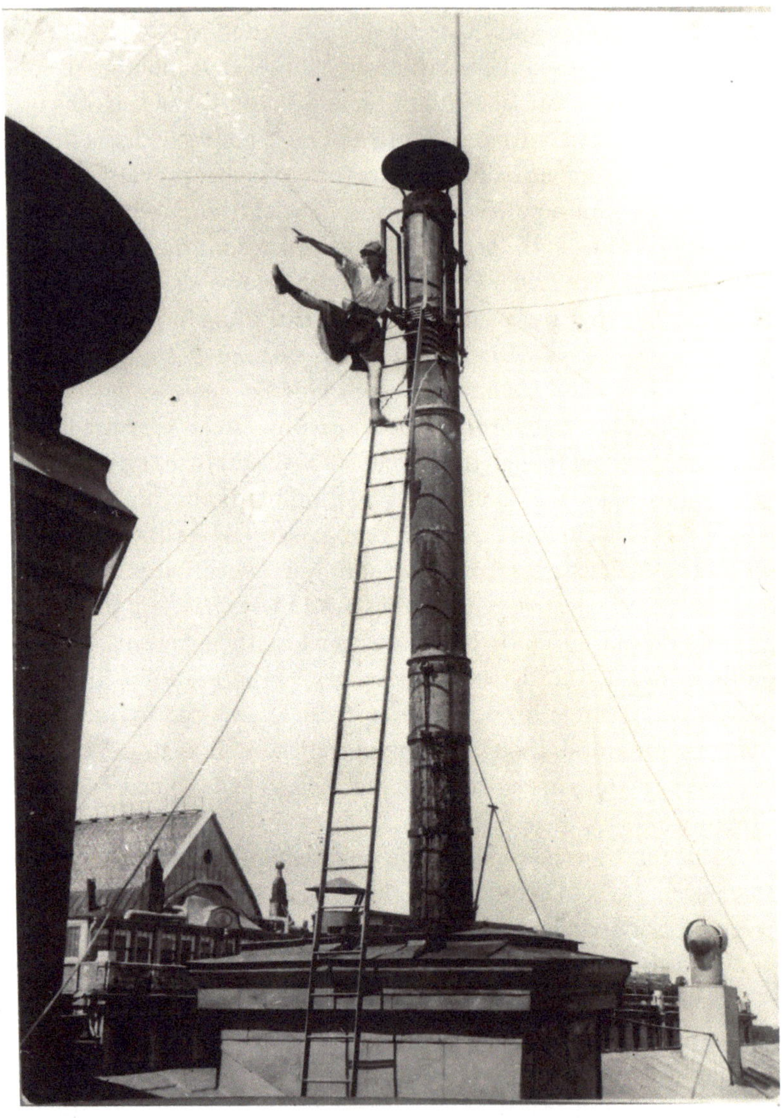

Figure 06. A still from the lost FEKS film *Pokhozhdeniia Oktiabriny* [The Adventures of Oktiabrina], 1924. Here, the titular character Oktiabrina chases her opponents along the rooftops of Leningrad.

to contend with—only an imperial history and a wide array of vernacular delights—from street theater to circus acrobatics—to juggle in their resistance against this weighty past.

Glumov's Diary and *The Adventures of Oktiabrina* are key texts, then, in the longer history of roofing, as they offer us actual examples of roofing from the early 1920s (that is, captured encounters between performers and rooftops designed to thrill a mass audience). More than this, however, they provide a theoretical framework for this mediatized encounter, which helps to define the full potential of the daring roofing hijinks captured via GoPro and selfie almost a century later. Both films enact a stark collision between the freedom of the acrobat actors, who chase speedily and gracefully across rooftops, and the fixedness of cities not yet ready for such slapstick encounters, what Alfonso Puyal refers to, using the language of a slightly older Eisenstein, as "this dialectic between the old and the new."[22] These films were produced before the theory for which Eisenstein is most known, in which he develops his ideas of dialectic, conflict, collision, and montage (terms which are only too apt to describe the power of roofing media). Nevertheless, the theoretical foundations of both films are highly significant for our purposes, particularly in light of two shared terms, the meanings of which have been contested ground for historians and theorists of media: Eccentrism and the trick, or the attraction.

In 1923, Eisenstein was working in the Proletkult theater and considered cinema to be an element that would assist in revolutionizing, or in his words, "abolishing the very institution of theatre as such."[23] To accomplish this, he devised "the *agitational theatre of attractions* (dynamic and Eccentric—the left wing)."[24] Kozintsev and Trauberg, meanwhile, had been working together since 1921 toward a similar mission, brandishing the term Eccentrism in Leningrad (or Petrograd as it was then named), where they founded FEKS, the Factory of the Eccentric Actor. The two young artists (aged sixteen and twenty, in 1921) had only recently arrived in the former capital from their hometowns of Kyiv and Odessa, respectively, but they found themselves aghast at the imperial backwardness of the city's culture, and dedicated themselves immediately to complete aesthetic and eccentric upheaval. This was announced via their manifesto—"Ekstsentrizm"—in which they declared Eccentrism to be "the art of the 20th century, the art of 1922, the art of this very moment."[25] The founding of their factory soon followed, and the artistic duo mounted plays, taught classes, and trained students in what they considered to be the Eccentric arts—from acrobatics to film history to courses on modernity.

This shared interest in the Eccentric is important to elucidate, especially as it can get tricky with all the slippery "isms" of the time period. On the one hand, Eccentrism falls quite neatly into the categories of "slapstick modernism" or "comedic modernism," terms deployed to clarify the collision of modernism and slapstick, or the "affinity for slapstick film on the part of the interwar European avant-garde."[26] In this sense, Eisenstein and FEKS are exuberantly accompanied by interwar experimental artists like Fernand Léger, Luis Buñuel, Salvador Dalí, and René Clair. But, as we have argued throughout, rooftop media cannot help but signify on the level of the nation, and thus the Soviet specifics are of vital importance. Puyal attributes Eisenstein and FEKS's desire to play with "city, machine and dynamism" to the influence of futurism in Soviet culture, and argues that "Soviet Constructivism turns the city into a stage upon which amazing deeds, burlesque situations and acrobatics are performed."[27] Eccentrism has been far less studied than these other movements, but emerges from these same traditions and negotiations.

It has been necessary to trace this artistic convergence between Eisenstein and FEKS because, seen from this vantage point, roofing extends entirely from the same impulses as Eccentrism itself: that is, a desire to use new media to visualize stunning new forms of expression and urban existence—a momentary freedom from gravity and the shock of an eccentric encounter with the landmarks and monuments that mark our otherwise fixed places. And if we accept this premise—that Eccentrism and roofing are the same tradition—we are then able to approach the ongoing theoretical concept at the heart of early cinema, slapstick cinema, Soviet cinema, and roofing media: that is, the focus on the *attraction* as the possibility for media to accomplish something truly transformational. For Tom Gunning, who coined the "cinema of attraction" in the 1980s, the term was useful to explore the ways that we were willfully misunderstanding early cinema and its unwillingness to tell a story over its impulse to display a set of views. But Gunning lifts the term from Eisenstein and, in this transposition, an essential component of Eisenstein's attraction is lost. For Eisenstein, the attraction is "*any aggressive moment in theatre... that subjects the audience to emotional and psychological influence, verified by experience and mathematically calculated to produce specific emotional shocks in the spectator*" (emphases in original).[28] Thus, Eisenstein deploys the attraction not for the capacity of theater or cinema to *display*, but to *shock* its audience *toward a political purpose*. FEKS, too, was working through this collection of attractions in their battle to upend tradition and the genres that were stabilized therein, as they participated in the avant-garde overhaul of culture that, in the post-revolutionary period, was united with the new Soviet project: an "October of the Arts." Seen from this vantage point, Mustang Wanted's stunt stands firmly in the tradition of Eccentrism that Phil Cavendish characterizes as "a broader phenomenon within Soviet proletarian culture of the early 1920s which sought to harness the carnivalesque energy of popular theatre for directly political ends."[29] Gunning acknowledges this Soviet setting partly, writing that "the source [for the term attraction] is significant." So too is the historical context; Eisenstein theorized the attraction as politically powerful in an article where he laid out how *Glumov's Diary*, his very first film, which also marks our earliest Soviet example of roofing, functions as the archetypal example of the attraction.

Conclusion

New media platforms such as TikTok, Instagram, YouTube, and the now deceased Vine have been warmly embraced by film historians in the classroom, as they restore an urgency to the study of early cinema's display of views and tricks. Like these early cinematic predecessors, TikTok refuses to absorb its user in a narrative, opting instead for the characteristics which have defined Gunning's use of the attraction: "direct confrontation of the audience, brevity of film subjects, a fascination with speedy and surprising special effects, a display of novelties, and sustained temporal and narrative development."[30] Disciplinary specifics have introduced new terminology into the mix, forcing a shift from audience to user, view to scroll, and tickets to "like and subscribe." But if this shift has asked us to reconsider the "cinema" part of the equation, I argue that we should also adjust our understanding of the "attraction" to include more than its Eccentric circus and fairground origins. As Maria Belodubrovskaya points out, the attraction was a stepping-stone to Eisenstein's "cine-fist," which, through its impact, was ultimately "about getting through to the audience and making an adjustment in them."[31] The trick is self-contained, but the attraction enacts a transformation beyond the bounds of the performance.

A general distrust of media and youth culture leads to a great deal of surprise at the political engagement and activism of teenage TikTok users or the use of new media platforms to disseminate updates from war fronts faster and more directly than our news channels. I do not argue that all new media attractions are laden with the same political or radical potential. Indeed, in his examination of the human flies of the early twentieth century, Smith also finds that "the thrill makers were remarkably adept at developing performance forms that spoke to a wide range of class constituencies and sustained multiple interpretations."[32] Roofing can, of course, be political provocation. It can just as easily be a pastime, a commercial venture, a brand, or, like the *Jackass* franchise to which it may draw comparison, a "modern manifestation of the medieval carnival" and a new vista for performance art.[33] Take Oleg Cricket, who provides a useful counterpoint for Mustang Wanted's overtly anti-Russian rooftop provocation. Cricket describes roofing as an activity that allows him access to views that would otherwise be reserved for the elite who can afford multimillion-dollar Moscow penthouses.[34] In addition to his multiple urban climbs, Cricket has performed roofing in the background of a music video and has transitioned his career into a lifestyle clothing influencer. Soviet literary theorist V. N. Volosinov might help us account for this wide variety of roofing in his development of the "multi-accentuality of the ideological sign" with regard to the cultural arena.[35] In this chapter, we have surveyed a litany of "multi-accentual" ideological signs—the flag, the skyscraper, the body in peril—all of which contain within themselves provocations that evoke an unstable history whose meanings and outcomes continue to hang in the balance.

Chapter 2

Sobre las Olas: Sheet Music, Radio Broadcasting, and the Popularization of a Mexican Waltz

Sonia Robles

On March 1, 1931, Rudolph Kuré, a self-identified "enthusiastic DX fan," wrote a letter to "Radio Station X.F.X." in Mexico City, Mexico, requesting that XFX send him a response verifying that he had tuned into their station from his hometown of Cincinnati, Ohio, in the United States. Though notable, this request was not unusual. Named after the amateur or "ham" radio code for distance (DX), DXers were tinkerers who belonged to an extensive community of operators across the world engaging in similar behavior such as building receivers at home or in their sheds or garages, and staying up late into the night calibrating the dials of their devices in search of distant sounds.[1] During the Golden Age of Radio (1920s to 1950s), the DX community in the United States often promoted competitions centered on tuning into as many stations as possible in the Americas, the Caribbean, Europe, or even Asia. The farther, the better. As a nocturnal activity, "DXing was a real adventure in mastering the unpredictable" and "success" was measured by the number of distant stations a DXer could tune into during a specific period of time.[2] Tinkerers would listen to a broadcast from a far-away location and immediately compose a letter hoping to obtain a response in the form of a verification stamp, card, or other official documentation that they could use as bragging rights, enter into their log books, or to participate in a local contest. Their late-night or early morning adventures across the ether were in vain, in fact, if the station they had tuned into did not write back with a response.

Mr. Kuré's one-page letter to XFX includes details and information DXers frequently included in their correspondence with foreign stations: the language or languages transmitted, the exact time the station broadcast a song via record, singer, duet, etc., at what time a speech was given, the station's call letters, announcements, the tone and volume of the transmission, details on the radio receiver used to listen to the broadcast, and whether there was static interference. Mr. Kuré noted that on the two occasions that he picked up station XFX he heard a "pretty Spanish melody," a "popular tune," and a "beautiful Mexican waltz." He recorded listening to the latter, titled "OVER THE WAVES", at "exactly 3:30 A.M., American Eastern Standard Time."[3]

This chapter traces the historical trajectory of the Mexican waltz "Over the Waves", or "Sobre las Olas" in its original Spanish-language name, across the various print and electronic media forms which disseminated it from the nineteenth century, when it was created, to the 1930s, when it was picked up by this amateur radio enthusiast in the US Midwest. It is unclear whether or not Mr. Kuré knew or was able to recognize "Sobre las Olas" when he tuned into XFX at dawn in the spring of 1931, or if the announcer told listeners its title before "the Spanish tenor" sang it.[4] And while it is probable that the amateur radio enthusiast had heard it before, I argue that the reason the waltz made it on XFX's playlist and the factor that made it recognizable thousands of miles away, decades after it was composed, lies in communication media's role in transforming a formal dance song into an international hit.

The chapter opens with a brief discussion on the history of Mexican music across three different time periods: the colonial era, which lasted three centuries (1521–1821); the mid-nineteenth century, when Mexico was invaded by the French in what is commonly known as the Second Mexican Empire (1864–1867); and the rule of President Porfirio Díaz in the late nineteenth century, which was the time when the waltz was created. Next, the chapter explains the different factors making this waltz a Mexican formal dance song, including the fact that the waltz's creator was a Mexican man of humble origins by the name of Juventino Rosas. In this way, the chapter builds upon recent literature on the multifaceted origins of Latin American music.[5] In the third and final section, I explain how sheet music and radio broadcasting, essential features in the print and electronic media revolutions of the nineteenth and early twentieth centuries, played a role popularizing "Sobre las Olas." Without sheet music, certain songs would never have been able to circulate within Europe or the United States. Likewise, radio broadcasting has allowed music of all genres—including waltzes—the ability to be global media forms since the first decades of the twentieth century. Focusing on communication media adds necessary layers to the history of Mexican music, songs, and artists, as it brings to the forefront media's role exposing, circulating, and preserving sounds.

Mexican Music from Independence, to the French Intervention, to the Porfiriato

"Sobre las Olas" is the name of a series of Viennese waltzes created in 1891 by Mexican violinist and composer Juventino Rosas. Understanding the historical events prior to the moment when they were written and the context in which they emerged helps explain the role and impact communication media had in diffusing, labeling, preserving, and popularizing this text.

Mexico's musical history is a multifaceted and extensive story given that the country is home to an array of unique musical sounds and traditions. What might be recognizable today as "Mexican music" is a byproduct of a long tradition of blending together pre-Hispanic Indigenous sounds, lyrics, and storytelling with both African and European melodies and rhythms.[6] In the twentieth century certain genres, such as *corridos*, which are lyrical ballads, and *canciones románticas* (romantic songs) were labeled "Mexican" because of their association with the popular classes and because their lyrics recounted stories familiar to the majority of the population during a specific historical moment. In this case, *corridos* and *canciones románticas* were byproducts of the Mexican Revolution of 1910.[7] In the aftermath of this time of vast social change, as Mexican historian Ricardo Pérez Montfort explains, there was an interest on behalf of the government to collect music from Mexico's vast regions and use it to give shape to a new national identity.[8] This dedicated pursuit to define Mexican music and associate it with a new national identity is in sharp contrast to one of the first English-language studies on Mexican popular music, which explained that "to the majority of people in other countries…Mexican music is not associated with a given artist or tune but with a certain type of orchestra, or rather, a particular sound."[9]

This sound, however, did not originate in the twentieth century. Decades before Mexico achieved independence from Spain in 1821, musicians and singers throughout the country produced local tunes and vernacular music. Scholars such as Yolanda Moreno Rivas claim that Mexican music has its roots in Mexico's colonial era (1521–1821). In the eighteenth century, Spanish authorities encouraged the colonial population in New Spain, as the colony was called, to demonstrate and pledge allegiance to the motherland through music. By the seventeenth century, the colony's multi-ethnic and socially stratified population consumed and created music in a variety of places: family parties, religious celebrations, outdoor festivals, the theater, and other public and private gatherings.[10] Any musical piece that was produced in one of Spain's most prosperous colonies was considered a "*son*". The word, in fact, became a blanket term to tag the rhythms or melodies created in what later became Mexico.

New musical expressions were born after independence, when the social interaction between the high-brow or elite and the popular classes became more common.[11] A distinguishable feature among Mexican society in the first half of the nineteenth century was that the "public was avidly musical," as historian Robert Stevenson explains. "High and low professed an overwhelming fondness for music."[12] Despite new forms of social interaction, class divisions did not disappear following independence and the elite began to characterize themselves by their taste in music and opera, prioritizing Italian, French, and Spanish styles. Communication studies expert Mark Pedelty notes that "opera, both tragic and common, became the rage among Mexico City elites, paralleling the growth of the urban middle class."[13] Another European import arriving in Mexico in the early nineteenth century was the waltz.[14]

Unsurprisingly, the military invasion of Mexico by France (1861–1867) was a chaotic and politically uncertain time for the young nation, which was recovering from a devastating war with the United States in the mid-nineteenth century that cut the size of its territory in half.[15] In the realm of culture and music, the "waltz circulated among the high court salons" of the Austrian Archduke Maximilian von Hapsburg and Queen Charlotte's tenure in Mexico between 1864 and 1867. The French imperial family aided high society's ease from only enjoying and accepting religious music to being open to European genres such as classical operas, signs of much larger cultural shifts occurring during a time of liberalism. The invading

French court also ushered in the practice of hiring Europeans and foreign-trained musicians, which became widely acceptable by the second half of the century.[16] And while the French did not stay in Mexico long, the importance given to classical music, opera, and waltzes remained in the nation for decades. From the 1860s onward, in fact, waltzes were accepted and diffused among different social classes.[17]

In the early 1890s, when Juventino Rosas composed "Sobre las Olas," European trends—clothing, art, music, architecture, etc.—still dominated Mexico. The nation was ruled by Porfirio Díaz, an authoritarian figure who came to power in the late 1870s and helped develop Mexico's railway system, implemented small-scale industrialization, opened the country to foreigners and their investments, and advanced a policy of "order and progress," most often through brutal repression. Díaz was in power for the latter half of the nineteenth century and finished his tenure when the Mexican Revolution erupted in the first decade of the twentieth century. His time in office, 1876 to 1910, is a historical era known as the "Porfiriato," after his first name.[18]

Musically, genres began to shift in the second half of the nineteenth century, particularly during Díaz's ascent to power. The government subsidized musical education and established the National Conservatory. There was a sizable and cultured population with the means to purchase piano sheet music. This feature set Mexico apart from many other countries, in particular, the United States. Despite fluctuating governments, political instability, and the rule of a dictator from the latter third of the nineteenth century to 1910, there was an undisputable "belief that music was important enough in national life to merit government support."[19] Both of these aspects—the government's attention to musical education and the advent of new musical genres—were vital elements of the origin story of "Over the Waves."

What Makes a Waltz "Mexican"

"Sobre las Olas" is celebrated as Mexico's first international hit.[20] Encyclopedia entries and scholarly articles and chapters mention its popularity briefly or in passing, yet disregard its connection to popular, folk, and other forms of nineteenth-century Mexican music. The song is recognized as Mexican despite the fact that it does not "sound" Mexican or

"Indian." On the contrary, one scholar claims that "if one were asked to define the particular qualities in 'Sobre las Olas' which distinguish it from hundreds of Viennese waltzes, the task might prove difficult."[21]

On one level, "Sobre las Olas" does, in fact, contradict the stereotypical Mexican musical categories recognized across the world today thanks to the film industry, restaurants, or the internet: mariachi, ranchera, *corrido*, and other music featuring an array of trumpets, string instruments, and wailing male and female voices. The waltz is a lively salon piece because its tune is in line with formal dance culture including waltzes and Czechoslovakian polkas, both mid-nineteenth-century European imports. Waltzes were romantic and quintessentially Porfirian musical pieces because they followed a rigid structure and also included heartfelt lyrics with nostalgic overtones, which, according to Ricardo Pérez Montfort, reflected the processes of political and economic decay during the dictator's long rule over Mexico.[22]

However, "Sobre las Olas" is considered Mexican and was recognized as a "beautiful Mexican waltz" by a radio amateur in the 1930s for other reasons. The waltz gave a nod to European styles and was a product of its time, but it paired those sounds and styles with long-suffering romantic lyrics of love and disdain. This invocation of sentimentality and its association with patriotism were foundations of what is known as "Mexican cultural nationalism," a government-sponsored movement spearheaded by the Ministry of Public Education in the 1920s.[23] "Sobre las Olas" fits well into the category of "*canción de autor*," or singer-songwriter song, which was part of a musical genre produced in the late nineteenth century by composers wanting to sell large numbers of sheet music. This genre was different because the composers who wrote *canciones de autor* also played an instrument. These were songs of longing and loving complaints and are also often categorized as "sentimental songs."[24]

Of course, another reason "Sobre las Olas" can be labeled "Mexican" is because its creator was born in that country. Juventino Rosas was born January 25, 1868 in the central Mexican state of Guanajuato. When he was six years old, his family left his village for Mexico City, a rural to urban sojourn millions of other people throughout Mexico have embarked on since the late nineteenth century. In the capital city, the Rosas family struggled to make ends meet. Juventino, who learned to play violin at a young age, joined his father and brother, formed a musical trio, and found work as itinerant musicians. The group performed in public venues throughout the capital city for a few years until the patriarch's passing, when they disbanded.

Next, Rosas enrolled in the *conservatorio nacional,* National Conservatory, a no-fee musical training school established during the Porfiriato. A career as a musician was a worthwhile and promising path for someone with a humble background like Juventino. "Even among the highest classes," Robert Stevenson notes, "music was regarded as a worthy vocation."[25] However, the violinist left the Conservatory and followed the demands of the growing entertainment industry. Rosas joined acclaimed opera singer Angela Peralta's company and traveled throughout Mexico until her untimely death, when he was out of work.[26]

Jumping from one musical gig to the next was not an uncommon existence for an amateur without formal training as a musician. During the second half of the nineteenth century, Mexican-born musicians and composers of different backgrounds wanting to succeed as musicians had to create music for the aristocratic class; that is, elite Mexicans familiar with Bach, Mozart, and Italian operas. Rosas was caught in a moment when Mexican music sought to resemble European models as much as possible.[27] Opportunities for amateurs were plentiful, and the chance to sell a piece of music available, but in order to earn a livelihood as a musician one had to produce music that obeyed a distinct business model by conforming "to the fashions of the period." A second requirement, especially for someone from a lower social class, was to acquire patrons.[28]

Juventino's lucky break came in 1885 when President Díaz heard him play the violin at one of Mexico City's most prominent theaters, the *Teatro Nacional.* The performance and recognition by Díaz served Rosas well. Afterwards, he was able to perform with formally trained elite orchestras, acquire patrons, and sell some of his original music. One of these aristocratic members of the Porfirian high society was Señora Calixta Gutiérrez de Alfaro, whom Rosas dedicated "Sobre las Olas" to when he composed the waltz at age twenty-three. Three years after creating the waltz, while on tour directing an orchestra in Cuba, Rosas died of a preventable illness.[29]

Juventino Rosas's life story—born in poverty in Mexico's countryside, forced to move to the capital to find work, struggling to make it as a student and hustling as an amateur until he struck gold, before dying at a young age—is both representative of migration patterns prevalent in Mexico both historically and to this present day and a vital component of stardom myths in Mexico. The fact that music or other cultural traditions from Mexico's provinces have to travel to Mexico City in order to be recognized and legitimized is a centuries-old trajectory that was subsidized and sponsored by the government for a number of years.[30] I propose that the examination of this popular Mexican waltz extend beyond the accepted and official narrative highlighting Rosas's premature death, the way in which he was paid a pittance for his internationally known song, or the fact that he was never able to enjoy a life of stardom. Juventino Rosas was a talented and young musician on the road to a bright future when he composed "Sobre las Olas," but it was the print and broadcast media forms accompanying the song's evolution that played a vital role in ensuring that the song become "a hit unparalleled in the history of Mexican music."[31]

Print and Electronic Media: Essential Components in the Story

Printed sheet music became an essential component in popularizing "Sobre las Olas." In 1891, when Juventino Rosas published the waltz, there was a local and international market in Mexico interested in publishing salon music. As many as 103 salon pieces were published in Mexico during the Porfiriato, most between 1870 and 1900.[32] "The enormous vogue of all this salon repertory in Mexico during the latter part of the 19th century," Stevenson notes, "proves how internationally minded the townspeople were. Their polkas, mazurkas, valses, and schottisches were all international dance types."[33] Piano and salon music—waltzes, polkas, etc.—were so prominent, in fact, that five publishing houses stayed in business during the mid- to late nineteenth century.[34]

A. Wagner and Levien Suc., the German publishing house that bought "Sobre las Olas," was a successful international enterprise with regional offices in Guadalajara, Puebla, Monterrey, Mérida, and other cities throughout Mexico and was responsible for publishing a wide variety of salon pieces: polkas, schottisches, mazurkas, marches, potpourris, boleros, *paso dobles*, meditations, and caprices.[35] After paying Juventino 17 pesos for the waltz, the publishing house exported "Sobre las Olas" to Germany, where it was known as "Über die Wellen." The Mexican waltz was also sold in the United States by 1895, just four years after it was created.[36] Calculating the amount of profit the publishing house made from the waltz is challenging. One scholar contends that because of its reputation and its ability to reprint and distribute the waltz widely throughout Europe, A. Wagner and Levien Suc. made more than a 100,000-peso profit from "Sobre las Olas."[37] The waltz was created in Mexico and traveled to Europe thanks to the international sale and exchange of sheet music, undoubtedly; yet it enjoyed a longer life because of other media forms, namely wireless broadcasting and the electronic communications revolution of the twentieth century.

Radio communication initiated with wireless telegraphy, using Morse code to transmit information without the cables and machinery that had accompanied the telegraph. This feat, which is credited to the work of Italian inventor Guglielmo Marconi, existed decades before the commercial use of radiotelephony, the transmission of voice and music.[38] Despite not containing any moving parts, radio is a complex machine, more than a camera, a typewriter or any of the other devices of the technological revolution, as Rubén Gallo reminds us.[39] Radio is also an electroacoustic medium. It shares this aural element with other sound media such as the telephone and the phonograph. The amplification of music and the human voice came about through a series of experiments and discoveries in the early 1910s, most importantly the development of the audion, a vacuum tube designed by Lee De Forest in 1907.[40] Once the practice of successfully sending voice messages wirelessly became widely known in the 1910s, "the entire world was seized by a radio frenzy."[41] Media scholar Susan J. Douglas explains that in the United States, "the word *miracle* was used repeatedly to try to convey the revolutionary, and mystical, properties of the device."[42]

The fact that an amateur radio enthusiast such as Mr. Kuré from Cincinnati, Ohio listened to "Sobre las Olas" decades after it was created and mentioned its title by name in his letter to station XFX reveals the international popularity of the waltz. In the first decade of the twentieth century, new technologies such as telegraphy and telephony caught the attention of amateur radio enthusiasts, many of whom began to construct and tinker with homemade radio receivers. Amateurs were key players in radio's early history and development in the Americas and Europe because they had access to the necessary resources to develop the medium and they had an interest in perfecting wireless communications. As Susan J. Douglas explains, long-distance friends were the "very first radio audience in the first decade of the century."[43]

For many radio enthusiasts, there was an unavoidable thrill in constructing an apparatus that had the capability to receive voices from unseen distant audiences. In the United States, hobbyist or "Ham" culture, as has been described by historian Kristen Haring, transformed into a unique "technical culture," a world of amateurs and tinkerers who joined clubs, subscribed to specialized magazines, participated in contests to earn trophies and recognitions for their abilities, organized and participated in technical conferences and regional meetings, and engaged in other masculine group behavior, as they were mostly male.[44] Mr. Kuré was certainly a part of a subculture of male hobbyists and that fact that he chose to write to Mexico City hours after listening to XFX's transmission suggests that for a ham operator, he possessed advanced skills. Before home receivers became widely available in the 1930s and 1940s, in order to operate a radio—either in private, as Mr. Kuré, or at a station—you needed to possess technical expertise and the time and resources to work with different components: a receiver, a transmitter, antennas, batteries, tubes, dials, and numberless cables, including the ones attached to your head, via earphones, which were required to listen to any transmissions at the time. In the spring of 1931 Kuré had calibrated the dials of the RCA Radiola 60 receiver and tuned into this particular Mexican station before writing them a letter.

The correspondence between the radio aficionados and the offices and stations they were in contact with in an effort to receive a verification report or reply was a vital component of hobbyist culture and was "at the center of two interdependent experiences relying on new technologies."[45] Mexico's Ministry of Public Education, the managing entity of station XFX, collected and counted English and Spanish-language correspondence from DXers and other radio enthusiasts from Canada, countries in the Caribbean and Central America, and every region of the United States. The radio department archived the correspondence and used it to calculate the range of the station's transmitter and highlight its power and reach. As historical archival sources, these reports are valuable for a number of reasons, since they contain written documentation, i.e. proof, of which stations were on the air, what they played, for how long, when, etc.

Electronic media helped popularize and preserve "Sobre las Olas" during the 1920s when Mexican radio station playlists prioritized Porfirian sounds and melodies. Radio played a number of roles in the history of this particular song: it exposed it to wide audiences, it circulated it across national borders, but it also preserved it for generations. Broadcast media helped the waltz maintain its "popular" status by including it in daily playlists long after waltzes lost their appeal. In the same way that sheet music's reproducibility took the waltz to Europe and back to the Americas, radio helped "Sobre las Olas" circulate within Mexico and be picked up by radio amateurs in the United States.

Conclusion

This chapter has attempted to bring into conversation the complexities of Mexican music and the challenges scholars face when we try to label music as "Mexican." "Sobre las Olas" became an international hit, was labeled a Mexican waltz, and received airplay over radio stations decades after it was created because of communication media's role in reproducing it and disseminating it throughout the world. Furthermore, it is Mexican because it can be defined by "multiple factors and actors" such as its romantic lyrics and the composer's nationality.[46]

Late-nineteenth-century Mexican waltzes such as "Sobre las Olas" are a window into understanding how communication media popularized musical genres and exposed listeners throughout the world to different sounds. Furthermore, as radio scholars Jason Loviglio and Michele Hilmes highlight in their collection *Radio's New Wave*, radio's global reach was taking place many years before the arrival of the internet, podcasting, and other forms of digital radio, when amateurs like Mr. Kuré were staying up late at night and tuning into far-away stations in an effort to win prizes, or simply out of boredom.[47] Only focusing on the waltz's sole creator, Juventino Rosas, overlooks the role that different forms of media played in popularizing this Mexican waltz. The story of the popularity and longevity of "Sobre las Olas" highlights the transnational power of different forms of media in making music appealing to local and international audiences.

Chapter 3

Secret Garden: The Fantastic, Melodrama, and Disenchantment in South Korean Television

Benjamin M. Han

In September 2014, a Facebook page titled "Queremos ver Secret Garden en la TV" (We Want to Watch Secret Garden on TV) was created to urge Latin American TV channels to broadcast *Secret Garden*, the popular Korean TV drama about a CEO and future heir of a large department store conglomerate and a working-class aspiring stuntwoman who swap bodies with the intervention of a magical spell. By October 2014, the page had 10,000 likes, and in January 2015, the Argentinian cable channel Magazine announced that it would air *Secret Garden*. In the same year, the Argentinian magazine *Revistas Noticias* published an article titled "Melodramas Exóticos: El Nuevo Boom Llega de Corea" (Exotic Melodramas: The New Boom Arrives from Korea) in which it discussed *Secret Garden* and further noted how a kiss is identical in all languages. A few months later, actress Ha Ji-won, the female protagonist of *Secret Garden*, addressed Latin American fans in a short video to commemorate the 6th K-Pop Latin American Contest. These examples not only attest to the growing significance of the Latin American market to the circulation of Korean TV dramas but also underscore how *Secret Garden* captivated the hearts of Latin American viewers.

While concepts such as cultural proximity, transcultural affinity, and transnational proximity have been employed to examine the contraflow of media from South Korea to the Global South,[1] this chapter explores how *Secret Garden* navigates the nebulous boundaries between the fantastic and magical realism to reinvent Korean TV dramas that speak to ambivalence toward global modernity.[2] In particular, the chapter analyzes how *Secret Garden*'s engagement with identifiable elements from what has been commodified and ethnicized as the Latin American magical realist tradition to reinvent the fantastic Korean TV drama reifies a problematic understanding of Latin America as the unknowable and marvelous. In doing so, the chapter explores the cultural intersections between South Korea and Latin America beyond the mere question of influence. Here I am interested in what Ella Shohat and Evelyn Alsultany have described as "complex itineraries" in cultural productions that subvert the uneven and dominant West–East binary.[3] In *Secret Garden*, the intervention of the fantastic in the form of a magical spell defies rationality rooted in science and materialism of Western modernity while simultaneously enabling the protagonists to recuperate from their disenchantment with modernity. During the process of re-enchantment, the protagonists actively engage in the process of translation to seek rationality, which also entails piecing together their fragmented memories to emancipate themselves from the painful past in order to be re-enchanted with modernity.

The Fantastic, Melodrama, and Affect

The fantastic has been historically more closely aligned with literature than media productions and yet has enchanted global readers and viewers. According to Cynthia Duncan, "the fantastic has proven to be an enduring source of fascination for readers decade after decade, in large part because of its mysterious and still undefined relationship to our understanding of the real."[4] In *Secret Garden*, the fantastic not only speaks to the nebulous relationship between what is real and unreal but also operates as a discursive mode to address ambivalence toward the past and future without strictly adhering to either fantasy and realism to address the characters' disenchantment with modernity. According to Bliss Cua Lim, "the dominant conceptualization of the fantastic as a question of belief versus skepticism is a rigid antimony between enchantment and disenchantment."[5] More specifically, "enchantment is an idiom of profound disaffection, a lived and felt register of resistance to the contradictions of millennial capitalism."[6] For Tzvetan Todorov, the fantastic "introduces some element into the text that strikes us as potentially supernatural, impossible, or inexplicable according to logic and reason."[7] Hence, in *Secret Garden*, the protagonists' re-enchantment with modernity is only possible through the intervention of the fantastic that not only reinjects mystery and wonder but also involves a self-reflexive process of translation to make sense of the ethereal forces, which becomes central to re-enchantment. As Joshua Landy and Michael Saler put it, the process of re-enchantment with the world encompasses not only the infusion of mystery and wonder but also order and purpose.[8] The process of re-enchantment requires the protagonists to actively seek out rationality to restore order to their chaotic lives while simultaneously discovering the purpose and meaning of their lives through the consummation of heterosexual romance.

Moreover, the fantastic becomes a transnational mode that addresses the complex configuration of colonialism, postcolonialism, and modernization. In *Secret Garden*, the fantastic interacts with the affective mode of melodrama inscribed in emotional feelings to address the complex and polarized understanding of Korean modernity while simultaneously providing the characters' disenchantment of the world in the form of social class disparities in the nation's path toward rapid developmentalism and modernization. The fantastic not only offers the audience a conflicting understanding of modernity but also allows them to recognize "that modernity is characterized by fruitful tensions between seemingly irreconcilable forces and ideas."[9] Thus, the traumatic experiences stemming from oppressive social and authoritarian powers are inflected in the personal struggles of the characters who cope with their own conflicting identities that stand in between the historical past and the present. Additionally, the fantastic is employed to "articulate contemporary anxieties without ignoring a realist perspective entirely."[10] That is, the fantastic interacts with the characters' traumatic historical pasts to help them reclaim their new modern subjectivities.

In the context of South Korea, the fantastic has been more discernible in Korean cinema than in television.[11] The fantastic in Korean cinema has often been linked to imaginaries, formulated through dream sequences. According to Soyoung Kim, "the fantastic mode of cinema in its powerful conjuration of the obstinate past also provides a rich platform on which to think about non-synchronous synchronicity and the working of the premodern modernity."[12] As a result, the fantastic became a discursive space to address clashing tensions between premodern and modernity in Korea. In particular, the fantastic in the form of magical aura or supernatural power is further interconnected to colonial modernization projects that depict the sacrifices of the older generations central to Korea's compressed modernity. In cinema, the fantastic often featured female ghosts and vampires as repressed figures who return to the present from the past, which speaks to how women were seen as threats to modernity, as their sexuality and desires for social mobility have been repressed under colonialism.[13]

Between the Fantastic and Magical Realism

The discussion of the fantastic cannot be disassociated with magical realism as they have been the subject of polemical debates among scholars. Magical realism as a literary genre had its first iteration in Europe with ties to the historical avant-garde movement of the 1920s. It became identified between 1949 and 1970 as "an emancipatory cultural discourse capable of expressing Latin America's historical particularity and desire to establish an aesthetic rhetoric independent of European modernism."[14] Magical realism became known as the genre of "literary identity politics," in which writers used to express the traumatic experiences of marginalized cultures and the underdeveloped world under different forms of oppression, including colonialism.[15] In the words of Homi K. Bhabha, magical realism is a "literary language of the emergent post-colonial world."[16]

As magical realism came to be thought of as an inherently Latin American genre, it received much criticism from Latin American writers and critics. Here, I echo Argentinian cultural critic Fernando Sdrigotti's critique that magical realism is a Western label coined to commodify and ethnicize Latin American literature. He writes:

> If this reduction were limited to literature the only problem would be inadequate criticism, mediocre books, confused readers, and some other minor catastrophes. But this imperative not only continuously shapes ideas of Latin American literature; in a more problematic way, it also shapes ideas of the region, well beyond the cushy world of books.[17]

Sdrigotti further claims that magical realism is a marketing label, "a reduction by means not of absurdity but of obfuscation—a crude simplification through fuzziness.[18] Therefore, it is more appropriate to mark magical realism as more exotic and foreign than the fantastic. As Sylvia Molloy observes, the United States's imaginary of Latin America has been replete with exoticism, ahistoricism, and postcolonialism through magical realism.[19] Therefore, *Secret Garden*'s intended or unintended oscillation between the fantastic and magical realism engenders a narrow and reductive imaginary of Latin America as the unknowable despite its desire to engage and appropriate magical realist elements found in popular Latin American cultural productions.

Magical realism has traveled well across national and cultural borders, including the Middle East and Asia, with literary scholars Lois Parkinson Zamora and Wendy Faris describing it as "an international commodity."[20] While the fantastic is a more appropriate lens than magical realism to analyze *Secret Garden*, the Korean TV drama oscillates between the two modes, thus deserving further historical contextualization of how magical realism was introduced to the Korean literature circle. Even before the influx of what was marked as magical realist literature in Korea, the concept of magical realism was discussed by Chungmoo Choi in her discussion of *minjung* (the people) movement when she wrote that "magical realism functions as an apt genre to address the supratemporality of history."[21]

The introduction of magical realism to Korea parallels its popularity in East Asia, further corresponding with the rapid economic development and growing cultural interactions between the West and the East.[22] In particular, the Latin American Boom, known as *Boom Latinoamericano*, a Latin American literary movement of the 1960s and 1970s, introduced Gabriel García Márquez's work to the Korean public. In 1977, Márquez's Nobel prize-winning fiction *One Hundred Years of Solitude* was translated into Korean for the first time by Ahn Jung-hyo.[23] Many readers interpreted Latin American literature of magical realism within the specific political context of Korea when the nation was under the authoritarian regime of Park Chung-hee, who espoused rapid industrialization and economic progress. As Ben Holgate explains, magical realism in East Asia "acts more as a shared approach to addressing contemporary issues that result from modernity, market-oriented economies, authoritarian political regimes and the erosion of traditional cultures and values."[24]

Therefore, it is no coincidence that Kim Eun-sook, a star TV writer, desired to engage with world literature that includes Latin American work. Most of her TV dramas have featured books as a narrative device that connects characters but also, in an interview, she explained that she read many books while working after graduating from high school, which was the only way to escape from reality.[25] Accordingly, in *Secret Garden*, there is a brief scene where we observe the books on the female protagonist's desk, which include global literature titles such as *1984* (George Orwell),

The Flounder (Günter Grass), and *One Hundred Years of Solitude* (Gabriel García Márquez), which particularly offered "a road map of the desire for modernization of Latin America" in order to speak to its own ambivalence toward its modernity.[26]

The introduction of Latin American literature into Korea made Márquez's influence more discernible in the Korean literature of the 1990s and early 2000s, especially with the publication of such titles as *Korae* (*Whale*, Cheon Myeong-kwan, 2004) and *Paek Nyŏnyŏkwan* (*One Hundred Years Inn*, Lim Chul-woo, 2004). The characters' struggle to make sense of the marvelous in their lives and distinguish between what is real or not signals how Korea's imaginary of Latin America is firmly embedded in neocolonial logic, as it reproduces the West's problematic use of magical realism to characterize Latin American cultural productions while ignoring the particularities that undermine the otherness of the region. Cuban novelist Alejo Carpentier argued that the marvelous could co-exist with the real in what he described as "*lo real maravilloso*."[27] Nonetheless, this term emanating from a Latin American scholar did not appeal to Western scholars. Instead, they borrowed the term magical realism from Franz Roh, a German art critic, who used it to describe a European art movement.[28] While the problematics of understanding magical realism inherently tied to Latin American media and culture have not subsided, what is more productive is not to come up with a clearly defined set of boundaries but rather to consider how a growing number of Korean TV dramas appropriate and engage with it, intentionally or unintentionally, in their desire to confront Korea's ambivalence toward modernity.

Secret Garden and the Fantastic

The broadcast of *Secret Garden* in 2010 on the terrestrial channel SBS followed several years of uncertainties and anxieties facing the nation. In 2007, Lee Myung-bak, a businessman turned mayor of Seoul and a member of the conservative political party, won a landslide victory in the presidential election, restoring the power of the economic elites and shedding the hopes of true democratic progress. Additionally, in 2008, the global financial crisis took a toll on the nation when the government announced a US$130 million financial rescue package to assist banks and stabilize markets. Given this uncertain political and social milieu, *Secret Garden* as a fantastic Korean TV drama not only provided escapist entertainment to Korean viewers but also allowed them to confront their own disillusionment with the experience of modernity.

Compared to other fantastic genres, *Secret Garden* does not feature female ghosts, vampires, or aliens but a socially privileged yet arrogant male protagonist who struggles to recuperate from a tragic event of the past, which continues to haunt him. The Korean TV drama uses the fantastic and melodrama to elicit affect, further enabling Latin American viewers to identify strongly with the characters. As Carla Marcantonio puts it, "melodrama continues to do significant work toward helping us make affective sense of a global environment that exceeds the legally demarcated contours of the state."[29] The interplay between the fantastic, magical realism, and melodrama not only speaks to the ambivalence toward the past and future but also addresses ambiguity, as "one of the defining characteristics of the [fantastic] genre" to explore "important philosophical, ideological, and social constructs."[30]

Secret Garden adapts conventional elements of a *telenovela* as its narrative centers on the romantic relationship between Kim Joo-won (played by Hyun Bin), who is the CEO and future heir of a large department store conglomerate, and Gil Ra-im (played by Ha ji-won), who is not only a member of the working class but also a stuntwoman aspiring to succeed in the film industry. With the intervention of a magical spell, their bodies are swapped, forcing them to experience each other's social class experience while revealing how their lives are far more interconnected than they have imagined.

The switching of the bodies not only interjects a fantastical element to the narrative but also functions as an opportunity to make an explicit commentary on social issues when the characters are occupying the bodies of the opposite sex. For example, in episode thirteen, as they arrive at Joon-won's home, they are surprised to discover Joo-won's mother waiting. The mother humiliates Ra-im with harsh words and actions, hurting her and ridiculing her socioeconomic background without knowing that she is indeed speaking to her son in Ra-im's swapped body. After the incident, Joo-won and Ra-im are in the car having a candid conversation about the incident back at home. Interestingly, as they speak to each other, the scene visually gives the illusion that their bodies have returned to their normal state. Joo-won apologizes to Ra-im about the incident involving his mother as he states, "But it's a relief that you didn't have to deal with it. It's the first time I was glad that our bodies were switched." Joo-won adds, "There is no need to be touched; this is called upper-class social conscience." Ra-im responds, "This is called lower-class rebellion." This scene poignantly captures the clash between the different social classes, and the conversation directed at each other in their original bodies resonates more with the audience as it offers the traumatic experience from Ra-im's perspective while also offering social commentary on the oppression of the female working class by the economically privileged class. It is only when the two characters' bodies are switched back to their normal state that there is the opportunity for a critique of patriarchal culture and *chaebol*.[31]

Instead of adhering to social realism to provide a critique of social and gender relations, the incorporation of the fantastic into social criticisms further illuminates the characters' disenchantment with social class hierarchies as an outcome of modernity. Additionally, the fact that the two characters are talking to each other in their own bodies undermines the otherness of this scene and successfully meshes the real and the fantasy world. In this particular scene, not only is the fantastic "understood as inhabiting an imaginative realm that was taken for 'real'," but the viewers also help to create reality.[32] In the subsequent scene, Joo-won visits Ra-im after hearing about the incident involving his mother. Instead of offering a sincere apology to her, Joo-won states that he does not know how to apologize. In response, Ra-im asks him to get out of her pathetic life and return to his pretty fairytale life. As she leaves him, the camera captures Ra-im in slow motion as one of the show's theme songs, "Reason," plays in the background to accentuate the emotional affect of the scene. Instead of highlighting Ra-im as a victim of social oppression, the camera employs different angles to capture Joo-won as he stands still in a state of shock. Joo-won does not speak a word and his facial expressions convey his sadness and heartache to the audience. The dramatic scene, further accentuated by the use of music, animates our emotional feelings and embodied experiences in the form of what Steve Choe characterizes as an "affective interlude."[33] Choe explains how the affective interlude not only implies "too lateness," borrowing from Linda Williams, but is the "culmination of the dramatic tension felt in the mismatch between how things are and how they, in the realm of fantasy, should be."[34] The scene not only elicits affect but also prompts the audience to further identify and establish a more personal connection with the characters, especially Joo-won.

As the interaction between the fantastic and melodrama requires active participation by the viewer to reflect on the past, cope with the present, and imagine the future, the drama also features many instances in which the act of reading a book becomes central to the characters' rediscovery of enchantment in order to affirm their romantic feelings toward each other. That is, the act of reading a text not only involves the process of translation but further requires reasoning. The protagonists participate in the act of translation in their attempt to seek an explanation for their unusual circumstances involving the swapping of their bodies and come to grips with their rational subjectivities.[35] In particular, the drama's explicit references to *Alice's Adventures in Wonderland* illuminate how the characters' disenchantment with modernity must be overcome through the intervention of the fantastic that defies rationality. The characters' re-enchantment with the modern world is only possible through the fantastic, which reinjects mystery and wonder, and self-reflexivity, which becomes critical to the process of re-enchantment. For example, the drama depicts how Ra-im and Joo-won cope with their conflicting understanding of fantasy and realism as each engages in their reading and translation of *Alice's Adventures in Wonderland*. In the process of translating the text, they encounter difficulty interpreting the magical forces that shape their romantic relationship. For example, in episode ten, Ra-im is reading *Alice's Adventures in Wonderland*, juxtaposed with a shot of Joo-won looking out through the large glass windows of his house while the intertitles on the screen read: "Like the fairy tale of *Alice's Adventures in Wonderland*, on a night when galaxies pass through each other, a bad boy stood there. Such a trivial melancholy. He walked at the speed of memories." While *Alice's Adventures in Wonderland* is set entirely outside the real world, *Secret Garden* depicts how the characters' own internalization of the fantastic enables them to cope with their subjectivities and identities in the modern world to rediscover enchantment. As Ra-im's voiceover in episode thirteen states, "There are things that seem like fantasies because they exist far away. That is how it is in the universe of stars. Just as very beautiful people do, they easily disappear." The voiceover underscores how rationality overcomes the fantastic as they come to terms with the historical consciousness of the past.

The protagonists' continuous struggle with ambiguity in the drama culminates in a fantastical climactic moment when the characters can finally confront and liberate themselves from their traumatic past embedded

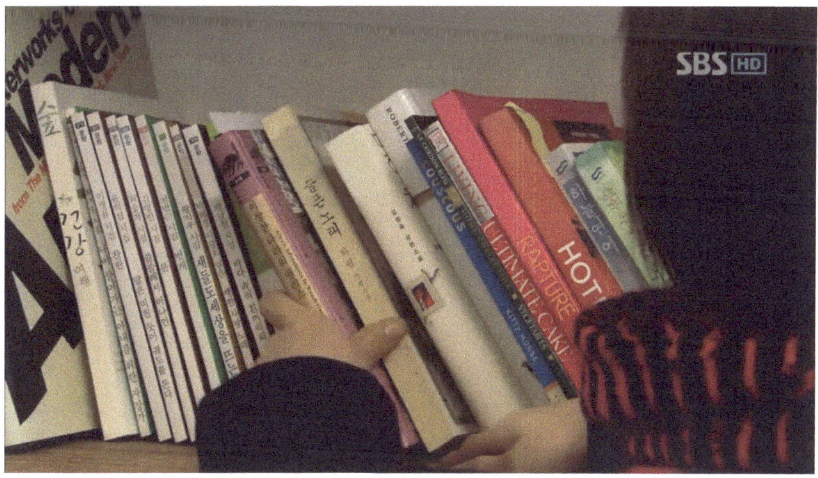

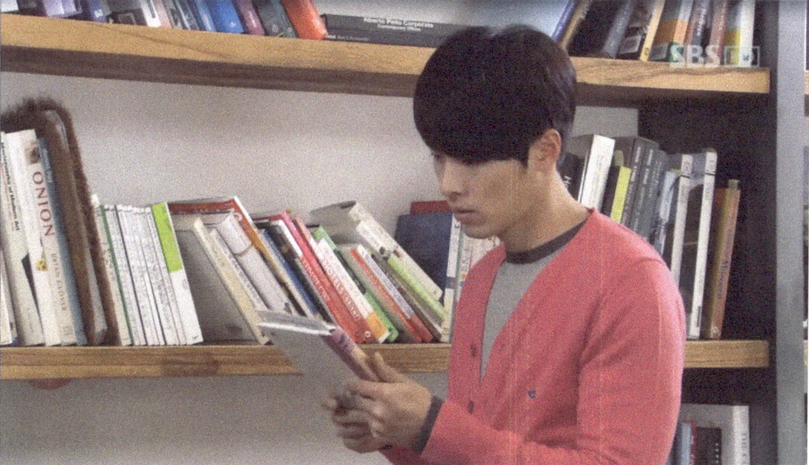

Figures 01.–02. The protagonists read *Alice's Adventures in Wonderland* to make sense of the magical spell and irrationality in their lives.

in painful personal memories. In episode seventeen, Ra-im gets into a severe car accident while doing stunt work on an action film. Joo-won, on the advice of Oska (his celebrity cousin), browses the books on his bookshelf for any possible clues that might save her. Interestingly, he discovers a sheet of paper inside the pages of *Alice's Adventures in Wonderland* containing a short story about a mermaid who falls in love with a prince.

According to the story, the knife in the little mermaid's hand trembled, and she flung it into the waves. As the knife fell into the water, the waves turned red, and the sun rose above the sea. The little mermaid looked at the prince with fading eyes and threw herself into the sea. She turned into foam and disappeared. As he is reading the story, the camera shifts back and forth between the close-up of his face and the actual text of the mermaid story. The scene is again accompanied by the theme song "Reason" as we witness Joo-won crying. This is a rare moment in the drama where Joo-won, rather than Ra-im, fully displays his emotions. Additionally, the song's lyrics "Even though my body changes, my heart remains here" suggest the transformation of Joo-won from an arrogant, individualistic, and unemphatic man to someone who can profess his love for Ra-im. Again, the use of the sentimental theme song continues to engender melodramatic affect while interjecting rationality manifested in romance.

After reading and translating the fairytale story, he places Ra-im's unconscious body in the car and drives into a rainstorm with the hope that their bodies will be swapped again to save her life. As expected, their bodies are successfully swapped as Ra-im regains her consciousness in Joo-won's body while he remains in a coma in Ra-im's body in the hospital. As Joo-won is holding Ra-im's hand on her hospital bed, there is a dreamlike sequence in which Ra-im's father appears and looks into a cup filled with a mysterious drink, which eventually converts into a hospital space where Joo-won and Ra-im are together. In the following scene, the two protagonists are sitting around a table. The voiceover narration of each character is interposed with a shot-reverse shot of the character that captures a medium close-up of their faces. Then, a man whom we recognize as Ra-im's father appears with a mysterious drink and explains that it is the beginning and end of the magical spell and pours it into the characters' glasses. The father tells Joo-won that it is okay to forget him because he has fulfilled more than what was promised. He tells the daughter to live and be loved and states that this is the end of the magic he has created, and they should manifest their own real magic in their romance. As the father finishes his statement, the background instrumental music converts into the romantic theme song "You Are My Spring" by Sung Si-kyung, a prominent Korean singer, followed by the characters' consumption of the drink. The scene again uses shot-reverse shots to capture the emotions on their faces as they look into each other without any dialogue. The visual aesthetics of the scene highlight the fantastical elements in which we witness rose petals falling from the sky to the ground. The interplay between the fantastic and melodramatic affect renders it difficult to distinguish what is real and fantasy as the audience actively must translate the affective interludes for themselves. After drinking the wine, their bodies are swapped back to their original state. It is the father's use of a magical spell that restores order and enables the characters to consummate their love.

Conclusion

Secret Garden enables us not only to move beyond a nation-centric framework to the study of global media circulation but also to explore the cultural intersections between Korea and Latin America through the specificity of the fantastic Korean TV drama. More specifically, it prompts us to move beyond the questions of cultural proximity, transcultural affinity, and hybridity to understand the intertwinement between the fantastic, magical realism, and melodramatic affect. The cultural interplay between the fantastic and melodrama as popular elements of contemporary Korean serial television speaks to how our disenchantment with the chaos and uncertainty of the modern world defies rationality and urges the need to rediscover our enchantment with the social world manifested in heterosexual romance and global modernity. Borrowing Kenneth Chan's words, "the fantastic serves the modernizing discourse of rationality as a negative example of what must be transcended, superseded and left behind in the course of a universal process of modernization."[36] *Secret Garden* as a fantastic TV drama that requires viewers to participate in an active negotiation between what is fantasy and real illuminates the complex itineraries through which Korean TV dramas travel across the globe. As Ella Shohat and Evelyn Alsultany note, "cultural production, consumption, and reception are ultimately intertwined, with blurry boundaries made ever more entangled within multiple itineraries" to highlight East–West, North–South, and even South-on-South cultural flows.[37] Accordingly, *Secret Garden* illustrates how "postcolonial dislocations and transnational cultural flows have generated collaborative artistic dialogues that go beyond the mere question of influence."[38]

As non-Anglophone media texts circulate transnationally, they not only accrue meanings but also are susceptible to the othering process.

Nonetheless, the entanglement between East Asian and Latin American cultural productions prompts us to reconsider how the interaction between the fantastic, magical realism, and melodrama allows the global audience to be re-enchanted with modernity. Hence, a critical analysis of the fantastic in *Secret Garden* illuminates its complex itineraries with other cultures, particularly Latin America, as it becomes a discursive mode to address ambivalent views on modernity while offering entertainment and pleasure to the global audience.

Part Two

The Global Tensions in the Local

Chapter 4

Beautiful Desolation: Finding Apartheid in South Africa's Video Game Futures

Rachel Lara van der Merwe

In the shadow of massive, well-funded industries like Hollywood, smaller national cinema and television industries have historically struggled to establish economic viability, let alone contribute culturally to the construction of national identities.[1] For video games with more extensive technological and infrastructural needs, the struggle has been even more difficult,[2] especially when in competition with the dominant North American and Japanese industries.[3] Nevertheless, independent game developers and publishers keep emerging around the world and with them burgeoning new industries. The existence of national video game *cultures* that contribute to the representation and construction of collective national identities, however, remains unclear and under-researched.

In my own home country, there is a distinct lack of "South Africanness" in the most successful video games produced here. South African (SA) game developers focus on designing games for a global audience while SA gamers primarily purchase foreign-made video games.[4] Research indicates that this dynamic is quite common around the world: in order to establish a successful national video game industry, game developers must appeal to a transnational audience first.[5] When game developers *do* choose to incorporate a sense of national identity into their games, this decision is unusual.

This chapter focuses on a game that does just that: *Beautiful Desolation* (*BD*), a point-and-click adventure puzzler and role-playing game (RPG) that begins when an alien technological edifice called The Penrose appears off the coast of SA. While exploring the structure, Mark Leslie is propelled into a future post-apocalyptic version of SA and must find a way home. The game was released in 2020 by SA studio The Brotherhood, run by brothers Chris and Nic Bischoff. It followed two successful independent games for the studio (*Stasis*, 2015 and *Cayne*, 2017), and built on this success by using Kickstarter to raise US$138,457 for game development. *BD*, however, was their first game to be set in SA with SA characters and explicit references to SA culture. While their previous games were only released on Steam for PC, *BD* was also ported to the PlayStation 4 and Nintendo Switch, signaling The Brotherhood's ability and desire to reach a much broader audience. Despite criticism about the quality of the console ports, the game was generally positively received and widely reviewed.[6]

While other reasonably successful and explicitly African RPGs exist, such as *Aurion: Legacy of the Kori-Odan* from Cameroon, most game developers have not had the means to port their games to console. This makes *BD* unique in its capacity to promote the SA video game industry on the global market *and* in its ability to contribute to national identity representation and construction. Using the former factor (industry success) as context, in this chapter I focus on the latter: how does *BD* imagine SA? I explore how the visual, verbal, and procedural rhetoric of a recent, relatively successful SA video game engages and performs SA national identity within the context and confines of existing global industries. My analysis reveals an imagining of SA infused with colonial and apartheid values that conflicts with contemporary struggles to more fully decolonize SA, and I argue the global video game industry encourages the continued production of games with such values.

Context: Building a Nation with Video Games

Foundational to my argument are three propositions supported by existing research. First, national media industries play a role in cultivating a nation's sense of self, and national identity serves a role both internally (internal cohesion) and externally (performing a cohesive identity to the world). Second, due to the cost and infrastructure necessary to produce video games, it is difficult to establish a financially viable national video game industry unless it garners significant engagement globally. This proves challenging due to the already dominant Japanese and North American media infrastructures. Third, the logics of many successful and influential triple A[7] games are fundamentally colonial even when they implement more diverse representation.

Before I weave these together into my argument, I will briefly unpack each, beginning with the first proposition: national media industries play a role in cultivating a nation's sense of self. By using the term "nation" rather than "nation-state," I focus on what Benedict Anderson described as an "imagined political community...conceived as a deep horizontal comradeship."[8] Anderson demonstrates how the modern nation was a unique political entity best understood not by examining borders and government structures, but by studying shared sociopolitical consciousnesses that emerge through the collective consumption of circulated media. Anderson points to the expression of an abstract "German-ness" or "Mexican-ness" in print media capitalism that facilitated the construction of these new political entities in the nineteenth century across large geographic areas and spanning disparate people groups.

His findings were followed by those who pointed to the fundamental role of the novel in developing national identities,[9] and those who extended these ideas to other media, such as the concept of "national cinema."[10] Scholars like Ziad Fahmy have thus proposed replacing Anderson's notion of "print capitalism" with "media capitalism," in order to acknowledge the broader media infrastructures and modalities that facilitate national imagining and in order to "make room for the aural and oral alongside the visual."[11] Andrew Higson further notes that national cinema, and by extension other forms of media used to imagine the nation, serve both internal and external functions.[12] They can unify a nation's population across varying interests and understandings of what the nation is or should be, and they can communicate to the rest of the world the nation's "unique" identity and values. Both functions serve to construct an imagined coherence of a unified state, though, in reality, national identities are seldom coherent nor unified.

Very little research, however, has been done to explore the relationship between video games and national identity, perhaps because video games tend to be associated with other digital forms of technology that are linked to transnational or global identities or perhaps because games have erroneously been perceived as niche media, not circulated widely enough to affect national identity. However, research demonstrates that video games *are* integral to mainstream culture and integral to the production of cultures,[13] and game scholars increasingly look to the relationship between games and local or national cultures.[14] This focus on games is vital because they "are cultural in their own terms, rather than as a result of their similarities to forms like film."[15] For example, Nick Webber investigates how national identity formation might operate when the interactivity of games allows for diverging possible narrative outcomes.

Returning to the word "imagined" is crucial because it reminds us to think about who is doing the imagining. On the one hand, there are the game developers cultivating an imaginary within their narratives, but on the other hand, players imagine their own narratives through their game choices. All media forms—even print media and novels—are subject to the agency and interpretation of the media user, so, in a sense, all media are interactive. But understanding the varying natures of interactivity for distinct media helps us to understand how processes of individual and collective identity construction take place. For video games, Webber suggests that "the imagined community is then created through wondering what others did when confronted with a dilemma, and in some cases realizing that many would have acted as you did because national enculturation led them along that path."[16] Nevertheless, player interpretation is limited by the choices of the developers; such dilemmas must be coded into the game with set outcomes. These decisions, along with those regarding landscape, character, and general narrative design, reflect how game *designers* instill their own sense of nation into a game, regardless of how a player makes decisions.

The second proposition is that due to the cost and infrastructure necessary to produce video games, it is difficult to establish a financially viable national video game industry unless it can garner significant global engagement. In order to understand this, we can return briefly to Higson, who demonstrates that national media operate within a necessary tension between the global and national. On one hand, national media are constructed through an inward gaze upon the nation's self, but on the other hand, the process of establishing national identity (and identity in general) is necessarily also about differentiating the self from the other. For cinema, this means "asserting national autonomy in the face of (usually) Hollywood's international domination,"[17] but the establishment of a new national film industry infrastructure paradoxically also requires reliance upon resources and recognition from Hollywood.

We see a similar tension in the video game industry for game developers and publishers operating on the periphery in relation to the dominant video game industries of North America, Western Europe, and Japan,[18] perhaps experienced more strongly due to how much more expensive and complex it can be to produce a video game. Mark Wolf outlines the necessary infrastructure for a video game industry from "basic needs such as access to electrical power, verbal and visual literacy, and lifestyles that include leisure time for gameplay"[19] to "corporate structures to stabilize and maintain an industry, the necessary investment capital, and a large enough user base to make larger-scale productions financially feasible."[20] To give a sense of how much game development costs: in 2023, a high-fidelity triple-A game, sold on a console like the Sony PlayStation 5, costs around US$200 million to make, not including a similarly priced marketing budget, and can take two to three years to produce.[21]

Recent digital initiatives have made game development and distribution more affordable for amateurs and indie game studios.[22] For example, the free-to-download Unity Game Engine used by many developers worldwide[23] (including The Brotherhood to make *BD*) provides a sophisticated interface and toolbox for simplifying the process of game production. The emergence of online platforms like Steam, the App Store, and Google Play also means that game developers no longer have to rely on "traditional gatekeepers, from console manufacturers to publishers and brick-and-mortar retail distributors" in order to sell their games.[24]

But with this so-called democratization of game design, there are new costs, both financially and in terms of creative liberty. Jennifer Whitson observes that the structures and systems that shape who can participate in the industry have simply expanded into different configurations of "exclusion and gatekeeping."[25] With a flood of new games on the market, success is dependent on your game standing out, which in turn is dependent on your ability to not only design something unique and engaging but also market it effectively.[26] Data-driven design becomes a key strategy to address these concerns but, as Whitson shows, it is time-intensive, costly, and minimizes a developer's capacity for creative experimentation.[27]

Instead of relying upon traditional game publishers, game developers who opt for these new production models now find themselves reliant on the priorities of data analytics companies, digital platform intermediaries (e.g. Steam and smartphone app stores), and the developers behind game engines like Unity. While these companies make it much easier to initially enter the world of making games, they simultaneously "lock-in how amateurs and professionals build digital content for platforms"[28] and create longer-term financial dependencies. For instance, with Unity, while initial download may be free, "Unity generates revenue by taking a percentage of earnings made by Unity and Asset Store developers, charging advertisers per ad placement, subscription-based analytics and reports features, licensing products to resellers, and charging partners for developing computer-aided design tools for Unity."[29] Chris Young also points out that now Unity Technologies has developed a game development infrastructure upon which many developers heavily depend, they are "closing the walls around these open gates"[30] and expanding their monetization of the product.

Many independent game developers are motivated not by large-scale commercial success but rather by "simply being able to keep the team together to make the next game."[31] In order to earn enough revenue to be sustainable, these developers need to appeal to as broad a player base as possible.[32] As a result, game developers on the periphery tend to eschew local or national culture in their games in favor of "globally recognized" cultural tropes and game styles. Game developers that do have the capacity to make games about local culture are often directly supported by governmental funds, for example in the UK, Ireland, and France, where grants incentivize creating games "judged to be culturally specific to a national or European culture."[33] It does not appear that the SA government is currently providing this kind of support.

Even when governments indicate support and/or preference for games contributing to a national imaginary, for game developers, a prioritization of global standards persists.[34] John Vanderhoef argues that indie games with national markers "are exceptions rather than the rule in a global marketplace that privileges genre tropes and innovative mechanics over cultural narratives embedded in specific geographies and cultures."[35] Describing what he calls a "transnational indie imaginary," Vanderhoef suggests that games are intentionally developed as "culturally ambiguous,"[36] with an emphasis on familiar types of narratives and mechanics, while innovation takes place within the general bounds of gamic legibility. I have found the same to be true for SA games.[37] Performances of "South Africanness" are located in the performance of industry success on the global market—not within the game texts themselves.

This leads to the third proposition: the logics of many successful triple-A games are fundamentally colonial even when they implement more diverse representation on the level of the audiovisual. Though a game developer might not be designing a triple-A game, if their goal is to make a game legible to a broader audience, as we observed in the previous section, then they will model at least part of their game upon existing financial "success stories." Thus, it is useful to consider the elements and values that constitute games regarded as commercial successes, and how those might shape understandings of gamic legibility.

I use the concept "imperial play" to describe the colonial ideologies embedded within the video game industry and many video game texts, focusing especially on the procedural logics in mainstream, generally triple-A, games to demonstrate "how so many of our basic assumptions of how a video game should work are fundamentally wrapped up in colonial attitudes."[38] In previously making this argument, I highlighted how textual analysis that operates on the level of audiovisual representation, i.e. observing what we see and hear taking place in a media text, is not sufficient for analyzing video games that also incorporate a procedural, interactive logic that significantly changes the meaning of text. We need our textual analyses to also engage on the level of *procedural* representation.

I analyzed the example of Naughty Dog's *Uncharted: The Lost Legacy*, the latest installment in a franchise featuring treasure-hunters who fight and puzzle their way through ancient monuments, generally found in exotic locations of the Global South. While *The Lost Legacy* replaced the franchise's White[39] main character Nathan Drake with Chloe and Nadine, two female protagonists of color, the video game maintained its previous exploitative and colonial game mechanics. Marc James Carpenter makes a similar argument about games like *Civilization*, noting that "even as these games have added indigenous polities, they have maintained core game systems that reinforce settler colonial assumption."[40] For example, the steadily expanding maps in videogames like *Civilization* and *Total War: EMPIRE* tend to be used as tools for mastering and traversing the gamescape much like maps were used during colonialism.[41] Without analyzing the procedural mechanics of these games alongside the audiovisual components, a scholar would miss key contradictory aspects of meaning-making embedded in these texts.

Addressing these deeper, procedural levels of representation is crucial to better understanding how players experience and make sense of video games and, in turn, how these representations might shape society. Ian Bogost notes that video games are "media where cultural values themselves can be represented—for critique, satire, education, or commentary", and that we scholars need to address "the social practices *of playing* the game", not just those "*represented in* the game."[42] My concept of imperial play builds upon this argument and those of other game scholars attentive to such concerns: Alexander Galloway describes algorithms of control in games;[43] Geoff King shows how such an embedded logic of control and mastery within games can reify the ideology that success in society entails mastery of one's body and environment;[44] Souvik Mukherjee argues "the video game might become a medium of subalternity";[45] and Christopher Paul points to the toxic meritocracy that transcends gameplay and characterizes the logics of the surrounding game culture itself.[46] The concept "imperial play" directly links these procedural patterns to the colonial capitalist ideologies that produce them.

Woven together, the three propositions raised above suggest that in order to accomplish global legibility and/or some form of commercial success, game developers are likely to model the logics of existing successful games, many of which tend to be inherently colonial. If creators also attempt to represent their nation, then one can infer that colonial values will likely be woven into whichever national identity and culture is depicted within the game. The nation itself is a colonial entity, so any construction of national identity necessarily participates in colonial structures;[47] however, for nations such as SA that are actively trying to decolonize within the limitations of a nation-state, introducing further colonial logics into the national imaginary is counterproductive.

Methodology

To explore how SA is imagined within *BD*, I conducted a rhetorical and critical discourse analysis through playing the game in its entirety and watching gameplay on YouTube. Rhetorically, I studied not just visual and verbal rhetoric deployed throughout the game but also procedural rhetoric, the "practice of using processes persuasively."[48] As Anna Anthropy notes, "Games tell stories…not just through their explicit content but through the logic of their design, and the systems they choose to model."[49] Even as I attended to how characters and gamescapes *look* and *sound*, I also asked what was possible in the game, and what choices was I given as a player?

Building upon the rhetorical analysis (the values and messages I perceived privileged in the game's representations and processes), I did a critical discourse analysis to see how those values and messages reproduce or challenge existing societal discourses.[50] In particular, I wanted to understand how SA national identity was constructed, and how it was related to apartheid and colonialism. I also investigated how other aspects of cultural identity (gender, race, socioeconomic class, and sexual orientation) were depicted as they inform expressions of collective identity, such as national identity. For this chapter, I focus on my observations regarding gender and race.

Analysis: Entering into the Beautiful Desolation

The video game *BD* plunges us into 1976 Cape Town on a stormy evening when a strange triangular structure abruptly appears in the sky. The arrival of the Penrose coincides with violent atmospheric conditions that cause a city-wide power outage, radio signal failure, and ultimately a powerful shockwave. We witness the disaster from the backseat of a couple's car, tossed through the air by the shockwave, but then travel forward ten years to learn that protagonist and principal avatar, Mark, survived the accident while his wife didn't.

The Penrose turns out to be "an object of untold technological abundance that would advance civilization on all frontiers: hunger and disease eradicated, energy mastered, immortality conquered,"[51] but Mark, an investigative journalist deeply shaken by the tragedy, harbors concerns about the Penrose. Determined to uncover where it came from and what the military is actually doing with it, Mark convinces his brother Don to fly him onto the structure. During this mission, the brothers are inexplicably transported into a post-apocalyptic future where new evolved alien civilizations have arisen in the wake of global self-destruction, catalyzed by societal struggles over the technological discoveries from the Penrose.

The majority of the game takes place in this future where our prime objective is to get home. None of the game is set in present-day SA and what little of 1970s and 1980s SA we see depicts an alternative history. While *BD's* SA is a speculative construct, its SA is nevertheless grounded in a familiar, existing SA. SA players will easily pick this up through various cultural signifiers scattered throughout the game; e.g. common Afrikaans terms and SA lingo are dropped into conversation ("Ja" for Yes) or used

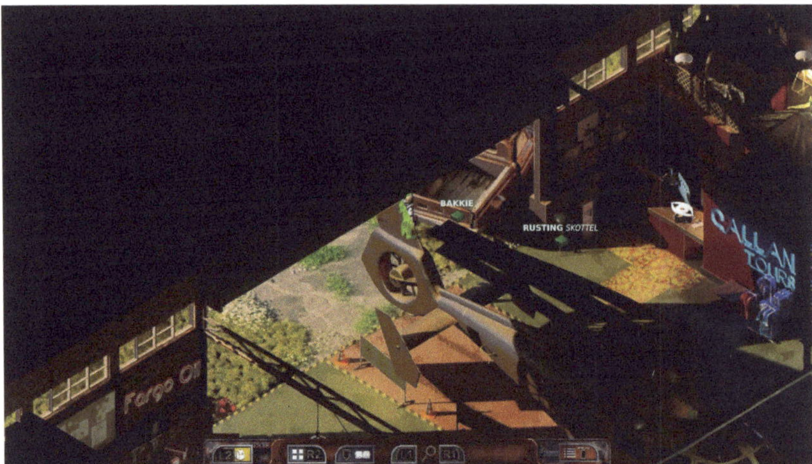

Figure 01. Callan Tours airfield shed in *Beautiful Desolation*. Screengrab by author.

to label items in gamescapes (for example in Figure 1, "bakkie": pick-up truck; "skottel": Weber grill).

Our protagonists in this game are both White men, and as we join them on their adventure, a White patriarchal vision of SA emerges. Though we travel into the future, ideologically we never leave 1980s SA and its apartheid national imaginary. I will begin by pointing to the colonial ideology embedded in the game's mechanics before addressing the audiovisual representations of race and gender that reify apartheid thinking.

Ideological mechanics in *BD*: White saviors and incidental genocides

There are no real puzzles or combat in this game, unlike many RPGs. Instead, most of the game entails running around a beautiful, strange world while trying to fix decades-old tensions between communities. By completing errands for new acquaintances, you gradually expand your map access and locate the spare parts you need to repair your ship. These tasks could be innocuous, but Mark and Don actually wield a significant amount of power and influence within this new world. Take for an example the conversation in Figure 2:

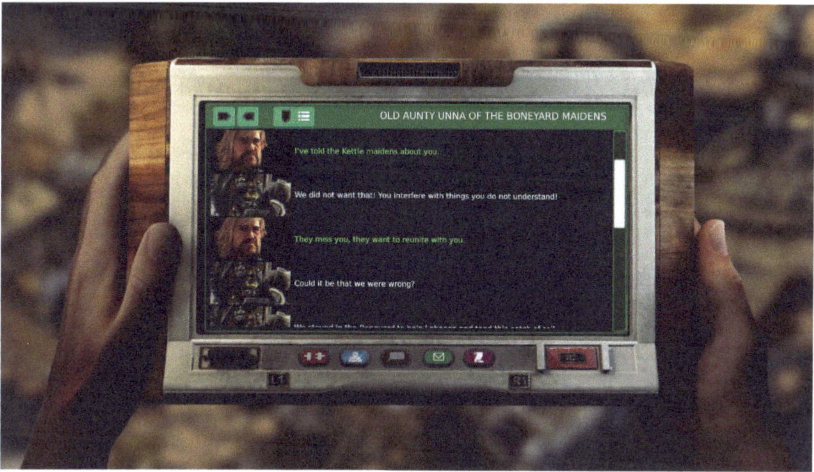

Figure 02. Conversation with Old Aunty Unna of the Boneyard Maidens in *Beautiful Desolation*. Screengrab by author.

The Boneyard Maidens were part of a larger community called the Kettle Maidens, but they had a disagreement years ago and left to start their own settlement. The two communities have been estranged, but in our journey, we engage with both. Each community agrees to help us so long as we respect their individual politics and history; however, the game makes it advantageous for us to interfere. We ignore the Boneyard Maidens' wishes for privacy and tell the Kettle Maidens where they are. Mark is a complete outsider meddling in issues he cannot possibly understand, but our brash interference is rewarded. Unna protests weakly before very suddenly declaring that the Boneyard Maidens were wrong and thanking Mark for his intervention. This is just one example in *BD* of the classic colonial White savior trope at play, where the White man, an outsider with no prior experience in the local context, comes in to save a so-called primitive, less intelligent people from themselves.[52]

Most of our errands are not simple acts of service or fair trades but amount to political maneuvering wherein the people we meet are reduced to pieces on a chessboard. Through Mark, we occupy a god-like position from which we determine the fate of entire people-groups; e.g. at one point we arbitrate between the Hanasi and the Chiznyama peoples and must decide to whom we will give map information. From what we learn in the game, the Chiznyama have enslaved the Hanasi for generations, so the groups hate each other bitterly. By giving the map to one group, we provide the means by which that group can destroy the other. Our companions, Don and Pooch (a robot dog), each offer opposing advice in these types of decision-making situations, such as arguing that the Hanasi were enslaved, so surely they deserve revenge.

This is not the only genocide that I facilitated while playing the game. Without fully understanding what I was doing, I made a "click-of-a-button" decision that murdered the Caecus people. Later in the game I decided between the lives of the Moss People, Dr. Anna, and the Nest hive intelligence. Genocides occurred not because of my ineptitude as a player, but because they were baked into the logic of the game. Besides the Caecus situation, it was not a question of genocide or not, but rather a question of *who* experiences genocide. Other forms of binary, "zero-sum" thinking also occurred regularly throughout the game. I was always playing sides, picking between this-vs.-that, and pretending to be everyone's friend, while my interest was instrumental or voyeuristically curious about the "other-ness" of this foreign world.

The most fundamental binary in the game is the "us-vs.-them" dynamic, and the driving force in gameplay remains trying to get "us" home, whatever it might take. In a side conversation, Don suggests that maybe we should stay and make our lives in this world. In response, we argue that we need to go back to our own time and prevent "all of this from ever happening." Mark refers here to the apocalypse that took place because humanity meddled with the Penrose. While at first Mark's argument seems to be a critique of techno-utopianism, implicit in his stance is the assumption that all the civilizations and lives that have emerged post-apocalypse do not deserve to exist: that 1980s SA (and the rest of the world) deserves a second chance more than this emergent world deserves to remain in existence. From what I could determine, it is not possible to choose an outcome in *BD* that allows Mark to remain in futuristic SA, short of refusing to play the game to completion. Thus, all genocides authorized throughout gameplay inevitably appear irrelevant in light of the mega-genocide we commit against this entire future timeline.

Race and Gender in *BD*: The Alien Everyone Else

The "us-vs.-them" dynamic mentioned above is integral for understanding how race and gender are depicted in *BD*. Though the game begins in a version of 1970s and 1980s SA, there are no direct references to an apartheid system that would have been in place at that time, or even depictions of a multiracial society, whether separated or integrated. However, the game *does* imagine a racialized and largely segregated futuristic southern African society.

Our protagonists, the "us," are White and male, and everyone else, who are not both those things, are coded as alien and strange. Mark's White wife Charlize dies in the opening scene, effectively erasing her from the narrative. In their abrupt time travel to the future, Mark and Don accidentally bring with them a robot designed to resemble a dog. The robot had been guarding the section of Penrose where they landed and wishes to return home. It agrees to travel with them, becoming a companion avatar we occasionally control in the game. But "Pooch" is clearly not of equal standing and is coded as "other" through both gender and in being not-human. While never explicitly gendered in the game, "Pooch" is marked with stereotypical and concerning indicators of femininity, such as a higher pitched voice and a nagging personality.

Once we begin engaging with the locals in this future, it is difficult to distinguish between who is human and who is alien, and perhaps who is both. We never learn the nature of evolution and settlement that took place after the apocalypse, so our encounters are largely dehistoricized. Everyone who isn't a protagonist is experienced as alien and other. The alien and unfamiliar is always a bit unsettling, but in the context of the game, such characters are often visually and aurally coded as disturbing (see Figure 3), and little is done to challenge or transform those perspectives. Mark does not treat these characters with respect, but rather as tools by which to get home. When Don or Pooch challenge him, they do so based on abstract ethical principles while "speaking for" these non-player characters (NPCs) without ever actually listening to or asking the NPCs what *they* want. The alien NPCs remain alien.

Furthermore, characters encountered are often coded racially. Jarek the Mechanic speaks with an implied Jamaican accent (see Figure 4). Intimidating guards protecting the Sanctuary of Witherberg speak a language that is visually depicted using unfamiliar symbols but aurally sounds quite similar to isiXhosa, a Nguni language from southern Africa that incorporates clicking phonetics. Thus, players encounter characters that are racially depicted as Black, regardless of the color of the character's skin, and that are simultaneously depicted as alien and disturbing—a very concerning combination reminiscent of colonial and

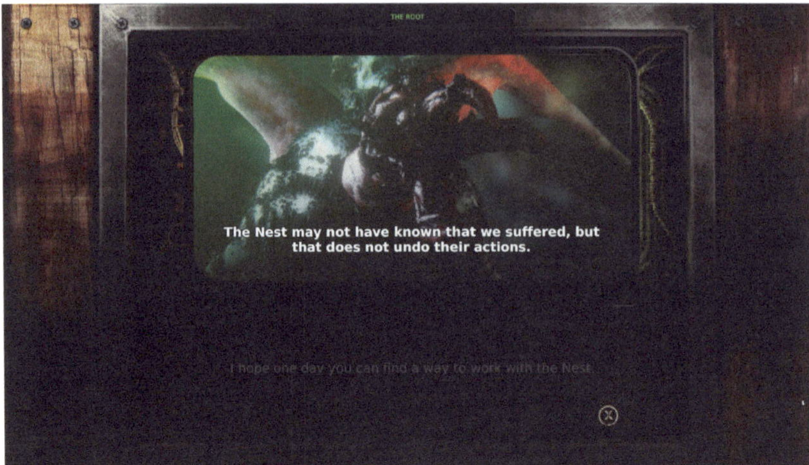

Figure 03. Conversation with The Root in *Beautiful Desolation*. Screengrab by author.

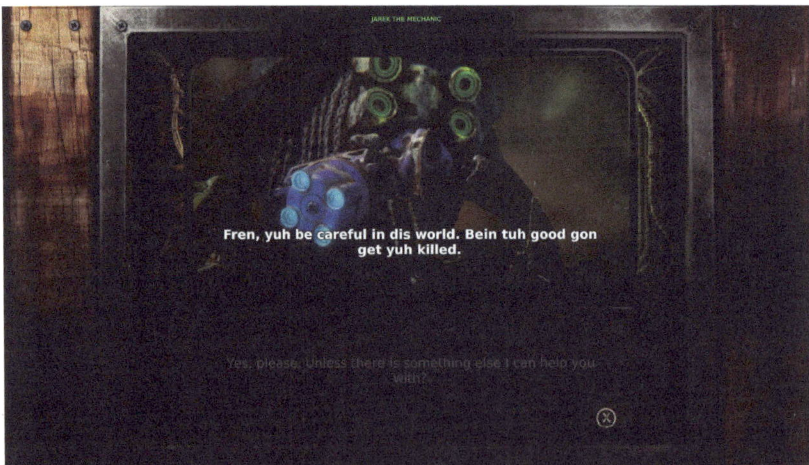

Figure 04. Conversation with Jarek the Mechanic in *Beautiful Desolation*. Screengrab by author.

apartheid narratives. For some characters, the associations of being Black with negative societal values are even more pronounced. The Hanasi people, implied to be Bantu descendants based on their accents, are portrayed as degenerate, lazy, and lacking moral values. They worship their dead hanging around the city, and the city itself is in disarray.

Many citizens are on drugs, and Don exclaims that the place smells like rotten meat. These unfavorable depictions hold an uncanny semblance to historical narratives that were used to justify colonialism as a "civilizing" or "redemptive" mission.

Even when characters are not coded with blatantly negative values, we are reminded frequently that the locals all need help. By design, they are non-playable characters placed throughout the game to serve Mark and Don while simultaneously Mark and Don sweep in as White saviors to fix their decades-old conflicts or to complete tasks that somehow these characters were unable to do themselves.

Conclusion

Beautiful Desolation's audiovisual representations of race and gender reflect colonial and patriarchal ideologies, and the game mechanics, which require players to play a White savior while simultaneously committing genocide, further reify the colonial values embedded throughout. Combined with the use of SA cultural markers and an absence of any in-game critical reflection or indication of satire, the national imaginary cultivated in this futuristic SA is one that centers Whiteness and masculinity, reminiscent of its apartheid past.

In trying to develop a video game that both embraces a SA context and might be legible to a global audience, the strategy that The Brotherhood took results in a game that (1) privileges White masculinity in its representations, perhaps catering to a presumed predominately White male audience, and (2) implements "imperial play," i.e. the colonial logics as seen in many successful triple-A games—although these choices contradict and even undermine the post-apartheid, decolonial identity that many South Africans are striving to build. One could argue that their game even encourages a return to a colonial imagining of the region.

As I have demonstrated above, scholarship indicates that indie game developers are deeply influenced by what constitutes success in dominant video game markets and these existing models are profoundly colonial in their values. *BD* exemplifies how the video game industry continues to sustain the production and success of male-centric games endowed with colonial values. At the moment of writing, this is the SA game most likely to circulate widely at a global level, meaning this is the story about SA that gamers will more likely encounter. What would it take to see instead enjoyable adventure RPG video games, with decolonial values reflecting a diverse range of cultures, find a global audience? Some success has already occurred with games like Iñupiat *Never Alone (Kisima Ingitchuna)*, but this is where scholars should consider partnering with indie, international game developers to explore strategies for breaking the industry cycle that privileges colonially informed games and marginalizes games instilled with decolonial, counter-cultural social imaginaries.

Chapter 5

Up North: The Re-Narration of Northeast Nigeria

Añulika Agina and Anthony Adah

The main concern of this chapter is how a popular Nigerian film, *Up North* (2018), "converses" with or ideologically "narrates" its themes, subjects, and social reality. Directed by Tope Oshin and set in Lagos (Southwest) and Bauchi (Northeast), Nigeria, the film reflects on the tensions between Bassey and his father, Chief Otuekong. After studying abroad, a recalcitrant Bassey returns home to discover the future imagined for him by his father. Otuekong intends to merge the family business with a bigger one and arrange a marriage between Bassey and his business partner's daughter to ensure the longevity of the company. Bassey's rejection of these plans causes his father to take punitive measures by freezing his bank accounts and insisting that he goes to Bauchi, Northern Nigeria (see the map of Nigeria in Figure 1 below), for the National Youth Service. Initially furious at the thought of Bauchi, but overpowered by his father's bodyguard, Bassey resigns himself to his new situation amid challenges and support from the locals. He coaches a group of schoolgirls while publicizing his activities through social media, thereby frustrating his father's efforts to redeploy him to Lagos. The film leads us to articulate the overarching question that the chapter engages with: *How does Up North dialogue with and re-narrate the location and people of Northeast Nigeria given the familiar visions of violence that the geographical area is known for?* Since 2002, mainstream media have been awash with details of the terrorist group Boko Haram and their insurgent activities in Northeast Nigeria. Such activities have mainly been to instill fear—through suicide bombings and kidnappings—in the citizens of the region to force them to

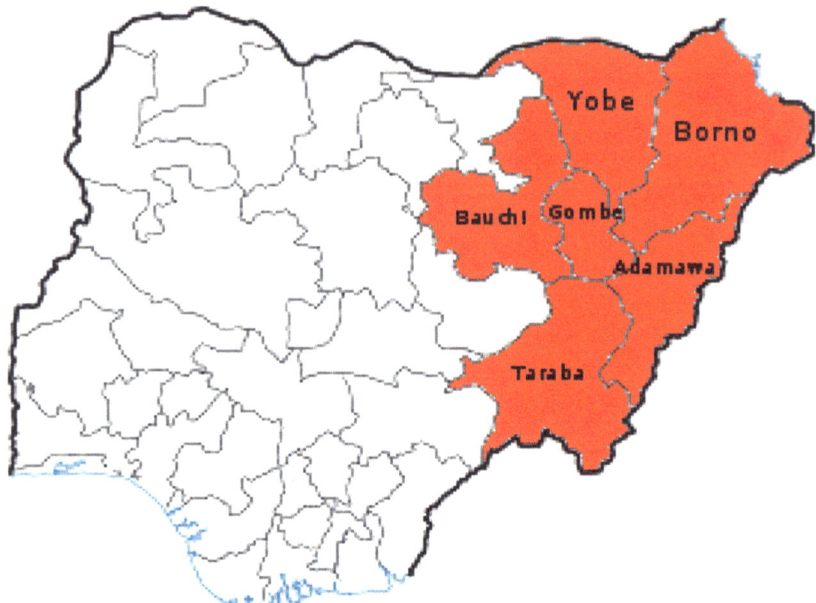

Figure 01. This map of Nigeria highlights the six northeast states from which Boko Haram activities take place.

do their bidding. The overall aim of this terrorist group has been to reject and eradicate infidels (i.e. non-Muslims) and to resist all influences of the West, including education and Christianity.

In 2014, Boko Haram kidnapped 276 schoolgirls from their dormitory in Chibok, Northeast Nigeria, and hid them in the Sambisa Forest in Borno State for three years. Efforts to liberate the girls from their captors proved futile at first. However, with a global outcry and social media campaign #bringbackourgirls, coupled with military and diplomatic assistance from the United States and especially from Europe, some girls were released but not without substantial mental health problems and physical abuse. Many of the returnees had been viciously indoctrinated, radicalized, forced to marry their captors or renounce Christianity, and given severe beatings whenever they tried to escape or challenge the terrorists. In their book-length treatment of this episode, Joe Parkinson and Drew Hinshaw observed that

> the Chibok Secondary School was meant to be an outpost through which Western education spread through Nigeria's conservative Northeast. But

> It was now almost the last of Borno State's 1,947 schools left open. For months, Boko Haram's men had been attacking campuses, torching at least 50 schools and murdering teachers they accused of polluting children with godless knowledge.[1]

The effects of the Chibok kidnap, the largest of its kind in the Northeast in terms of the global outcry it sparked, heightened the national security problem in the region, accounting for mass migration to other parts of the country, closure of schools and churches, and an end to public gatherings. Visits to the north by southerners became a thing of the past since the operations of Boko Haram spawned several other (counter)attacks by the ever-increasing Islamic fundamentalist *cum* terrorist groups, sub-factions, and the Nigerian military. What made the Chibok episode particularly traumatizing is that parents and teachers had debated the wisdom behind leaving the school open, given the rising militancy in the region. After much deliberation, the parties agreed to keep the school open just for the duration of the senior students' final exams. But with the kidnap, schools and education were never heard of again in the region, and many became abandoned.

So when a southern Nigerian film crew, driven by Lagos-based Anakle Films and Inkblot Productions, moved northwards to shoot a film, *Up North*, it was considered "a feat that has never been attempted in the Nigerian film industry."[2] A chance meeting between Anakle Films CEO Editi Effiong and Bauchi State's governor at the time, Mohammed Abdullahi Abubakar, was pivotal to the actualization of the film, which had over 25,000 background actors, five cameras, and a crew of 160 people, including over 50 security personnel. *Up North* needed a large number of people for a re-narration of prevailing news stories in the popular press of mass murder, militancy, and kidnap in Borno and Bauchi, both in the same geographical area. The film injected a refreshing practice into Nigeria's mediascape because it was a cross-regional production (south and north of Nigeria) and it offered an alternative story of Northeast Nigeria. The term alternative media has been used to identify diverse ideas and practices. Chris Atton observes, for instance, that while the term could be used to map media that "generate non-standard, often infractory, methods of creation, production and distribution," it is also possible to think of alternative "content."[3] Similarly, and closer to our usage of alternative media, is Mitzi Waltz's assertion that the term refers to "any form of media which constitutes an alternative to, or positions itself in opposition to, widely available and consumed mass media products."[4] Within the context of this essay, we understand alternative media to include films that draw attention to significant but ignored regional/national stories, thereby enabling, in a Gramscian sense,[5] a counter-hegemonic narrative that interrogates and rebalances mainstream media portrayal of Northeastern Nigeria, while offering a different possible national future.

We chose *Up North* because it envisions an alternative Northern Nigeria, which has been previously unseen in the dominant narratives of brutality that daily make the headlines in local and international news media. It subtly challenges and critiques Boko Haram's Northeast by drawing in the uncommon practice of political endorsement through the figure of the state governor who made a cameo appearance. The film's setting is not a place of bombings and kidnaps but a beautiful and culturally rich location that values and defends education and religion and openly welcomes visitors. It uses the same instrument rejected by Boko Haram: the education of the female to offer alternative visions of people and place in the 99-minute-long film. By this choice, we argue that the popular Nollywood film functions as alternative media by providing social commentary on women-enabled education, thus tacitly entering broader discussions of Nollywood's ability to comment on social disintegration and political change.[6]

In the following sections, we briefly examine Nollywood, the Nigerian film industry, to show how the popular and commercial film culture it birthed became a powerful and alternative media outlet. This is immediately followed by a brief exposé on the activities of Boko Haram, the terrorist group operating in parts of Northern Nigeria, especially Borno and Bauchi, where *Up North* was set. The section on Boko Haram is important because of the main argument of this chapter, which is that *Up North* re-narrates a Northeastern Nigeria pillaged by the terrorist group. In the final section, we offer a reading of the film through its stylistic and other aesthetic features.

Nollywood: Popular, Alternative, and Subversive

The Nigerian film industry, referred to as Nollywood, was born in 1992, with the production of a family drama titled *Living in Bondage*. This period marked a major turn in the history of filmmaking in Nigeria because it launched the home video boom, made films available on VHS cassettes in people's homes, and attracted larger audiences, all thanks to available new digital technologies. The filmmaking period from the 1970s to the early 1990s was less known even though it produced a crop of filmmakers who had previously trained and worked in the popular Yoruba traveling theatre and television industries. But fewer Nigerians at home and abroad ever got to see the celluloid films that the likes of Francis Oladele, Ola Balogun, and Eddie Ugboma made. Our attention in this chapter, however, is focused on the period from 1992, which triggered the growth of what currently exists today.

Growing out of popular expressions of the self and community, creative enterprise and storytelling, Nollywood represents the ways through which ordinary people denied official channels of communication respond to societal issues such as those raised in *Up North*. Based on his interactions with television producers who later migrated to filmmaking, Jonathan Haynes documented the following: "Even if you shared thoughts in the public space...as we were all drinking, you could be taken into State Security Services for questioning for two or three days...It was that bad, not to talk of reproducing things like that on television."[7] This lack of freedom of speech and artistic expression, a feature of the military regimes from 1966 to 1999, meant that people either had to focus on apolitical themes on television (and film) or seek alternative channels of expression, where the government was unlikely to look. Nollywood was therefore self-censored until the post-military era, when it began to produce political critiques.[8] Prior to 1999, Nollywood filmmakers were criticized by scholars such as the historian Biodun Jeyifo and elite Nigerians including the executive director of the Censors Board, James Ademola, for not engaging with the deep sociopolitical conditions of the state in their narratives. It was Jonathan Haynes who tied this absence of politically conscious narratives to the stiff censorship of the military period, revealing the shift since the end of military dictatorship from apolitical to political themes. From 2000, filmmakers felt free enough to explore political topics again. By 2009, critics were making the point that Nollywood was boldly addressing sociopolitical themes and denouncing a host of illegal wealth obtained through institutionalized malfeasance.

Nollywood is today the largest film industry in sub-Saharan Africa, with over 2,500 titles per annum, according to UNESCO, and a significant contributor to Nigeria's gross domestic product. The films are mostly financed locally through self-sourced funding (between N5 million and

N100 million = US$12,000 and US$240,000), and since 2011, federal and state governments have shown more interest by offering minimal funding to a handful of filmmakers. To a large extent, Nollywood's self-financing model allowed filmmakers to tell stories without external control. On very few occasions, however, the National Film and Video Censors Board (NFVCB) banned films for containing potentially incendiary images or dialogue.[9] Its huge popularity distinguishes Nollywood among local and continent-wide audiences, a feature that sets it apart from its antecedents not only in Nigeria but also in various parts of Africa. Due to small budget sizes, most productions are completed within a month in Lagos. To have a film crew move out of Lagos in the Southwest to the North is noteworthy. Produced on a budget of N94 million (US$225,600) and judged one of the best films of 2018, *Up North* featured among the top twenty-five films of all time according to FilmOne Entertainment, the leading cinema chain in the country and publisher of the Nigerian Box Office Yearbook.

Using Chris Atton's alternative media as a conceptual tool,[10] we examine through textual and contextual analyses the Nigerian film *Up North* as an introduction to and a re-narration of an often-ignored vision of Bauchi State, which shares a border with Borno State, the den of Boko Haram, the Islamic insurgency group. Atton's use of alternative media in reference to non-official mainstream media (community, grassroots or radical media, electronic and internet-enabled modes of communication) and Tony Harcup's perspective[11] provide some insight into our reading of *Up North* as an alternative version of the same geographical location now known for violence and hostage-taking, among other extremist activities. According to Atton, the range of media products and activities understood as alternative media includes a hybridized field that comprises artistic and literary practices, which admit of extremes of transformation in products, processes, and relations. Refocusing their gaze from the dominant and wealthy, alternative media would encompass pamphlets of the less dominant, whatever is not accepted, permitted, or available in mainstream media,[12] or activist AIDS videos as politically expressive forms of low-budget community engagement.[13] Alternative media in this sense challenges the status quo while evoking a call to action from the various perspectives of dissident and underrepresented people.

Our use of alternative media goes beyond the concept of the press to include Nollywood films, most of which seek to challenge and change society in discernible ways. Interestingly, by engaging explicitly in sociopolitical national subjects, Nollywood could be said to perform as a national cinema practice. Although slippery to any fast definition, the concept of national cinema loosely functions as a placeholder for filmmakers, institutions of filmmaking, film texts, and their audiences within some generalized geo-social space. Whereas theorists such as Andrew Higson deemphasize the critical value of the concept given intensified globalization,[14] others such as Susan Hayward and Stephen Crofts suggest that national cinema may still be mobilized for significant heuristic benefits.[15] To Crofts, for instance, the concept should be nimble enough "to challenge the fictional homogenisation of much discourse on national cinema, and in others to support them."[16] If Boko Haram's efforts were to provide a homogenizing narrative of a violent Northeast Nigeria, *Up North* offers an alternative counter-narrative. The fact of traveling northwards to shoot the film and collaborating with local talent is, in itself, alternative and subversive, refusing to accept the familiar images of the north while inviting viewers to rethink the location through beautiful shots of the landscape, its people, and festivals. At the end of the film, popular sentiments about the north, which are mostly those of fear, anger, and disgust, give way to touristic longings and a desire for social change through education. For Nancy Kranich, the term alternative media is used to describe the collection of small independent publishers seeking to complement mainstream or corporate media.[17] A similar arrangement can be seen among Nollywood filmmakers. Nollywood as described by Haynes has never functioned like the studio system in North America but has been made up of pockets of culture entrepreneurs who raise meager sums for film productions, make little profits on them, and move on to other film projects. The model is risky since the failure of one project could be ruinous to the small-scale entrepreneur, but the industry has been sustained by numerous entrants coming and going at will.

As an alternative vision of Northeast Nigeria, one that embraces education, sports, dialogue, culture, and development (elements rejected by Boko Haram), we read the social issue film as a tribute to a ravaged and insecure people and place. *Up North* follows MIT graduate Bassey (Bankole Wellington, aka Banky W.), whose wealthy father, Chief Etuekong (Kanayo O. Kanayo, aka KOK), gets him deployed to Bauchi for a year-long national service (notice the t-shirt worn by the lead character, printed NYSC—National Youth Service Corps) to both punish him and coerce him into taking over and ensuring the longevity of the family business. Bassey resists but gets to Bauchi and manages to thwart his father's plans by falling in love with the people and the city through his work in a secondary school. When *Up North* was released in December 2018, popular Nollywood and media blogs were brimming over with positive reviews because it featured one of Nigeria's pop music icons, Banky W., in the lead role with other celebrity actors like Kanayo O. Kanayo and Adesuwa Etomi, and was the first Nigerian film to cast an incumbent state governor to play his official role. This meant an institutional endorsement of the film, including the deployment of state security apparatus for the protection of cast and crew from threats to life and property. Setting aside his official duties to audition for the role, Mohammed Abdullahi Abubakar's appearance on set was a powerful testimony of the role and position that Nollywood has come to occupy in the Nigerian imagination and specifically in the publicity of an alternative, re-imagined Bauchi. Prior to the production of *Up North*, Nollywood stars were the endorsers of politicians and corporate entities, but with this film, we witness a reversal of roles in the politician's (or state celebrity's) endorsement and appropriation of the film. Without a doubt, the film was at once inspirational and resistant, invoking new forms of collaboration between filmmakers in the north and south and simultaneously defying Boko Haram and the fear it instills.

Boko Haram and the Rejection of Western Education in Northeast Nigeria

Although the group called Boko Haram emerged in 2002 under the leadership of Mohammed Yusef,[18] its beginnings go further back to the activities of another controversial self-proclaimed Muslim prophet, Mohammed Marwa (aka Maitatsine: "the one who damns"), who, with his ardent followers, terrorized Northern Nigeria from the late 1970s until his capture by the police and death in 1980. Like Maitatsine, Boko Haram (translated as "Western education is forbidden") eschews all things Western, including books and communication technologies (radio, television, cars, etc.), but ironically uses social media to broadcast its threats to the government and people of Nigeria. Given these goals, it is not surprising that the only way to practice the lifestyle the sect advocates is to create its own Caliphate. That said, Boko Haram as an iteration of violent religious advocacy is different from the movement Maitatsine championed because the focus of the latter was to foreground poor economic conditions and uneven distribution of wealth.

Since 2009, Boko Haram has terrorized Nigeria (especially pockets of the Northeast) with bombings, kidnappings, banditry, and extortions. In the public's consciousness, news, and social media circulations, Northeastern Nigeria swarms with Boko Haram's violent operations. In the US State Department's travel advisory to Nigeria, the Northeast is clearly marked out as a "Do Not Travel To" zone (travel.state.gov). While such warnings might come off as a tendency to exaggerate violent conditions in developing nations by the "developed" world, Nigerians are just as concerned and, perhaps, do little to nuance or counter the stereotype of Northeast Nigeria as a Hobbesian environment.

Scholarly discourse on the emergence, history, and actions of Boko Haram abounds, is varied, and is cast along Islamic, class, ethnic, and political lines. Framed as one of the world's deadliest jihadist groups in the world, Boko Haram's terrorist activities have left tens of thousands of people in Nigeria (and neighboring Niger, Chad, and Cameroon) dead and millions displaced. Several extrajudicial killings including that of the leader, Mohammed Yusuf, in 2009 precipitated counterattacks with deadly repercussions for the military, civilians, and members of the group itself. As Atta Barkindo observed, what was originally a peaceful existence of a group desirous to propagate Islamic ideology, albeit questionably as in to Islamize the Nigerian state, morphed into violent extremism due to the state's misrepresentation of the group. In his words, "A massive national and cross-border military deployment supported by the Civilian Joint Task Force, mercenaries, local hunters and vigilantes has failed to eradicate the group."[19] Instead, the group's recruitment effort—even of highly educated individuals—its operational tactics, and its exploitation of Islamic and cultural history to spread its ideology in Northeast Nigeria intensified, leading to a takeover of the region. The result is a heightened security threat among civilians and the military and the use of terror to instill fear.

Locals in the north and elsewhere in the country have their lives ruled by this fear, although the impact of the terrorist activities is less felt in the southwestern region, where many Nollywood filmmakers work. To justify its operations, Boko Haram alludes to the environmental degradation and corruption among government officials that plunge indigenes into deep poverty; hence its efforts to seek justice.[20] In spite of this narrative, locals are doubtful of Boko Haram's intentions as the violent attacks seemingly wreck more havoc on civilians, who are easy targets and without the security apparatuses mounted by the military and government officials.

In this social context, therefore, to be transferred to Borno State or anywhere Northeast is to be sent to one's death. This mainstream popular opinion of Northeast Nigeria as a Boko Haram hotbed provides an opening into Bassey's initial refusal to take up national service in Bauchi.

A brief look at the NYSC scheme is essential to provide some background to Bassey's mandatory year of service in Bauchi and narrative adventure. Following the Nigerian Civil War and from 1973, the Nigerian government established the scheme as a unity project. It entailed deploying fresh Nigerian graduates to locations within the country where they neither studied nor originated from. The youth spent the first three-week period undergoing paramilitary training to withstand physical and other relocation challenges. Thereafter, they received primary assignments for a year and held weekly and monthly meetings with peers and officials of the scheme "with a view to the proper encouragement and development of common ties among the youths of Nigeria and the promotion of national unity."[21] The scheme was a laudable project, comparable in merit to the reconciliation projects of post-war or politically divided countries like Rwanda and South Africa. But its execution was a different ballgame. The failure of political institutions to boost security and guarantee the welfare of the youth contributed to ruining the scheme's objectives. Children of wealthy or influential parents compromised the process, and with deteriorating security in the country, serving in the Northern states as depicted in *Up North* became anathema to many. Given his parents' economic class, Bassey expects redeployment upon learning about his posting to Bauchi State, but that did not happen. Instead, his father insists that he go to Bauchi to teach him a lesson—traditional respect for the patriarch. He orders his redeployment to Lagos only when the chief learns that Bassey is making the most of his Northern experience.

Formal and Stylistic Features of *Up North*

While the audience may seize upon their knowledge of terrorism as a crutch to interpret dramatic situations in the Northeast, it is worth recalling that Boko Haram's initial fight was against Western education and culture. Part of the film's success is focusing the narration on a generalized sense of the West that most Nigerians can understand. When the film opens, the protagonist, Bassey, is introduced with what would become his sound motif, a popular Nigerian hit song, *Omode Meta Sere* by Tony Tetuila. Based on a folktale, the song not only establishes Bassey (Olubankole Wellington aka Banky W.) as a cool "baddest" guy, but it also hints at the three major challenges Bassey must overcome as the narrative unfolds. In the Yoruba folktale, *Ọmọdé Mẹta*, three kids playfully boast that they can climb a palm tree without any tools, swim across the ocean, and hit the heavens with an arrow respectively. Challenged by the king for their audacity, the kids tearfully begin their tasks, failing in the initial attempts, but after some prodding and cheering from the wider community, they finally succeed. Similarly, Bassey must overcome three challenges: succeed where his father expects him to fail, convince his Northern hosts of his genuineness and industry, and persuade Miriam (Rahama Sadau) that his love is wholesome and not exploitative. *Omode Meta Sere*, therefore, sets up Bassey's challenges and invites the community to be allies. Stylistically, *Up North*'s use of folklore in a popular commercial medium shows how a Nollywood film can be a site of convergence for exploring folklore, popular music, and film and providing a multilayered intertextual practice that is yet accessible to various audiences.

The narrative structure of the film is linear, with forward progression once Bassey's father punitively thrusts him into a challenging journey to Northeast Nigeria. Up north in Bauchi, Bassey meets initial resistance and must learn to navigate local social and religious mores. His primary NYSC assignment is to teach in an all-girls high school. When he tries to engage the students in athletics, he encounters resistance from a conservative religious father who insists that sports are not for girls. Bassey, therefore, must reassure the Islamic parents and his collaborator-love interest, Miriam, about the wholesomeness of his intentions.

From the outset, it is obvious that *Up North* utilizes elements of parallel structuring. For example, just as the Northern father "protects" his daughter from Bassey's southern Nigerian (Western) influence, so does the chief, who believes his son is pampered and spoiled because of his Western education (he is an MIT graduate and carries an air of American "arrogant" attitude) and needs to be reined back into traditional ways. In one scene very early in the film, Bassey appears in tight sporty attire to a business and marriage arrangement meeting hosted by his father, clothing inappropriate and disrespectful to the occasion. Similarly, Miriam initially rebuffs Bassey's friendship on the grounds of what might be called Western privilege.

Such a narrative parallel also extends to aspects of style, particularly the mise-en-scène. Setting, which is rich in range and depth, is pivotal to *Up North*'s narration and renarration of Northeast Nigeria. Generic glamorous aerial shots of Lagos are balanced by equally spacious drone shots of Bauchi. The parallel structure also governs the dazzling sartorial codes of North and South. However, interior spaces are more contrasted. Interior scenes in Lagos tend to be in tight framing (perhaps suggestive of the father's high-handedness and traditional stuffiness), while interiors in Bauchi are in open frames and utilize more offscreen space. Even more striking than the images described above, the film offers viewers a stunning visual spectacle of the Northeast: vast landscapes of gorgeous rolling hills and valleys; lakes and pools; the international tourist attraction Yankari Game Reserve; iconic architectural structures such as the tomb of Tafawa Balewa (Nigeria's first prime minister); and the brilliant colors of the Emir's Durbar.

These scenes are shot in expansive, deep-focus cinematography. Not infrequently, especially with the nature shots, the images function as *attractions*. Tom Gunning uses the term to refer to images that provide "a series of views to an audience, fascinating because of their illusory power... and exoticism."[22] Such images, as provided in *Up North*, invites the viewer's attention, excite curiosity, and offer spectatorial pleasure rather than dramatic action (in fact, they retard it). Overall, rather than the swirling dystopian images of the Northeast circulating in mass media, the film offers a visual spectacle that re-narrates Northeast Nigeria as idyllic, peaceful, understanding, and loving.

Up North equally delivers a national unity message using other popular media arts: film, music, and social media. Casting Banky W., a famous Nigerian musician and actor, as the protagonist, Bassey, helps not only to market the film but also to participate in an ongoing effort to leverage the economic potential of the popular arts in Nigeria. Banky W.'s star power in *Up North* echoes Stephen Neale's explanation of the relationship between content creators (auteurs) and viewers. Neale argues that the "name of the author can function as a 'brand name,' a means of labeling and selling a film and of orienting expectation and channeling meaning and pleasure..."[23] *Up North* benefits from the recent accelerating synergy between

Nollywood and the popular music industry in Nigeria by exploiting Banky W.'s star "brand" for marketing purposes and disseminating an imagined and unified Nigeria that defies Boko Haram's terror and divisive rhetoric.

Furthermore, Bassey becomes the conduit through which the world knows of a "new" Northeast. Broadcasting from "up north" on social media as "Bauchi Boy," he uses social media platforms to transform perceptions of Nigeria, with an anonymous consumer public "liking," "loving," "querying," and "commenting" on his posts and cheering him on. About three-quarters into the film, it is not only local allies cheering him on. Like the broader community that encourages the three boys in the folktale, a wider international community is now involved in ensuring that Bassey succeeds. Bassey's documentation of his experiences in Northern Nigeria stands in sharp contrast to what the popular press offers. Whereas Boko Haram uses social media to disperse citizens and instill fear, *Up North* mobilizes it to reconnect and unite them. After the kidnap in 2014, Abubakar Shekau, the terrorist leader, circulated videos on YouTube in which he swore to maim and kill Nigerians. He also promised to sell the abducted girls through a series of videos. This contradictory feature of social media was echoed by two journalists from *The Wall Street Journal*. Parkinson and Hinshaw's account of how musicians, Hollywood actors, politicians, and other influencers used social media, particularly Twitter, to promote the "#bringbackourgirls" campaign revealed the inherent paradoxes of social media use and effects.[24] The authors argue that the rescue efforts of the Nigerian government were thwarted by the increasing use of tweets and retweets, which apparently led to an overexposure of rescue efforts and compromised the girls' safety. The result is that they ended up in captivity longer than was strictly necessary. Through his social media posts, Bassey documents in *Up North* the location that had been forgotten and silenced, so much so that he incited comments from his on-screen followers such as "This is absolutely magnificent" or "I'm feeling homesick for Bauchi."

Conclusion

Jude Akudinobi observes that Nollywood narratives tend to be topical, noting that "Nollywood's penchant for the quotidian and its focus on life lessons inevitably intervene in the social and political imaginaries not just through its narrative premises but also in terms of how its narratives unfold as bearers of meaning."[25] So, what are the life and national unity lessons in *Up North*? Since Nigeria's independence, different administrations have tried to forge a wholesome and enduring imagined "national" community. Examples include the establishment of unity schools and the NYSC. Perhaps we could say that *Up North* advances that project by suggesting the role popular arts and culture play in nationhood.

Up North re-narrates in the following significant ways. Boko Haram displaced people and their livelihoods; *Up North* reinstates them by offering Bassey and his girlfriend a new location and jobs to settle down to. Boko Haram caused the loss of Bauchi's touristic value with the mindless bombings and torching of schools, churches, and government buildings; *Up North* restored viewers' confidence in the aesthetic values of the environs where the film was shot. Boko Haram ended festivals and crowds; *Up North* re-started them through the lavish Durbar Festival as well as drawing attention to the geographical attributes of the state, which mainstream media had long forgotten. Boko Haram made women despise schools as it was reminiscent of the Chibok girls' worst nightmare; *Up North* rekindled the love for education and sports, turning girls into school and state champions through the "She Runs Bauchi" competition. In significant ways, *Up North* offered a different and welcoming view of the northern region, where the sounds of guns and bomb explosions gave way to the boisterous sounds of girls in school fields and a referee's whistle.

The importance of *Up North* in re-telling a dominant Nigerian story among local and international news media cannot be overlooked. Through the film, Nollywood becomes a vehicle of resistance and subversion, illustrative of the use of alternative media in a national context, and for once, viewers do not hear gunshots, bombs, or any of the devastating stories that have come to define the Nigerian Northeast in mainstream media. Instead, the voices of schoolgirls and their teachers are heard. Given that the film was set in Bauchi, which shares a border with Borno, we read *Up North*, in the first instance, as an alternative vision of Northeast Nigeria, one that embraces education, sports, dialogue, culture, and development. However, in doing so, we are also keenly aware that *Up North* is not a localized narration limited to Northeast Nigeria. Rather, the film enables a revitalization of concepts of national cinema and film's role in national unity projects.

Chapter 6

Santa & Andrés: The New, The Old and The Queer in Postsocialist Cuban Cinema

David Tenorio

In this chapter, I articulate the idea that twenty-first-century queer Cuban cinema has directed our eyes to the emergence of what I am referring to as "postsocialism" in Cuban cultural politics. Postsocialism, I argue, refers to a marked distance from state-funded models of socialism that shape and inform sociocultural arrangements in Cuba. By tracing a postsocialist turn in twenty-first-century queer Cuban cinema, I redirect the "political actions and feelings" to expand on a method that "shed[s] light on ongoing socialist legacies in new ethical collectivities and networks of dissent opposing state- and corporate-based military, economic, and cultural expansionism since the end of the Cold War."[1] Furthermore, I seek to unsettle a Cold War paradigm that continues to pervade cultural criticism on the island and abroad, as well as in discursive practices that construct a dichotomous onto-epistemology between unreconcilable categories such as revolutionary/counterrevolutionary, public/private, local/global, socialist/capitalist, and homosexual/heterosexual. More than cinematic productions, queer films in postsocialist Cuba extend a queer critique from the global south that, following Bogdan Popa's notion of queer postsocialism, "seeks to imagine a new temporality that moves away from a Cold War narrative of progress, emancipation, and development."[2]

Queer and trans cinema in a postsocialist turn teases out conventional scripts of representation, challenging the very legacies of the Cuban revolution's sexual politics. Carlos Lechuga's feature film *Santa & Andrés*

(2016) is a case in point through which to trace the complicated and contested intimacies between queer ways of life and Cuban revolutionary affects, as they become entangled in a globalized network of consumption, distribution, and production. These affective entanglements reveal an ongoing tension shaping a sexual culture built on suspicion, shame, and distrust in the Cuban context. By establishing a sensorial engagement with the film, that is, an attunement to the film's sonic, haptic, and material registers, which do not always appear as distinct elements of images in motion, I extend three axes of a queer media mixology, that is, a critical interaction with various media artifacts carrying a queer sensibility, to help situate a postsocialist turn in Cuban cinema today. In doing so, this queer media mixology sends out a sexual feeling that, evoking Eve Sedgwick's articulations, moves beside and alongside queer formations that disrupt Cuban heteronormative frequencies of global postsocialism.

Grappling with the political persecution of sexual and gender nonconforming folk, *Santa & Andrés* invites critical viewers to examine the contested relationship between queer dissent and Cuban revolutionary politics through a film that, far from portraying a reconciliation with the past, restages the very conflicts leaving queer people astray. This drama centers on the development of an unlikely friendship between a gay writer, Andrés, and a revolutionary farmworker, Santa. Preoccupied with the threatening possibility of talking to the international press, local revolutionary officials task Santa with watching over Andrés for three consecutive days until an international peace summit held in their small town concludes. Rather than developing an antagonistic plot set in 1980s Cuba, the film centers on the mistrust each share for the Cuban revolution, while interrogating the patriarchal structures of a once-thought redemptive social struggle. As such, the camera follows the chase between two strangers who become friends amid a lush countryside. In the end, Andrés rushes to the shoreline, making sure no one trails behind him, as he hastens to the beach to catch an escape boat. An expansive shot shows Santa catching up to him at the edge of a cliff. "Don't go," she exclaims, hoping to change her friend's decision to flee. This farewell scene is not uncommon to members of the queer Cuban diaspora, who constantly entertain the hypothetically improbable supposition of staying on the island. *Santa & Andrés* thus reconsiders how revolutionary legacies continue to shape new forms of media production in a global Cuba.

The New

Cinema in Cuba is shaped by changing laws and policies that, first and foremost, seek to protect the integrity of the Revolution's cultural interests. Officially launched in 2019, Cuba's Law 373 (Decreto-Ley no. 373) sought to respond to the emergence of "independent" film and audiovisual creators.[3] Making a direct reference to the creation of independent collectives, the law not only represents a significant amendment to the vigorous Law 169 (Decreto-Ley no. 169) from 1959, which determined the creation of the ICAIC, Cuban Institute of Cinematographic Art and Industry, two months after the triumph of the Cuban Revolution, but also stipulates the creation of a registry for independent creators, *Registro del Creador Audiovisual.* Registration would depend on a successful evaluation made by two admission committees spearheaded respectively by the heads of the ICAIC and the recently created Cuban Institute of Information and Social Communication. Some critics of Law 373 effusively outcry the requirements for the admission process, as well as the arbitrary composition of the evaluation committee since the head of each institute unilaterally selects its members.[4]

While Law 373 seeks to recognize independent cultural production, the sociopolitical and economic practices it enacts seem to further enshrine ICAIC's core ideological values than aid the production, exhibition, and distribution of independent film and audiovisual production in Cuba. Tellingly, Law 373 reinscribes the importance of ICAIC by attributing full control, regulation, and execution of programs that guarantee the distribution, production, and commercialization of independent audiovisual materials that solely align with the "artistic characteristics of the Cuban cultural tradition and the means that sustain it through the Revolution to ensure a climate of creative freedom."[5] In other words, it is the role of the Revolution's cultural institutions to define what constitutes "independent" audiovisual creation inasmuch they regulate, surveille, and profit from its production and distribution. Law 373 not only represents a new regulatory measure to ensure that independent audiovisual production stays "in line" with revolutionary ideals, a mission that ICAIC has translated into specific thematic, aesthetic, and visual codes, but the law also presents a new fiscal measure through which independent filmmakers are taxed appropriately for their labor and external sponsorship.

Enmeshed in the cultural policies of Cuban postsocialism, Law 373 points to the polemic surrounding the government's censoring of Carlos Lechuga's *Santa & Andrés*, a film that received the 2014 Havana Film Festival's "Unproduced Script Award," as well as production funds from Programa Ibermedia, Fundación SGAE, Proimágenes Colombia, Cinergia, Hubert Bals Fund, Wouter Barendretch Film Foundation, and the Embassy of Norway, among others. Along with its critique against the persecution of gay Cuban artists, Lechuga's second film was made possible through substantial nongovernmental support, which positioned it as an independent production. The trend in the Cuban film industry of securing funds beyond state institutions has been consistently growing since the turn of the twenty-first century and has received the attention of Cuban cultural institutions considering various reforms geared toward remediating a collapsing national economy. Specifically, ICAIC recognized this shift in film production by creating the young filmmakers' festival, Muestra Joven ICAIC, in Havana in 2000.

After being screened at the 2016 Toronto International Film Festival, the film was scheduled to debut during the thirty-eighth edition of Havana's Film Festival that year, but its screening was abruptly canceled by ICAIC, forcing its exclusion from the competition due, allegedly, to its revisionist outlook on political dissidence and homosexuality. ICAIC also banned the film's circulation and distribution in Cuba, but international acclaim made it a top contender within a global circuit of international festivals including Chicago, Guadalajara, San Sebastián, Zurich, Miami, Göteborg, and Cartagena, where it garnered various awards. By reducing the film's theme as simply counterrevolutionary, that is, standing in complete opposition to revolutionary ideals, ICAIC's prohibition of *Santa & Andrés* within the island paradoxically participates in its distribution and commercialization, both at home and abroad.

Despite ICAIC's banning of the film, audiences across Cuba were able to watch the film outside the state-sponsored network of cinemas and through an underground network of audiovisual and web content circulation commonly known as *el paquete semanal*, a one-terabyte collection of digital content curated by individuals with access to internet and media outlets.[6] *El paquete semanal* usually features national and international TV shows, YouTube videos, podcasts, music, and news from around the world, and retails for US$2 or $5. Media scholars have emphasized the "human infrastructure" on which *el paquete semanal* relies for its

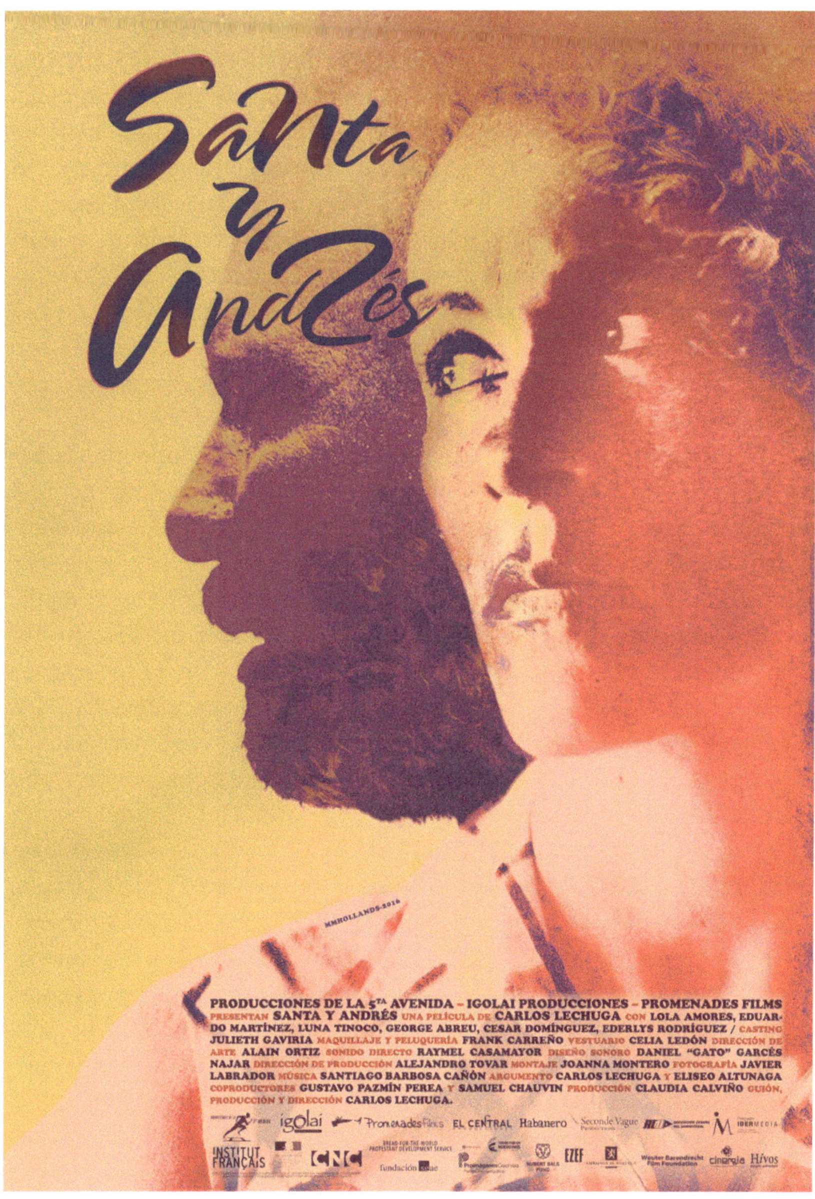

Figure 01. Film poster for *Santa & Andrés* (2016), courtesy of Habanero Film Sales.

circulation, noting that "human infrastructure [not only] consists of the people, relationships, and organizations that underlie the foundation of a system or network, [but also involves people] in creative practices, social processes, and flows of information and materials" beyond the material artifacts it interacts with.[7] In principle, government officials only allow *el paquete semanal* to circulate if it leaves out content considered counter-revolutionary, such as pornography or blunt political propaganda against the government, but that is not always the case.[8] From USB flash drives to hard drives, passing through improvised screens, *Santa & Andrés* has traveled through an alternative data-sharing network that exceeds state-run infrastructure through which banned audiovisual and media products go around the island at an affordable price.

The debate around Carlos Lechuga's blacklisted film pinpoints a larger governmental infrastructure that looks for ways to generate internal revenue from taxing alternative and experimental media, digital, and audiovisual practices with and through ongoing state control. In the absence of a market regulating the cost of goods and services according to supply and demand, the Ministry of Finance and Prices and the Ministry of Communications set their own pricing, controlling many of the island's markets. In 2021, for instance, the Cuban government announced a 500% increment in energy costs to residential customers, leaving marginalized populations, such as Afro-Cubans, sexual minorities, single mothers, and elders, in strained economic positions.[9]

Like Law 373, these economic measures reveal a new axis of government taxation and revenue for audiovisual production that bear resemblance to other state-run service providers, like ETECSA, Cuba's only telecommunication company charging for internet and phone services. The revolutionary government has stretched its socialist mission for over sixty years and prides itself on equal and free access to education, health care, and social welfare. However, this has not applied to digital inclusivity and broad internet access. The cost of Wi-Fi internet per hour is about US$2 when the average Cuban earns about US$20 per month, making it more of a luxury commodity than a subsidized necessity good.[10] In this sense, Cuba's service companies have operated under an economic model that protects the interests of a military elite, constituting state-run monopolies, while proclaiming a socialist model that, in practice, is no longer tenable.

Santa & Andrés highlights the contradictions of such seemingly opposed economic models by inserting an excerpt from Fidel Castro's

Figure 02. Santa eating and watching Fidel Castro give a speech on national TV. Movie still from *Santa & Andrés* (2016).

infamous speeches about making personal sacrifices for the greater revolutionary good. Santa's precarious living conditions shown in this sequence, exactly when having dinner while watching state TV, serve as counterimages to articulate a strong critique in the now about the economic failures of the revolutionary apparatus.

Castro's tone inscribes the imagery of sacrifice, of making "an extraordinary effort" to solve the economic issues of third-world countries, and those of Cuba to be more precise. Castro's socialist rhetoric of economic development creates a sense of national belonging by assigning personal responsibility to everyone fighting for the Revolution. At the same time, Castro's speech participates in the construction of an imagined enemy that must be defeated and shamed to maintain the legitimacy of Cuba's socialist project.

The politics of Cuban audiovisual and media production reveal a present context situated beyond Soviet socialism, that is, a turning point that moves toward assemblages of local economic practices, state monopolies, and foreign investment, sustaining the emergence of a postsocialist cinema. Beyond juxtaposing images of underdevelopment, the film restages the failures of an old Cuban socialist model, especially when considering that an anti-nationalist sentiment has been growing in the last two decades, pointing to the largest protest staged in 2021 as part of the J-11 movement.

The Old

Centered around the surveillance of Andrés, a gay Cuban dissident writer, *Santa & Andrés* uncovers the intimacies of suspicion affecting Cuban sociality, both rural and urban, since the onset of the 1959 Revolution. Santa, a devoted revolutionary and farmworker, is instructed by Jesús, the head of the Popular Council, or Consejo Popular, to keep a close eye on Andrés during a three-day peace summit in a small town in eastern Cuba where the foreign press will be present. Created in the 1980s, Popular Councils are local organizations that represents the interests and needs of a particular municipality. They are also in charge of developing job programs and other activities for the towns they represent; in the case of Santa, she works in a farm collective.

According to the words of Fidel Castro, the Popular Council would represent an essential link for the smooth functioning of the socialist state. Aside from their bureaucratic functions, Popular Councils are part of a larger affective machinery that aims to regulate everyday life in tandem with the CDRs, or Consejos de Defensa de la Revolución, yet another device for surveilling Cuban intimacies. These socialist apparatuses operate through a human infrastructure comprising neighbors, family members, and friends that seeks to patrol everyday life to ensure loyalty to socialist ideals. Those who dare critique or not comply with any of the tasks assigned as proof of their devotion to a revolutionary dogma are subjected to public humiliation by their close acquaintances through Public Acts of Repudiation, state-sponsored practices that Amnesty International has continuously denounced as human rights violations.[11]

Such acts aim to bring shame to those suspected of being counterrevolutionaries by unleashing the punitive force of the Revolution; a force embodied by those who are intimately entangled with their target, such as family members, friends, or loved ones. Following Sara Ahmed's notion of "affective economies,"[12] the shame and rage directed at socialist defectors shape and inform a sense of national belonging, or, as I contend, a socialist affect. In the film, the act of repudiation brought upon Andrés precisely captures the wave of violence with which the socialist state has treated most of its fervent critics, including many queers. The state has devised mechanisms of ideological control to foster an affective attachment to Cuban socialism, through which sexual shame acts to maintain gender and social binaries, as well as craft the fantasy of a public enemy.[13]

Santa & Andrés thus exposes both the affective charges that animate such state machinery and the gendered dynamics that inform its functioning. The film opens with an expansive scene in which Santa walks in the middle of the open road holding a chair, which is later used as her seating post to watch over Andrés. At first, Santa embodies the socialist regime's technologies of surveillance, as the camera establishes a marked distance between the physical space characters take. Not only does Santa position herself away from Andrés's humble home, but she purviews with askance her immediate surroundings. The distance between Santa and Andrés, framed through low- and high-angle shots, also choreographs a sense of suspicion, as the camera lens tracks Andrés's everyday movements and contacts across the rural environment. As such, the film draws us into a feeling of being watched. Santa treads suspiciously into counterrevolutionary territory, looking for what she knowingly fears: becoming intimate with a queer dissident.

As viewers become familiar with the precarious living conditions of rural Cuba, the film's framing of Santa and Andrés's everyday interactions debunks a public/private dualism. Taking into consideration the role CDRs and Popular Councils play as state devices in regulating Cuban intimacy, the personal and the political appear less as distinctly separate spheres than as irreducibly entangled relational planes. But the ideological

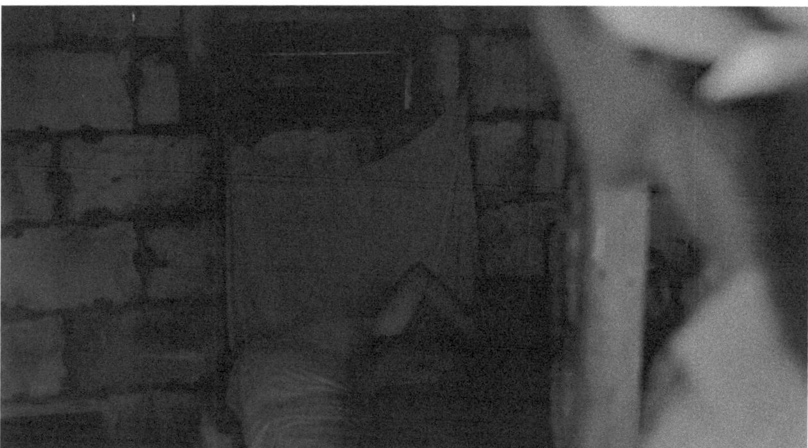

Figure 03. Santa glancing over at Andrés's shack on her way to the outpost. Movie still from *Santa & Andrés* (2016).

frictions make more evident the affective flows that intervene in generating such fields of intimacy.

Placed within the fields of suspicion, mistrust, and shame, Andrés evokes a fearful anxiety that is felt throughout the film. I locate this affect in the various shots that hide and expose Andrés's writings, which caused much alarm at the prospect of being discovered, prompting his confinement, and detonating a personal encounter with Santa. While the film frames suspicion as a critical affect circulating through Cuban rural sociality, its revisionist approach highlights the failure of the state's emancipatory project that, disguised as a socialist utopia, turns into a masculinist military dictatorship. In this context, suspicion is thus directed at those who either fail to embody "the new man," or engage in any activity considered counterrevolutionary, such as voicing a critique against the socialist regime through writing. The flowing intensities of suspicion thus depend on a gendered embodiment of revolutionary ideals. While belligerent masculinities mark those bodies who are seen as able to fight for the Revolution, the feminization of other-than-revolutionary justifies the acts of violence against those who are perceived as weak, queer, and counterrevolutionary.

Although Santa serves as a sentinel of the Revolution, her entering the space of queer dissidence makes her initial suspicion shift toward developing a sense of empathy for Andrés. Chipping away at the solidified exclusion of queer dissidence in Cuban sociality, the film beautifully dialogues with what Eve K. Sedgwick has referred to as *beside*, "the law of the excluded middle [whose] interest does not depend on a fantasy of metonymically egalitarian or even pacific relations. *Beside* comprises a wide range of desiring, identifying, representing, repelling, paralleling, differentiating, rivaling, leaning, twisting, mimicking, withdrawing, attracting, aggressing, warping, and other relations."[14] The possibility of other relations outside the Revolution's national affect is continually performed each time Santa and Andrés come closer together. These moments of queer encounter are captured in scenes in the shadows, like in the moment when Santa takes shelter with Andrés from the roaring storm, or when the queer dissident writer consoles Santa after a rowdy night out. Through smalls acts of caring, the affective charges of suspicion veer away from the regulation of intimacy to the fostering of a queer friendship between a custodian and her counterrevolutionary dissident.

The Queer

In the last axis of this chapter's queer media mixology, I situate *Santa & Andrés* within a larger genealogy of queer Cuban cinema, as well as interact with its sonic, haptic, and material registers, as they force us to confront an unresolved and contested queer past. Set in 1983, *Santa & Andrés* grapples with two queer specters of the Revolution, namely the 1960s UMAPs, or Military Units to Aid Production, the forced labor camps where counterrevolutionaries, including homosexuals, were supposedly sent to be reformed, and the 1980s Mariel Boatlift, an exodus that sent out the so-called "scum" of Cuban society to Florida. Around 125,000 Cubans, many of whom were queer and who later changed Miami's queer night scene, arrived in the United States.[15]

Inspired by the biopics of Reinaldo Arenas, René Ariza, and Delfín Prats, respectively, the film follows cues from Julian Schnabel's *Before Night Falls* (2000) and Manuel Zayas's *Seres extravagantes* (2004), particularly the expansive takes of nature, or the close-up scenes between characters, which help craft an epitome of Cuba's queer dissident writers through the protagonist Andrés. Film journalist Alejandro Ríos notes that Carlos Lechuga's film borrows elements from Lavernia's documentary on René Ariza, as well as one of Ariza's confessions about his own marginalization as a queer Cuban artist.[16] In this sense, the film reveals a dark episode in the history of the Cuban Revolution that, despite the long years of internal socioeconomic and cultural reforms, has not been officially acknowledged or publicly recognized. Apart from the film's political undertones, a sense of queer from below emerges through the registers of music, touch, and caring that exist alongside shame, suspicion, and mistrust.

In the early scenes when Santa arrives at the shack, Andrés begins to play a cassette tape of Martha Strada's romantic ballad *Viento*. The replay of Strada's music begins to irritate Santa, but the song sieves a sense of queer loss, setting the tone for the characters' impending friction, physical contact, and eventual goodbye. Charged with dramatism, Strada's heartbreaking song reinscribes her own heartbreak with the Revolution. At the peak of her career in the 1960s, Strada is invited to perform at The Olympia, a legendary concert venue in Paris, but the invitation is turned down because the Revolution does not allow the luminary of the Cuban ballad to travel abroad.

Viento's melodic registers gesture at the longing of a distant loved one through a slow musical tempo that oscillates between jazz, romantic ballad, and opera. Its repetitive dramatism, transmitted as Andrés switches a music tape over and over, begins to dislocate Santa's fantasies of monstrosity associated with queer counterrevolutionaries. Strada's mezzosoprano tones sounding through the old cassette tape player channel a sense of queer loss that will be pivotal in bringing into contact these two ideologically different characters.

While Strada's song points to a queer relationality emerging from Andrés's surveillance, Cuba's natural landscape, often characterized in revolutionary imaginaries as rustic, raw, masculine, and as the birth site of the Rebel Army, is also queered by the decibels of queer loss. The playing of Strada's song in the middle of the rural landscape creates an out-of-place ambience that queers the rural, as well as indexes nightlife as a queer site of care and communion. In other words, the song plays with a queer femme sensibility through its soundwaves to re-imagine a space filled with images of revolutionary masculinity.

Although brief, the night bar scene in the film functions as a site where Santa's revolutionary stoic traits collapse, revealing her vulnerabilities, and where a sort of queer relationality highlights some contradictions of the Cuban socialist state, namely a corrupt judicial system, the criminalization of sex work, and the public control of private life. The erotics of the night, in this context, also appear as a filmic space for social contestation, a revolutionary aesthetic value of film-as-critique that is subverted by filmmakers who veer away from the exaltation of socialist ideals and realities, such as Sabá Cabrera Infante and Orlando Jiménez Leal's *P.M.* (1961). Portraying the nightlife scene in the ports of the bay of Havana, *P.M.* also represents the first instance of Cuban cultural institutions banning a film for its counterrevolutionary appeal.

Queer sexualities and the night are two sites that reveal the programmatic logics of revolutionary censorship. On the last day of her surveillance mission, after Santa helps Andrés recover from a violent attack from his mute lover, she finds herself unwilling to let him go. Santa prolongs her cheer and care for Andrés, as the film shows how their interactions begin to crack at suspicion, and through those cracks, empathy flows through sharing their pain. Santa's heartbreaking secret—spoiler alert!—binds her feelings to Andrés's sense of shame. Drawing from such dissidence, *Santa & Andrés* thus portrays the contested intimacies of Cuban queer relationality, an underground social tectonic that, like nightlife, exists under the masculinist gaze of the Revolution.

In this sense, the film's engaging the green exuberance of rural Cuba does more than just make nature an omnipresent protagonist but also seeks to undo the masculinization of the rural space accomplished through early Cuban documentary, such as *Historias de la Revolución* (Gutiérrez Alea, 1960), *La primera carga al machete* (Gómez, 1969), or *El hombre de Maisinicú* (Peréz, 1973), in which revolutionary men take siege of and conquer the untamed jungle, while planning to overthrow Fulgencio Batista's government. One of the first revolutionary fantasies places rurality as the first territory won by the Rebel Army led by Fidel Castro and Che Guevara. As Lauren Peña has noted, "the revolutionary discourse fostered the idea that rural space was the ideal stage for the guerrilla and later on the stage for social struggles and revolutionary victories."[17] Yet the presence of a queer dissident writer within the rural space dislodges the triumphant version of the revolutionary guerrilla, while queering nature.

The Cuban countryside as a site for queer eroticism has a specific visual referent in Reinaldo Arena's poetics, which serve as inspiration to develop the script in Julian Schnabel's biopic of this queer writer in *Before Night Falls* (2000), which also plays with the visual registers of Cabrera Infante and Jiménez Leal's *P.M.* in the credits. Throughout Schnabel's film, nature, and particularly the countryside of eastern Cuba, appears

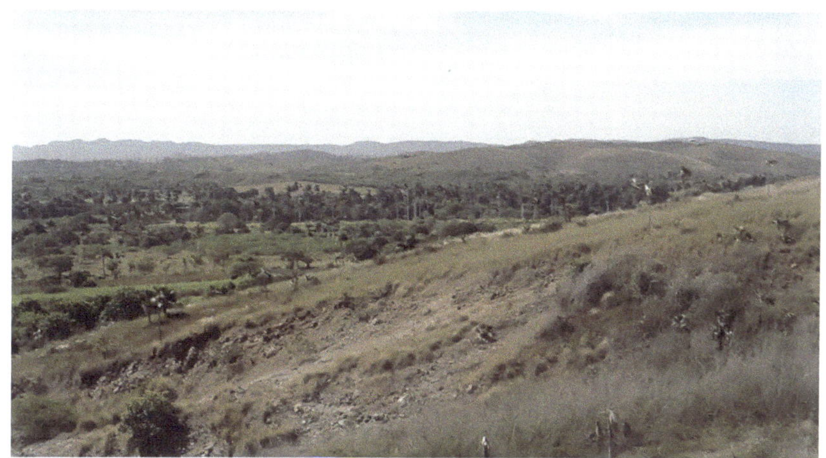

Figure 04. Expansive shot of the Cuban countryside in *Santa & Andrés*.

unbound, flowing, and erotic. The camera frames with detail the movement of trees, the falling of rain, and the dampness of the soil, as well as the rich greenery surrounding Arena's early childhood. In a way, Carlos Lechuga's *Santa & Andrés* pays tribute to Schnabel's adaptation of Arena's hyperbolic memoire, namely through a series of aerial shots that pan out the uncontainable eroticism of the countryside, of exposed trees that, according to Arenas himself, hold magical worlds within: "Trees have a secret life that is only revealed to those willing to climb them. To climb a tree is to slowly discover a unique world, rhythmic, magical, and harmonious, with its worms, insects, birds, and other living things, all apparently insignificant creatures, telling us their secrets."[18]

In these films, the Cuban countryside functions as an erotic queer geography that undoes the masculinist imaginaries around the rural landscape. Borrowing from a queer ode to nature found in the opening sequences of Schnabel's *Before Night Falls*, *Santa & Andrés* finds a metaphor in filming birds flying across the sky. Lechuga thus plays with an allegory of queer resilience in the face of marginalization and public shaming—the word "pájaro" in Cuban slang is used as a slur to shame queer people. The presence of "pájaros" traveling through "viento" are queer gestures that point to a queer immanence, as well as to a queer-nature relation, beautifully expressed in Arenas's words as a world of sexual excess: "...There is no

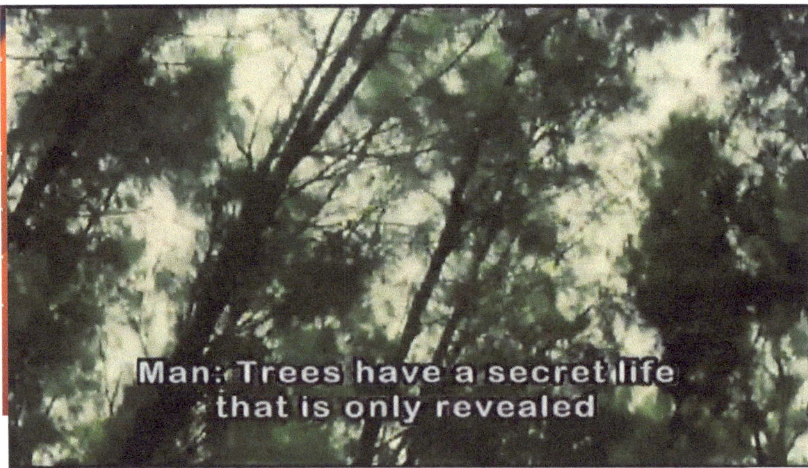

Figure 05. Opening scene in Julian Schnabel's Reinaldo Arenas-inspired film, *Before Night Falls* (2000).

truth to the theory, held by some, about the sexual innocence of peasants. In the country, sexual energy generally overcomes all prejudice, repression, and punishment. That force, the force of nature, dominates."[19] The convergence between the sexual and the natural gives life to a queer force shaping Andrés's sexual encounters with his mute lover, who later turns on him after being pressured by state police.

Santa & Andrés makes evident the emergence of other affects that are possible beyond the socialist machinery of control. After spending time with one another, of getting to know their traumas, their fears, their dreams, and their suspicions, Santa and Andrés begin to see each other more as equals than as ideological rivals. Even though mistrust continues to exist in their interactions, as the camera tilts emulating the feeling of being watched, care is nonetheless central to the restructuring of a gendered Cuban sociality captured in the film. Their intimate acts of care, whether they take place in a hospital, a shack, a bar, or a dark room, embody other ways of relating beyond revolutionary ideology.

While hanging out at a local bar, Santa and Andrés share their disappointment with men, as they are literally confronted by heartbreak. Andrés must endure watching over his mute lover hanging out with an older guy, who seems to be a sugar daddy. Contrastingly, Santa faces the drunk driver who killed her son in a car accident. The protagonists' unraveling following the bar scene concludes in a physical embrace between Santa and Andrés. In this sense, touch makes possible the fracturing of socialist walls by allowing the characters to feel the complicated textures comprising their heartbreaking experience with revolutionary masculinities. Like in the case of Martha Strada, Santa and Andrés have also been hurt and disappointed by the men of the Revolution. As the film nears its end, Andrés takes to the sea and flees the island in a furtive vessel, finding in exile the only way of stopping state harassment. In a final scene, Santa and Andrés face each other one last time, framing their hug as a cathartic event of sensations. In their embrace, they challenge the affective registers of the Revolution. As they say their goodbyes, they insist on taking care, while the wind carries their loss away, echoing Strada's windy queer redemption.

By exhuming the queer ghosts of the revolutionary past, Carlos Lechuga's *Santa & Andrés* debunks the idea that, far from opening a civic dialogue, official cultural institutions, including the film industry, have replayed the scripts of censorship, but this time, such repression rehearses a

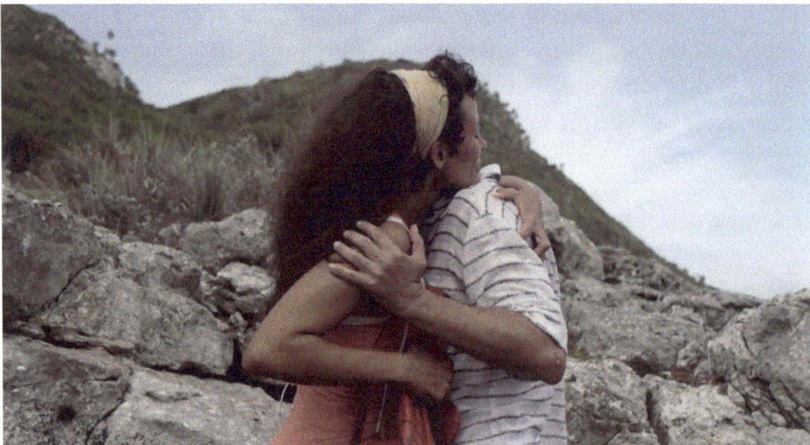

Figure 06. Santa hugging Andrés as a goodbye gesture. Movie still from *Santa & Andrés* (2016).

new market ideology anchored in state monopolism beyond postsocialism. As such, Carlos Lechuga's film makes evident a new configuration in cultural politics that departs in some ways from the old state machinery of socialist relationality, giving way to a mix of state-funded initiatives, alternative networks, and foreign investments that sustain media production in Cuba today. The final hug in *Santa & Andrés* precisely embodies an ideological irresolution between queer dissent and state institutionalism, embracing indeed a queer way of negotiating media contradictions.

Part Three

Transmedia Figurations

Chapter 7

A Necklace of Songs: Transmediating Hindi Film Music

Kuhu Tanvir

For popular Hindi cinema, the arrival of sound was significant not only for its ability to enhance the film's verisimilitude, but also because it enabled the inclusion of songs in the films, a tradition that continues to this day. In the first ever Indian talkie, *Alam Ara* (1931), director Ardeshir Irani had his actors sing on the set, recording the audio and the visual together using the Tanar single system camera. However, for *Shirin Farhad*, the industry's second talkie released later that same year, director J. J. Madan did away with the practice of recording songs on set and instead recorded the audio separately. Two years later, in 1933, the record label His Master's Voice (HMV)[1] took a major step in commodifying film music by recording songs of R.S. Choudhary's 1932 film *Madhuri* for distribution as a gramophone record.[2,3] Until this point, the repertoire of gramophone records consisted largely of classical and folk music by Indian musicians and Western classical music. With this turn, film songs became a part of the repertoire of musical media objects available for purchase. Perhaps inadvertently, by formalizing the separation of the sound and the image of the film song, J. J. Madan paved the way for the transmediation of Indian film songs, allowing them to be consumed outside the movie theater, beyond the filmic text, in domestic spaces, and through a range of media.

One of the first documented uses of the word "transmedia" is from 1991, and is attributed to Marsha Kinder in what she called the "intertextual super system" of media for children which consciously maintained intertextual connections across film, television, and videogames.[4] The term gained most attention in 2006 with Henry Jenkins's treatise on what he called "transmedia storytelling," which he defined as "a process where integral elements of a fiction get dispersed systematically across multiple delivery channels for the purpose of creating a unified and coordinated entertainment experience."[5] Since then, the conceptual and industrial scope of transmediation as a practice has proliferated,[6] but with very few exceptions, this literature consists largely of work in the Euro-American context. The goal of this chapter is to examine transmediation in the Global South by studying the circulation of Hindi film songs beyond the text and context of the film they are from. To this end, I trace the transmedial journey of film songs as they separate from the original film's text and circulate across radio, gramophones, television, computers, and cell phones.

The grammar of Hindi film music is particularly suited to a study of transmediation, as songs go on to have rich afterlives more or less independent of the film they were in. In the process of transmediation, the song object continuously transforms itself and also the medium to which it travels. While the vehicle for this study is the afterlives of songs from popular Hindi cinema, my aim is to illustrate the various processes of fragmentation that engender forms of transmediation so the broader argument about this fragmentation's productive potentials will be relevant to other geographical and historical media cultures.

The Hindi film song itself has received sustained critical attention from scholars of Indian cinema. It has been studied as a remnant of the commercial Parsi theater tradition that was an aesthetic model of sorts for popular Hindi cinema, and it has also been studied for its complex relationship with the film's diegesis,[7] and as a manifestation of excess, to express feelings and situations that the prosaic cannot contain, be it love, sorrow, aspiration, etc.[8] Scholars have paid sustained attention to the politics of music[9] and voice.[10] In the post-Liberalization era, scholars dealt with the song as a vehicle for both finance and its role in shaping the ever-growing Indian diaspora's relationship to India.[11] This chapter extends the work on circulation of the film song by focusing on the transformations of these songs as they appeared first on Indian radio and then on Indian television.

Sonic Separations: The Film Song on Radio

As gramophone records of film songs became available, radio started playing Hindi film songs. For the first few years, at least on the basis of radio program schedules, there was no consistency or particular organization to when or how these songs were played. In the latter half of the 1930s, there are some stray listings on radio for programs that were innocuously called "Songs from the Screen" or "Hits from Films" or "Film Hits," etc. By 1936, there are occasional slots dedicated to the broadcast of songs from single films. There is, for instance, a seven-minute slot for "Wahan (film music)."[12] At the same time, there are also slots for individual songs from some films. There is, for instance, a curiously specific listing On November 11, 1938, for the Peshawar radio station that reads, "A song from the film *Alam Ara*."[13] The specificity of playing just one song from the film, seven years after its release, raises questions about how film songs were being used, at least in terms of programming, given that there was no standardization of a regular timeslot or any explanation of the basis on which these songs appeared on radio. Since individual songs were played and songs often had awkward timeslots of eight minutes or twelve minutes, etc., it could be that the songs were being used as inserts that would work as fillers to ensure the more traditional programs—such as the news—remained in their usual schedule. It could also be due to a relatively small repertoire of records to pick from.

Radio's lack of commitment to film songs didn't last long, and by the early 1940s, film songs comprised a significant portion of what was referred to as "light" content or entertainment programming on radio. In 1952, a few years after independence from British rule, India's first Information and Broadcasting minister, B. V. Keskar, announced a policy to reduce film songs on radio to a maximum of 10% of the entire content. This would mean a massive cutback from the nearly 60% of the content on radio that film music accounted for at the time.[14] He cited two reasons for this decision: one, that film songs were "vulgar" and therefore had adverse effects on young minds and, two, the need to promote classical music—mostly Indian but not entirely—as the appropriate choice.[15] The Indian Motion Pictures Producers Association, IMPPA, took offense to the charge of vulgarity, and decided to revoke the permit they had signed with All India Radio (AIR) back in 1943 that allowed the latter to play film songs.[16] Thus, what began as an attempt to reduce film songs amounted to a complete removal of film songs from AIR. In the popular imagination, the semantics of "reduction" and not "termination" were of no consequence, and the widely held notion was that Keskar banned film songs from radio. It was during this time that Radio Ceylon took the opportunity to fill the gaping void that listeners felt, and began *Binaca Geet Mala* or Binaca Song Garland, which was a weekly program of film songs sponsored by the toothpaste brand Binaca (subsequently Cibaca) and hosted by Amin Sayani. Exasperated by Keskar's didactic move of forcing classical music as entertainment, listeners turned in hordes to Radio Ceylon, skyrocketing its popularity.

While radio had played film songs before, *Binaca Geet Mala* was the first formal packaging of film songs as a regular program scheduled for a set slot every week. It became a weekly event that people looked forward to and made time for in their schedules. The program consisted of Sayani sharing tidbits leading up to each song. Though Sayani announced the name of the film the song was originally from, as a product that was audio only, and comprised new combinations of film songs every week, on this show, the song's separation from the film was decisive. This is also because songs were selected for their popularity, which was calculated based on record sales from music stores across the country, and not box office sales. Thus, in the transmediation of the songs from the movie theater to the radio, the songs didn't just enter a consumption economy different from that of the film, but also became a part of an entirely different genre: that of a collection of songs popular in the moment. The garland metaphor seems particularly apt given that the songs ran in something resembling a loop based on their rising or falling popularity. While the popularity of a song often reflected the popularity of the film, that wasn't always the case, as songs could remain on the garland, so to speak, for longer than the film ran in the theater.

In the shift from film to audio, technically, the songs lost their visuals; however, I would argue that it was a loss that allowed the song to adapt to the specifications of a different medium, thus also reaching a different audience whose association of the songs could be entirely removed from the film and its narrative. With large parts of the Indian population not having easy access to a movie theater,[17] there would inevitably be listeners who heard the same songs week after week on radio, but had not watched the film and were therefore entirely free of the visuals attached to the song as well as the original narrative context that the song was a part of, while still having an intimate familiarity with the song. Conversely, it can also be argued that the visual is never perfectly lost as the aura of the visual—either the actual visuals that went with the film or visuals imagined by someone who hasn't encountered the film, and has just heard the song could accompany it even as it was experienced through a sonic medium. In other words, a sonic experience doesn't have to be framed as a loss even though the media object was originally imagined with visuals. It can instead be considered a transformation that enables an afterlife that exceeds the song's original framing.

Television's Encounters with Film Songs

The film song's transmediation expanded with the expansion of AIR's responsibilities due to the arrival of television in India in 1959 as an extension of AIR. AIR, however, was not entirely prepared for this new role of managing a visual medium like TV. The day after TV service was announced in New Delhi, the Director General of AIR "warned" the public to not expect "programmes of a very high standard" since the available resources would still prioritize radio.[18] AIR provided very basic training to the employees who were asked to manage TV. These were people trained in the technicalities of radio and were essentially forced to learn the workings of television on the job, leading to recurring mishaps and programming errors that cultural commentators remarked upon in their weekly columns. The programming of the first decade of television betrayed its workforce's radio background, with programs that were more conversation-centric with a basic visual of people sitting across from each other. It is therefore not entirely surprising that TV leaned heavily on film-based programming to fill airtime. Telecasts of popular films began as early as the mid-1960s, and for almost two decades were telecast over two consecutive weekends, with half the film being shown on one Saturday or Sunday and the other half the following weekend.

Film-based programming was second only to the news in terms of content that received a degree of stability on television in the late 1960s and 1970s when broadcast was limited to a few hours a day. Along with the feature film, the film song-based show *Chitrahaar* had a dedicated weekly slot, certainly by August 1970, though presumably before that since an August 1970 column refers to it as TV's most popular program. *Chitrahaar*, *chitra* (picture) + *haar* (necklace) translates to a necklace of images. This title requires some deliberation. First, I would argue that the use of "haar," or necklace, is heavily inspired by radio's *Binaca Geet Mala*, which translates to Song Garland. While *Binaca Geet Mala* was transmitted by Radio Ceylon and not AIR, the popularity of the packaged set of film songs format was arguably the impetus behind *Chitrahaar.* Even though AIR lifted its ban on film music, such as it was, the damage had been done, and there was no substitute for the union of *Binaca Geet Mala* and Amin Sayani, not only because it had rescued listeners from Keskar's diktat, under which they would largely only get classical music on radio, but also because Sayani and the show had hit star status with their listeners and had become a part of their weekly routine. It is also no coincidence that *Chitrahaar* aired on the same day and time of the week as *Binaca Geet Mala*. While *Chitrahaar* may have taken inspiration from *Binaca Geet Mala*, including the word "chitra," which means pictures or images, it foregrounds what it had over *Binaca Geet Mala*: i.e. visuals. Thus, while radio had a garland of songs, TV had a necklace of songs and images.

Until 1972, Delhi was the only TV center in the country, and the only city that got a TV signal, so *Chitrahaar* was meant for Delhi audiences only. In 1972, the second TV station opened in Bombay, and they began their own version of a program presenting film songs. This show was called *Chhaya Geet*, which translates to shadow and song. The reference to shadow play of the filmic image combined with song is all too clear here as well.

While Delhi's television center maintained some degree of authority over subsequent regional centers, Bombay had an upper hand when it came to film-based programming because most film producers, directors, stars, etc. lived in Bombay and that was also where a significant amount of film production and distribution activity took place. By the time the Bombay TV center opened, TV had been in India for over a decade, and had established itself as a serious player in the media landscape, despite its limited reach at the time. With the population of Bombay having access to TV, film producers could keep a regular eye on any potential copyright violations, so the transactions for showing films on the Bombay station had to be entirely transparent, which it hadn't always been in Delhi. The producer of *Chhaya Geet*, Yakub Syed, told me in an interview that, luckily for the Bombay center, producers were more than eager to have their films shown on TV.[19] The process, Syed explained, entailed producers sending their films to the Bombay center. The Bombay center then paid to get a fresh copy of the film print made, which they then telecast. After the film was telecast in Bombay, the print was sent to thirteen other TV centers as they came into being. Each center that telecast the film sent a check to the film's producer, thus making TV one of the earlier sources of additional collections for the film beyond the box office.

Keen to establish *Chhaya Geet*'s own identity, and stand out as distinct from *Chitrahaar*, its producers decided to organize songs based on a theme rather than attempting to play only the latest or the most popular songs. In doing so, they also managed to separate themselves from the comparison with *Binaca Geet Mala*. Themes ranged from songs about motherhood to more season-specific ones such as "barsaat ke geet" (songs of the rain). The theme for the following week was announced at the end of every episode of *Chhaya Geet*, which served the function of creating some degree of anticipation in the audience, and more importantly, served as a "call for songs" directed at film producers, notifying them that the Bombay TV center was accepting songs based on said theme. This led producers to send in songs from their films to be featured. The songs played on *Chitrahaar* were more contemporaneous than the ones on *Chhaya Geet* because they were picked for their popularity at the time. Thus, even if the songs were from films that weren't playing in theaters anymore, the films were a part of the popular imagination. With *Chhaya Geet*, its thematic structure became a part of the metanarrative that housed the song, rather than the film. Invoking nostalgia with songs from older films that many listeners may not have heard in a while and giving them an entirely new framework became the conceit of the show. *Chhaya Geet* thus not only evoked nostalgia for the song, but in fact repackaged it, renewing the memory of the song much more substantially than the memory of the film. This occurred to me during my interview with Syed as he remembered songs by the theme he had selected them for back in the 1970s, rather than the film the song was from.

The theme of the show, however, was not the only anchor for the renewed memory of the song. Having the visuals from the film meant that, on *Chhaya Geet* in particular, the songs also featured the stars of the film. The renewed interest in the song and corresponding renewed memory cycle could easily be anchored in the repertoire of a star's songs. For fans of movie stars especially, getting to see their favorite actor on screen by means of the song played on *Chhaya Geet* could be a source of pleasure that is marked by its unexpected nature. Further, seeing an actor in more than one song played under the aegis of a particular theme could also classify an actor within that theme. For instance, the *Chhaya Geet* episode that was played on July 17, 1980 had the moon as its organizing theme. Three songs selected for that theme featured the actress Mala Sinha.[20] For someone not intimately familiar with Sinha's body of work, encountering this episode could create an association between Mala Sinha and the kinds of love songs that compared the female protagonist to the moon. This isn't entirely different from watching a number of songs picturized on the Hindi film actress Helen and putting her in a sociocultural category that evokes nightclubs and vamps.

In a period where programs like *Chitrahaar* (in Delhi), *Chhaya Geet* (in Bombay), and the weekly film were the only means of accessing film-related content outside the movie theater, these programs were the first time many viewers "saw" the song. Several of these viewers may still have heard the songs on radio and been familiar with them in a largely sonic way. By the late 1970s, there were approximately one million television sets in India, more than half of which were in Delhi and Bombay. This is barely 1% of the entire population at the time.[21] These figures, however, represent only the number of TV sets, not the number of people who watched TV. Accounts of the first two decades of television in India are replete with anecdotes and cultural commentary in newspapers and magazines that describe TV as a social medium, wherein the homes of those who did own TV sets became quasi theaters, with people from the neighborhood gathering in their living rooms to watch specific programs. Not unlike *Binaca Geet Mala*, *Chitrahaar* and *Chhaya Geet* became the means for people who weren't inclined to or couldn't watch movies in the theaters to access film-based material.

Transmediation and the Politics of Fragmentation

Central to this articulation of transmediating film songs was the material separation of the film and the song and also the visuals of the song from its audio means for the afterlife of the film. First, as with any instance of transmediation, the shift from one medium to another inevitably transforms the media object either as material or as content. Second, relatedly, each of the receiving media have their own ontologies that define what kind of material they can accept from another medium and, by extension, how the media object has to change to correspond with its new media destination. I'll add that this doesn't discount that these shows were conceived in accordance with the possibilities for changing the film object.

Further, it was not just the film object that underwent a transformation, but the receiving medium as well. The very arrival of film-based material on TV changed that medium in the most profound manner. In the case of film songs on radio, songs had to be extracted from the film and packaged as gramophone records, and then played on-air for the listeners. We could consider this selection a separation wherein the song is extracted from the finished film product, or we could think of it as going back to an earlier and incomplete stage of the film before the sound strip was added to the film, or, in other words, to a stage when sound and image were separate elements that had yet to even merge. In either situation, there is a separation of the audio from the visual, and that separation is crucial to the song's ability to be conducive to a sonic medium like radio. Third, both radio and television had to alter the song in some way to fit the format of the shows they had envisioned, first by selecting songs for extraction and then by further breaking them down in numerous ways. Both radio and TV often edit songs that are too long to fit with the format of the program—*Binaca Geet Mala*, for instance, was a one-hour program that played sixteen songs in that hour each week. It's not uncommon for songs to be between four and five minutes long, so even if the songs were played back-to-back with no commentary, sixteen full songs wouldn't fit in an hour, and Amin Sayani's commentary and anecdotes preceded every song. Each of these changes can influence the relationship between the song and the film and what the listener or viewer understands of the entire film from this one snippet.

Another factor altering the relationship between the film and the song in the process of transmediation was censorship. With visuals of the film included on TV, the lyrics of songs about love and longing that Keskar found vulgar, perhaps for suggestions of physical intimacy or even the idea of sex, became significantly less abstract. To combat this, TV producers often edited out some of the sexually suggestive imagery from the songs that were telecasting. Yakub Syed recalls asking producers to insert stock footage of two roses or a bird into songs to remove evidence of risqué content. This is curious since both radio and television could only feature songs from films that had received a censor certificate. I argue that the additional and usually ad hoc edits occurred because expectations of something playing in the circumscribed space of a movie theater that is built to subsume the spectator in darkness, and by extension in anonymity, are different from how it is watched in a domestic space, especially in broad daylight surrounded by family, neighbors, and children. It reflects a socio-spatial aspect of medium specificity as it brings attention to the need or desire to alter content based on where and how it is being watched.

With radio, the song stands more independent because it is without the visuals that attach it to the film. However, when visuals from the film are attached to the song, as they were in *Chitrahaar* and *Chhaya Geet*, is the relationship between the song and the film reestablished? The answer of course is necessarily subjective, based on a variety of factors, not least of which is whether the spectator has encountered the song as a part of the film at any time. When radio first started playing film songs, it was the only sonic medium for audiences to access even parts of the movies outside the movie theater. This was also the case for film material on TV. Therefore, from the 1930s until the arrival of VHS and cable TV, a spectator's ability to watch the entire film after encountering a song on radio or TV was quite limited. With more channels on offer after 1992 and most neighborhoods in the metro areas having their own cable operator sourcing movies that they showed on a local channel, there were more options. The caveat to having options is that it was again a minority of the population who could afford either video record players (VCRs), individual movie tapes, or even cable. Therefore, while these options certainly did exist, they didn't drastically change the centrality of television or of Doordarshan—the state-run channel—which continued to remain free while cable services cost extra.[22] The landscape of knowledge, curiosity, and access to film material of course exploded with the arrival and growth of the internet.

The thematic nature of *Chhaya Geet* also mitigated the connection between the film and the song, particularly for those whose first encounter with the song was on TV. If the theme was rain, the particularities of the entire movie became less relevant, but the content of the song, i.e. the lyrics and the visuals, did. Even for those who had watched the film before, the song with its visuals that usually featured big stars became little units of entertainment that offered the song, the stars, and visuals of the film. By the late 1990s, we see films including songs that appear to be staged the way they are precisely to fit into the structure of television for easy extraction. Thus, transmediation, specifically to television, became a part of the logic of film production. Consider the song "Koi ladka hai" (There is a boy) from the 1997 film *Dil Toh Pagal Hai* (This Heart Is Crazy, 1997).[23] The film presents a classic love triangle between Rahul (Shahrukh Khan), Pooja (Madhuri Dixit), and Nisha (Karishma Kapoor); Nisha is in love with Rahul who falls in love with Pooja. The song begins in the courtyard of what is presumably a home for orphans or poor children that Rahul and Pooja enter to escape a downpour. They then join the children, who are already doing a choreographed dance routine. The entire song is four minutes and forty seconds long. Of this, the first two and a half minutes are just Rahul and Pooja dancing with the children. Roughly halfway through the song, the setting changes to the lawns of the hospital where Nisha is recovering from a broken foot. She is brought out in a wheelchair while Rahul and Pooja (both dressed in different clothes) are dancing with a different group of backup dancers (adults this time). At some point, Nisha—with her foot in a cast—hops out of her wheelchair to go join them and the three of them lead the dance. The change of scene from the original location to a different one is not uncommon in song sequences; however, here, the change allowed the third star to join the dance, making it the one time the three stars are dancing together. I contend that this song was imagined this way—despite the fact the film narrative had Nisha wheelchair bound—to have a song that would feature its three stars, and could therefore be a vehicle to promote the film on television. In other words, the song was a package meant for easy extraction with the song, the dance, and the stars as its key offerings.

What then have the permutations of separation of the audio and visual tracks of a film meant for the afterlife of the film and the song? To an extent, we can argue that the affordances that these permutations introduced are crucial to making film music its own industry. This industry thrives because of the possibility of separating the song as a media object that can circulate independently of the film, both physically (as the packaged soundtrack available for purchase) but also as independent of the fate of the film. The ability to further break the song down into two media objects, one that is purely sonic, and the other that also has visuals from the film, multiplies the possibilities of transmediation. The sonic media object has circulated on radio, gramophone records, through cassette tapes, CDs, as mp3 files, and streaming, while the media object that includes the visuals with the audio has circulated through TV, VHS, DVDs, and the internet as YouTube videos or videos on other online platforms. These separations have allowed a dispersal of filmic material across other media, raising questions not just about the afterlife of the film song, but about the afterlife of the film itself as well.

Chapter 8

O'odham Dances: Soundscapes and Landscapes of Indigenous Resurgence

Angelica Marie Lawson

When reading Ofelia Zepeda's poetry, one is immersed in the language and the landscapes of the Tohono O'odham, the Desert People, of the American southwest and northern Mexico. Her elegant and concise "song poems"[1] allow the reader to briefly imagine the ephemeral moments of changing cloudscapes and desert rains. To read her poetry is to engage in a world unfamiliar to many, and to hear her read a poem is an opportunity to experience an Indigenous language rooted in the desert and long-standing traditions. Zepeda's poem film *O'odham Dances* invites the audience to briefly experience visually and viscerally the enchantment of the Sonoran Desert, a place of ceremony and song, gentle rains, and torrential floods. Aerial views of desert landscapes, ambient wind, and bird song entice the viewer to participate in what is about to begin. Through the poem's verses, they are called to join a ceremony to bring rain and fix the earth. However, the film does not depict ceremony with visual specificity. Instead, it immerses the audience in a soundscape of ceremony and images of the desert. A ceremonial leader calling their community to gather, a gourd rattle, a song in O'odham, and ambient sounds create an affective encounter with humans and other-than-humans, inviting the audience to participate in the experience. The film privileges an Indigenous perspective, ethically protecting sacred ceremonial knowledge by abstracting elements from ceremony to create an immersive moment while refusing to recreate the ethnographic spectacles of past film and media.

This chapter illuminates the poem film's contribution to a matrix of Indigenous resurgence practices and how they can connect creative work to the essential work of building and sustaining Indigenous community. It brings into conversation Indigenous digital media and critical Indigenous feminisms to consider how Indigenous women's creative work functions in tandem with their community engagement to produce projects of resurgence. These creative projects perform the critical work of centering voices and perspectives of historically silenced and continually marginalized groups. The majority of North American Indigenous media, and in particular film, does not look like mainstream film in that, aside from documentary, there is only a small body of feature films and very few are distributed to theaters for extended periods of time. Access to mainstream media production, specifically the Hollywood industry, has largely been denied to Indigenous writers and directors.[2] Meanwhile, there is a considerable body of work created by Indigenous artists and filmmakers shared online through various platforms such as Vimeo and YouTube. This work sometimes premieres in theaters and at festivals, but is ultimately distributed through less traditional channels, thereby creating greater access to the work. Importantly, these Indigenous authored works have created an outpouring in new media production by Indigenous people, delivering more truthful historical and contemporary representations. These counter-narratives intervene in settler colonial stories and stereotypes about Indigenous people. *O'odham Dances* is but one short film within a large body of Indigenous digital media available online, which can be extremely varied in terms of style and content, yet such works represent hidden treasures that deserve the attention of film and media critics, as well as the general public.

When considering the place of Indigenous film in the larger scope of global media we must consider more than the aesthetic hallmarks of this work. Frequently, this media includes Indigenous language with an emphasis on community and connection to place. Building on Annishnabeeg feminist scholar Leanne Simpson's work, Aubrey Hanson (Métis) in *Reading for Resurgence* claims artistic practices are essential to community resurgence, where resurgence is, in part, "the growth of Indigenous communities from strong roots towards strong futures, building upon tradition and heritage through processes of revitalization and reclamation in order to create healthy vibrant, self-determining nations."[3] As a linguist at the forefront of Indigenous language revitalization, Zepeda's poem film contributes to what I call Indigenous resurgence media, media that both reflects, and contributes to, resurgence practices. According to Simpson, resurgence theory derives from "Indigenous thought systems, intelligence systems that are continually generated in relationship to place."[4] Ceremonial practices are often place-specific and reflective of Indigenous ethics and values. The continuance of these ceremonies contributes to resurgence practices, which Zepeda shares in an abstracted and artistic way through her poetry and poem film collaboration. As such, the linguistic elements as well as ceremonial aesthetics of the film will be considered here.

On Poem Films

The poem film *O'odham Dances* debuted in Tucson, Arizona on April 25, 2017, and was a collaboration between Tohono O'odham linguist, scholar, and poet Ofelia Zepeda and filmmaker Johnathan VanBallenberghe for the Western Folklife Center's series "Moving Rural Verse: Poem Films from the Deep West." While the exact origin and definition of poetry film, or "poem film," is somewhat debated, the Center's emphasis on the "artful fusion of poetry and video" coincides with Herman Berlandt's definition in his 1977 essay "What Is a Poetry Film?," where he emphasizes a "collaboration between poet and film-maker" to create a film that "seeks a symbiotic relationship of image, music, and work; uses filmic rhythms as well as the tempo of music and meter to maintain mood and continuity."[5] This is reflected in Zepeda and VanBallenberghe's short film, which employs music, song, poetry, and film footage of the Sonoran Desert to draw the viewer into a meditative and rhythmic feeling of ceremonial participation.

The goal of the "Moving Rural Verse" series is to produce "poems that powerfully communicate contemporary rural issues, ideas and insight—and, in particular, the subject of water in the West...[to] nurture a deeper understanding of rural America and kindle important conversation."[6] Zepeda's creative approach to this theme highlights Indigenous perspectives on water, which are notably different from settler colonial perspectives. Rather than focus on issues typically associated with water in the West such as rivers, dams, or drought, Zepeda's poem alludes to O'odham ceremonies for bringing rain and fixing the earth. Zepeda notes that the visuals by VanBallenberghe help express an O'odham perspective that may benefit contemporary desert dwellers: "The scarcity of water is something that has always been there, so try to live accordingly, the way you are supposed to live in a desert."[7] In her article "Confluence: Water as an Analytic of Indigenous Feminism," Joanne Barker states:

> Water teaches us to be mindful of our relations with one another, including other-than-human beings and the lands and the waters on/in which we live together. It decenters human exceptionalism when considering issues of life and well-being requiring practices of responsible care in understanding the world and its varied, place-specific ecosystems that extend beyond the centrism of humans.[8]

O'odham dances are ceremonies conducted to invite water to the desert, but importantly, the ceremonial texts also remind humans of their interconnectedness to all living beings. This interconnectedness is at the center of the ceremony's importance. The poem film pushes back against simplistic notions of water scarcity in the West as a recent phenomenon. As a people thought to be one of the longest inhabitants in the Sonoran Desert, the Tohono O'odham language speaks specifically to water, and ceremonies to address it.

On the Indigenous O'odham Language

Much of *O'odham Dances* is in the O'odham language, contributing to a growing body of Indigenous art in Native languages. As a linguist and figure of critical importance in global Native language resurgence, Zepeda has made invaluable contributions to the general field of American Indian Studies and specifically to Native language revitalization. Even before becoming a professor at the University of Arizona, Zepeda participated in projects to encourage language revitalization and literacy. One of the many projects she spearheaded was to encourage students of the O'odham language to write original stories, poems, and essays in their language. Many of these students were educators themselves and were teaching at bilingual schools. Zepeda's original goal for writing and eventually publishing in the O'odham language was to help build an O'odham literature base in order to increase literacy: "As a language teacher, and having been a student of my own language, I saw how limited the literature was as far as anything that could be used in a classroom setting, for adult readers of O'odham especially."[9] Zepeda's efforts to produce literature in O'odham led to collections of student poetry and stories, sometimes collected informally, and in the case of *Mat Hekid o Ju/When It Rains: Papago and Pima Poetry* (1982) collected and published by the University of Arizona Press.

Zepeda is a lauded and highly recognized linguist whose work with the Tohono O'odham language has garnered many prestigious awards including a MacArthur Fellowship in 1999. Her academic and creative works are published in numerous journals, books, and anthologies and her contribution to the revitalization and publication of the O'odham language is significant. Her published creative works are also substantial. She has published several books of bilingual poetry, including *Ocean Power: Poems from the Desert* (1995), *Jewed 'I-hoi/Earth Movements: O'odham Poems* (1997), and *Where Clouds Are Formed* (2008). Naturally, Zepeda is aware of the significance of creating work in the O'odham language:

> It is language, of course, that orders, carries, and expresses [our] experience and...transmits it to future generations. But this implies more than simply language capacity or language as speech. The meanings, symbolism, shared history, and experiences of a people within a landscape all reside within individual languages.[10]

Language revitalization, a critical component of Indigenous resurgence, is an important part of current Indigenous movements. As such, Zepeda's bilingual poems contain significant amounts of untranslated O'odham. In her introduction to her premiere book of poetry, *Ocean Power: Poems from the Desert*, she says:

> As for the pieces that are written in O'odham, for the moment I will simply say that O'odham is my first language. I feel confident in the language and so am able to create pieces solely in my first language... The O'odham pieces could be meant for the small but growing number of O'odham speakers who are becoming literate. Here, then, is a little bit of O'odham literature for them to read.[11]

However, despite her modest assertion that these poems are merely "a bit of O'odham literature for them to read," her publication of these untranslated poems is a poignant political statement regarding the legitimacy and significance of the O'odham language—a statement that speaks to Indigenous resurgence and resistance to attempted Native language eradication by settler colonial institutions, such as boarding schools which were designed to eliminate Indigenous languages and cultures.[12] Zepeda's poem film *O'odham Dances* does important work in its contribution to language resurgence while also emphasizing the importance of ceremony.

Zepeda was raised in an O'odham community in the Sonoran Desert. In this setting, Zepeda states, "our community organization replicated the traditional O'odham village community" and "even in the unlikely setting of cotton farms the traditional beliefs were held on to steadfastly. Many traditional practices were carried out in these communities."[13] Zepeda's upbringing led to poems referencing these practices, such as ceremonies for "pulling down the clouds," ceremonies to bring rain and "fix the earth."[14] As a child, she heard about the ceremonies from her parents, and when she was older, she was able to participate. Observing O'odham oratory, she notes: "The O'odham have a great deal of oral tradition that speaks to the topic of rain. The oral tradition, whether it is in the form of song, oratory, speech, prayer, or story, can speak of the moisture and other minute instances of it in the most poetic way."[15] The inclusion of Indigenous language, in addition to the sounds and images in the poem film *O'odham Dances*, conveys the longevity of these important ceremonies and the language in which it is grounded.

The "Vanishing Race" and Ethnographic Refusal

However, the poem film does not feature ceremony with visual specificity and, as such, refuses to share sacred knowledge with the audience. This is a significant refusal which resists popular and historical depictions of Native Americans in film. Since the early days of cinema and Thomas Edison's invention of the kinetoscope, Native American ceremonies have been captured on film. Edison's vignettes, sometimes referred to as "actualities," included ethnographic short films of Native American ceremonies including "Hopi Snake Dance" and "Sioux Ghost Dance," and while these ceremonies were likely inaccurate, they were promoted as authentic and viewers believed they were seeing slices of real Native American life.[16] These films were part of a larger movement in both academia and the arts to capture the ceremonies of the exotic Other before they disappeared.[17]

The assimilation policy period, marked by both the passing of the Dawes Act in 1887 and the first off-reservation boarding school for Native

Americans in Carlisle, Pennsylvania in 1897, led many to believe that Native Americans were doomed to disappear. The United States goal to individualize and detribalize Native Americans was backed by official US policy and forced assimilation placed special emphasis on eradicating Indigenous languages, with boarding schools forbidding the use of Native American language, along with customs, clothing, and spiritual practices, often inflicting harsh physical punishment for digressions.[18] The boarding school era contributed to both the rapid decline of Indigenous languages and the belief that Native Americans were going to "vanish," if not literally, then culturally, launching anthropological research on Native Americans and establishing careers for artists wishing to capture the vanishing race before their demise, the most famous of whom was Edward Curtis. In 1906 Curtis used moving pictures and photography to record ceremonies, events, and portraits of Native Americans. The opening photo for his multi-volume, decades-long photographic project *The North American Indian (1907–1930)* was titled "The Vanishing Race" and in Curtis's words was meant to convey how "the Indians as a race, already shorn of their tribal strength and stripped of their primitive dress, are passing into the darkness of an unknown future."[19] Curtis, revered for his work, captured the sentiment of the era, one that was also expressed in major motion pictures.

In 1925 Paramount Pictures released *The Vanishing American*, directed by George Seitz based on a novel by Zane Grey. This epic silent western was meant to be a sympathetic portrayal of Native Americans; however, the script was rewritten to include a prologue not included in the original material. The prologue shows the conquering of one people after another beginning with what appear to be cavemen and ending with Kit Carson taming the southwest. The setting for the remainder of the film is a fictional reservation with a fictional tribe (clearly based on Navajo people) and ends with the tragic death of the hero and protagonist Nophaie. The prologue hints at this inevitability as "Nophaie and his people represent a noble but doomed race," allowing the viewer to "feel deep sympathy but without responsibilities since the Indians are soon to be no more."[20] This notion of a Vanishing Race/American has persisted into the present; however, Indigenous filmmakers, writers, poets, and artists are working to resist these destructive narratives, and instead highlight living, vibrant Indigenous people and their languages.[21]

Indigenous resurgence includes reclaiming and revitalizing Indigenous languages, and recently filmmakers have been foregrounding Indigenous language in their work. Hopi photographer and filmmaker Victor

Masayesva's short film *Hopiit* (1981), and later *Itam Hakim Hopiit: We, Someone, The Hopi* (1984), are both films entirely in the Hopi language and feature contemporary Hopi communities and storytelling. Zacharias Kunuk's breakthrough fiction feature film *Atanarjuat: The Fast Runner* (2001) made headlines and won awards as the first full-length feature film in the Inuit language. As more Indigenous filmmakers are creating work to be circulated both in theaters and online (though more frequently online), we are seeing a proliferation of films that feature Indigenous language, including the work of Amanda Strong, Missy Whiteman, Lisa Jackson, Johnathan Thunder, Sky Hopinka, and others.

As Native American filmmakers and artists actively resist the myth of the vanishing race, many also refuse to divulge sacred information in their art, thus refusing to participate in ethnographic spectacle. This collaboration between Zepeda and VanBallenberghe is no exception. The poem film *O'odham Dances* resists the narrative of disappearing while also indicating the living vitality of Indigenous people and ceremony. Yet, even as it refuses to share ceremonial knowledge with visual representation of O'odham dances, the film invites the viewer in to share the experiential affect of this significant ceremony. It does this through notable visual and audio cues throughout the film.

O'odham Dances

As the poem film begins, a close-up of prickly pear cactus fills the frame before transitioning to a hillside dotted with luminous Saguaro. The viewer is immersed in the sounds of the desert. Birds chirp and insects buzz as the camera eyes a wary tortoise before closely scanning teddy bear cholla and fading to black. The title card "O'odham Dances" appears on screen in tandem with the poet's voice. As she recites the initial lyrics in O'odham, the viewer re-enters the desert landscape from a bird's-eye view. They float back into the scene to a soundscape consisting of the poet's voice and ambient wind until we hear the first note of a gourd rattle. Soon, the rhythmic shaking of the rattle is accompanied by a song in the O'odham language. Zepeda emulates a ceremonial leader through the refrain "oigo, oigo," calling the audience to gather, as a ceremonial leader would call to their participants. The song remains in the background as the poet continues. Switching to English, she says, "it is time for the ritual." The desert setting, song, ambient sounds, and poem lyrics make one feel as though they are there, as though they are part of the event. The affect of this soundscape and the visual re-entry from a bird's-eye view is one that invites the viewer to participate. As the scene fades from day to night the images mirror the language of the poem:

Throughout the night,
a night too short for such important work,
the people converge energies

As Zepeda switches to English interspersed with O'odham, she maintains a poetic ceremonial aesthetic that echoes concepts from an O'odham worldview, providing a glimpse of the meaning of the previously untranslated words. A hallmark of Zepeda's poetry is her ability to manipulate the English language to better reflect O'odham oratory. The poem is written and spoken with attention to cultural patterns from O'odham ceremonial traditions. The steady refrain of "Oigo oigo," in addition to repetitive phrases throughout, emulates O'odham ceremonial texts. Zepeda states, "Linguistically, this piece has some O'odham phrases which I pulled from how traditional singers and ritual language handle calling people together around water."[22] In this way, Zepeda is able to speak to an O'odham ethic that insists on the importance of ceremony and ritual. In commenting on the importance of the rain ceremony to the O'odham, Zepeda states, "We believe that this ceremony and many others must be continued in order that everything be right. Should the ceremonies end, we believe that the world as we know it would not be the same."[23] Zepeda speaks poetically to this concept in *O'odham Dances* and artistically expresses this ethic in an aesthetically pleasing way. In addition, Zepeda's use of parallelism mirrors the form and structure of ceremonial oratory:

They call upon the night.
They call upon the stars in the darkness.
They call upon the hot breezes.
They call upon the heat coming off the earth.
They implore all animals.

The ceremony is meant to invoke an event and ceremonial texts often include repetition as a way to build power. Importantly, they are also place-specific. "They" in the poem refers to the O'odham community, who have for centuries lived in the Sonoran Desert reaching from the southwestern United States and across northern Mexico. This home has, naturally, inspired many songs about rain. "The songs deal with the holiest of all things to the desert people, rain. To them rain is...life itself."[24] As the poem concludes, images of clouds gathering and a soundscape of heavy rain evoke monsoons familiar to those who live in the desert—the specific rains that are called for in the ceremony. The concluding soundscape of heavy rainfall implies the success of the ceremony:

From the dark dryness of the desert,
on that one night the call of the people is heard.
It is heard by the oceans, winds, and clouds.

The final audio creates a pulsing sound like ocean waves, alluding to *Ocean Power: Poems from the Desert.* This seemingly incongruent pairing of ocean and desert in the title is a reference to the salt pilgrimages historically performed by O'odham men, who would travel by foot across the desert to the ocean to ask for rain. Again, this ceremony indicates a consciousness of delicately balanced ecosystems, and recognizes that the waters of the world are intricately connected. Our actions in one place may affect what happens in another. In this way we are urged to consider our interconnectedness and interdependence on larger ecosystems beyond our own specific location. Despite being a very place-based poem set in the Sonoran Desert, both the ceremony and poem acknowledge the oceans along with "all the waters of the earth."

The concluding images capture a morning sunrise as the poem ends. Halos gather around the prickly spines of cholla and other cacti as we hear footsteps and Zepeda walks into the light. She recites:

With the dawn we face the sunrise.
We face it with all our humility.
We are mere beings.

O'odham humility acknowledges that people are one small part of a greater ecosystem, one that must be carefully balanced. As Barker states, "It is not quaint when Indigenous people tell water stories or perform water ceremonies. Water represents that humans are not the preeminent life force in the universe."[25] *O'odham Dances* reminds us of our interconnectedness and interdependence for survival. In "converging energies" through ceremony and calling humans and other-than-humans together, the ceremony conveys teachings around water.

However, community emphasis on ceremony does not imply a lack of political action on the part of the O'odham and other tribal nations who have fought to assert their water rights and sovereignty regarding those rights for decades. Indeed, the surge in Indigenous activism regarding water protection, from Idle No More to Standing Rock, prove that water teachings and knowledges work together with political action to assert Indigenous understandings and movements around water.[26] This activism is rooted in knowledge systems regarding care and kinship, and works toward strengthening self-determining nations. Resurgence media contributes to these efforts, and in their creative approach to collaborating on a film about "water in the West" Zepeda and VanBallenberghe bring a perspective both ancient and new to the conversation.

Part Four

Intersectional Politics in Global Media

Chapter 9

Intimidades de Shakespeare y Víctor Hugo: Discomfort at Elderly Women's Intimacies

Lilia Adriana Pérez Limón

Media representations of old age have proven to be complicated in Mexico, and the issue has only become more urgent. A frequent undercurrent of the crime and horror genre throughout Mexican cinema is a general anxiety about aging women, and this subgenre reveals concerns that are specific to disability culture. The increased media emphasis on the possible dangers presented by aging and the easily corruptible elderly population betrays a discomfort with the increased isolation of Mexico's older population. This isolation is presented as being akin to criminality given that it opens the door for transgression of generational roles. In this chapter, I explore the presence of disability and criminality in the representation of intimacy in old age by situating the absence of proper aging in the work of Yulene Olaizola's 2008 documentary, *Intimidades de Shakespeare y Víctor Hugo* (Shakespeare and Victor Hugo's Intimacies). This reading is heavily invested in questioning stereotypical representations of old age, arguing that current depictions in film and television contribute to harmful ableist attitudes, which in turn justify practices that reproduce the social and material conditions for old age to be considered a pathological disability.

In the tradition of disability studies, gerontology, and cultural studies, Sally Chivers's *The Silvering Screen: Old Age and Disability in Cinema* examines several films about aging, demonstrating how Hollywood repeatedly conflates representations of aging with representations of disability.[1] Following Chivers in further problematizing some of the dominant trends in the representation of aging, Timothy Shary and Nancy McVittie's *Fade to Gray: Aging in American Cinema* examines social attitudes toward

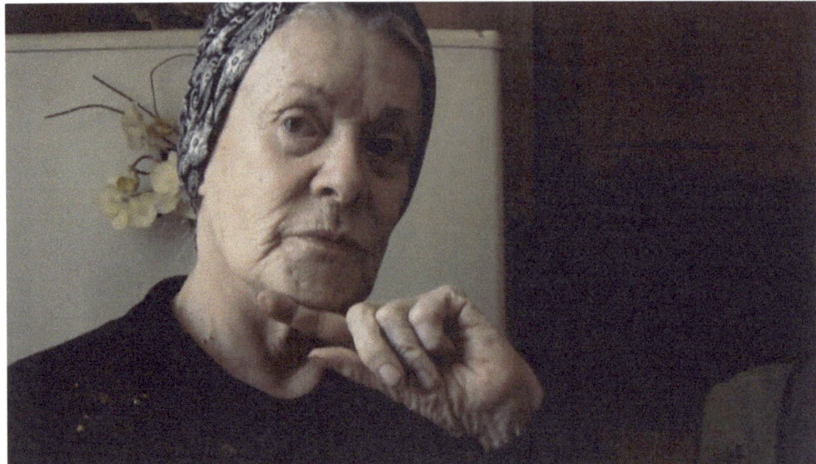

Figure 01. Rosa Carbajal is remembering Jorge Riosse telling her he was twenty years old, but he was twenty-five and she was fifty-five years old.

aging through an analysis of the social and political motivations for negative cinematic portrayals of the elderly.[2] In line with Chivers, Shary, and McVittie, my analysis of Olaizola's work shows how the documentary replicates the negative traits that categorize aging characters as pathologically disabled in media.

Intimidades de Shakespeare y Víctor Hugo is a documentary about the tenants of a house located on the corner of Shakespeare and Víctor Hugo streets in Colonia Anzures in Mexico City. The film goes back twenty years to when Rosa Carbajal, the filmmaker's grandmother and owner of the house, met Jorge Riosse, a young guest with whom she became very close. The man lived there for eight years, during which he always showed himself to be a talented and calm person. However, after Riosse's abrupt death, unique details of his personality came to light, such as the fact that he occasionally cross-dressed and went out at night without anyone knowing his whereabouts. Later, his name was linked to the murder of several sex workers in La Merced, a neighborhood in Mexico City. The journey the film takes through the labyrinths of memory garnered Olaizola significant acclaim.[3]

Emphasizing a thematic examination of the veracity of the story, the narrative is built around conversations with Rosa Carbajal, her housekeeper Florencia Vega Moctezuma, a lodger who knew Riosse, and Rosa's son and sister. From its very beginnings, socially committed filmmakers in the New Latin American Cinema movement embraced documentary approaches as a means of cultural exploration that allowed them to express a raw realism. The upsurge of Latin American documentary,[4] in the context of Mexico, includes an increase in documentary festivals[5] and a growth in alternative distribution channels with widespread digital technologies becoming more available.[6] The relatively inexpensive types of documentary filmmaking made possible by portable media presented an advantage to documentary filmmakers for presenting urgent social, economic, and political issues.

The Rise of Mexican Commercial Documentary

Documentaries of social representation are typically non-fiction, and they aim to give viewers a tangible representation of certain aspects of the world. According to the initial understanding of the documentary narrative, the film has an ideological function, but its merits transpire in its artistry. Documentaries make the stuff of social reality visible and audible, according to the acts of editing, selection, and curation carried out by the filmmaker. Documentaries also convey truths according to the filmmaker, and the audience must assess their claims, assertions, and arguments in relation to the world as we know it and decide whether they are worthy of belief. Social documentaries offer us new views of our common world to explore and understand.[7]

Ignacio Sánchez Prado argues that the social documentary has long been the dominant form in Mexico even though they are often only seen by relatively small audiences. Sánchez Prado attributes the success of Mexican documentaries in the neoliberal market to their vague political messages that appeal to a diverse audience.[8] Within this framework, Olaizola's 2008 documentary encompasses a narrative that is in concordance with the state's vision of older people and shows older women in the same depictions of old age that have worked historically. Following the example of non-subversive cinema, *Intimidades de Shakespeare y Víctor Hugo* continues Mexican cinematic depictions of older women by either not including them at all or by grouping them in categories of older women in traditional roles (caregivers who are dependent and selfless) and by generally providing a negative image of older female characters, who are often portrayed as unbearable mothers-in-law, mentally deteriorating, perverse, and/or deranged.

Alba Nidia Sánchez Baltazar's study on postmodern cinema says that this type of cinema does not intend to show reality but also does not reconstruct it.[9] Rather, postmodern cinema looks for new ways to explain reality; it relativizes it in partial truths according to the subjectivities of those who intervene and those who present themselves in the film. Sánchez Baltazar understands this as a crisis of representation where the possibility of knowing reality or giving voice to others is brought into question. Ultimately, this cinema foregrounds the need to contextualize the producer and the film. Connecting back Sánchez Prado's logic to Mexican documentary films' success in the neoliberal market, Sánchez Baltazar understands these documentary films as seeing reality from their own and individual positions, but with concerns that transcend the regional and come to be positioned as part of global cinema. This cinema is situated between the most independent and experimental trends and those aimed at mass commercial consumption. According to Sánchez Baltazar, more diverse films are proposed using realism as a narrative strategy, the use of subjectivity, and breaking with conventional structures. To this end, Lauro Zavala's study on new Mexican documentary understands the unprecedented distribution and exhibition as the result of the production of materials closer to formal experimentation and the exploration of equally undocumented themes, especially in relation to gender studies, migration, exile, and personal reflection.[10]

Understanding how Olaizola's documentary represents the historical world by giving audible and visual shape to a perspective on Mexican society is key to understanding Olaizola's grandmother. The topic of intimacy in old age being linked to pathology is normally a controversial issue. If one considers the reception of the film, it becomes apparent that its art festival success directly had to do with its lack of a direct approach to aging intimacies. Rather, it centered on the prominent narrative of a different elder–youth relationship in Mexican cinema, the filmmaker's pursuit of resolution through an internal odyssey with her grandmother. The voice of the documentary conveys a sense of urgency to pathologize Jorge Riosse for the violence he committed against women combined with archival footage that shifts the attention away from the elderly grandmother's intimacy. As Sánchez Prado puts it in his study, the documentary's politics on aging might come off as ambiguous enough to enjoy good art cinema distribution because they appeal to a diverse audience. However, unlike *En el hoyo* (In the Pit, 2006), the film subject of Sánchez Prado's study, this documentary participates in the art cinema circuit, although its subject matter does not directly critique the dominant stance on Mexican aging intimacy, nor does it outwardly support any stance that condemns violence against women. This documentary achieved success not because of its social-political ambiguity but because of its alliance to normative cultural narratives on proper femininity and aging. Yet the topic of aging is not the main focus of the film, nor is the narrative of gender violence. The dominant culture proposes a conventional way of understanding old age, but some directors, knowingly or not, propose alternative forms. Olaizola's documentary does not. At first sight, the film generates a plurality of voices that counteract the dominant values proposed by media in Mexico, mostly from a young, masculine, able-bodied vision that does not accurately represent women or aging. However, in further analyzing this exploration of loneliness, longing, and intimacy in old age, I read her film as yet another contribution to the normative ideas of aging in Mexican media.

According to Bill Nichols, there are six principal modes of documentary filmmaking: poetic, expository, observational, participatory, reflexive, and performative.[11] *Intimidades de Shakespeare y Víctor Hugo* falls under the participatory mode, as the interaction between the filmmaker

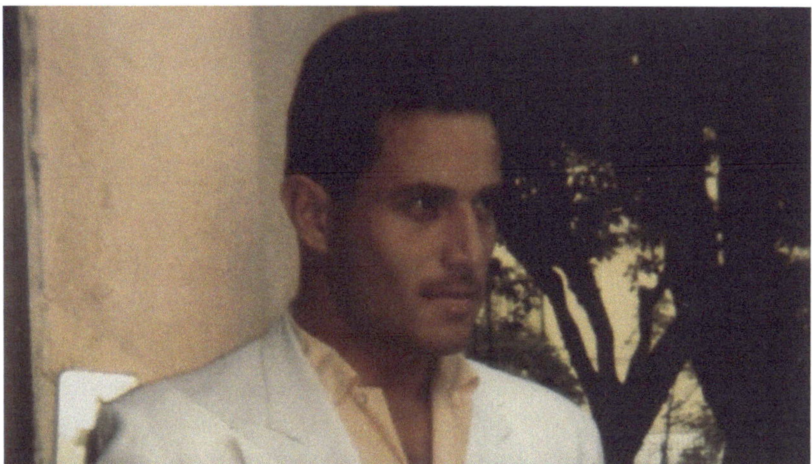

Figure 02. A picture of Jorge Riosse that Rosa Carbajal has in her home.

and the subject, her grandmother, allows the filming to take place through interviews or other forms of conversation. Much of the documentary is coupled with archival footage examining the historical crimes of "the killer of the Merced." The title *Intimidades de Shakespeare y Víctor Hugo* suggests a personal approach, an investigative report on a family history.[12] Olaizola presents Riosse in a complex way, from various points of view. In doing so, the film moves away from the classic ways of representing crime stories through an expository mode and instead analyzes Riosse's personality from multiple angles in order to better shape a more informed image of the grandmother's intimate friend.

As previously mentioned, the documentary does not attempt to offer a direct political reading of old age or give a critique of May–December romances. Instead, the documentary's rhetoric falls under a supposed subjective approach to contemporary Mexican reality by placing the camera in the domestic space, allowing for a personal and intimate view of the family. With references to official discourses on violence against women, it proposes the idea of authenticity. These domestic scenes are what make the documentary appear as a vital source of evidence about the world and its discourses on violence against women.

In that same vein, audiences saw Olaizola's 2008 documentary as interweaving between interactive and reflexive modes of narration. Her committed filmmaking approaches the documentary form as her primary tool in the search to discover and define the submerged, denied, and devalued realities of her grandmother, yet she always represents her as an old and fragile woman. She takes as a starting point the intimate structure of domestic life. The documentary explores the mysterious history of Jorge Riosse, a lodger who resided at Rosa Elena Carbajal's boarding house. The film is an early 1990s portrait of Rosa, who unashamedly gives her granddaughter and the viewer a tour of her home and of her past relationship with Riosse, the suspected "killer of the Merced," a precarious neighborhood in Mexico City. Interlaced with the mystery plot is a platonic love story. The documentary narrates the relationship Olaizola's grandmother had with Jorge Riosse, a man who filled her life with art and love, but whom she also suspected of murdering a dozen sex workers.

Films such as *Intimidades de Shakespeare y Víctor Hugo* demonstrate that, as elderly people become more numerous and commonplace in twenty-first-century Mexican life, elderly characters in Mexican films often fall into recurring types: saintly grandparents, out-of-touch seniors, and admirable pillars of the community. In contrast, Olaizola portrays her grandmother as infused with mystery and scandal and is always careful not to linger on the subject of her grandmother, instead shifting the focus toward Riosse's criminal endeavors. Through interviews, the documentary reveals her grandmother's close relationship with the much younger Riosse, a man who lived a withdrawn life, shutting out a past he rarely spoke about.

The Mexican film industry and culture at large are deeply invested in repressing aging femininity and intimate romantic desires as dangerous or comical. Despite cultural myths around aging, the need for intimacy, excitement, and pleasure does not disappear in old age. The discomfort that elder intimacy provokes has been reflected in film and treated as a pathology for a long time. The puritanical ethos of Mexican culture imposes a moral innocence on intimate practices among the aging. The perception of romance or intimacy among the aged has been reflected in films that treat these otherwise healthy relationships with suspicion and apprehension. Despite this, some more recent Mexican documentaries have depicted elder relationships without the trappings of the pathology *Intimidades de Shakespeare y Víctor Hugo* fails to escape.[13]

Dehumanization and objectification of elderly people sets the stage for many Hollywood cinematic representations: the comedic trope, the elder odyssey, the May–December romance genre device, the geriatric death trope, and generational conflict in which elderly people are hindrances, helpers, or recipients of care. Like the examples of commercial and critical success in Hollywood representations, *Intimidades de Shakespeare y Víctor Hugo* uses the female aging trope to promote anxiety and discomfort of aging femininity as disturbingly disabled. The grandmother's friendship with a younger man has ominous consequences for any transgressive desires.

Documentary's Private Matters

The opening scene of *Intimidades de Shakespeare y Víctor Hugo* features an exterior long shot of the Colonia Anzures, zooming into a bedroom window that a few seconds later we will find out is Rosa's, and the zoom is accompanied by a male voice heard coming from an audio recording. The voice is reading part of the *Manual de Urbanidad y Buenas Maneras*

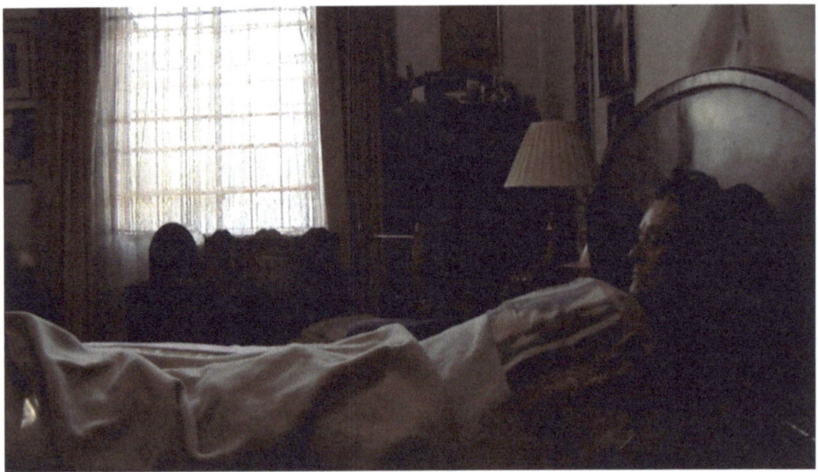

Figure 03. Rosa Carbajal is waking up listening to the news on the radio about the feminicides in Ciudad Juárez.

(Manual of Urbanity and Good Manners) by Manuel Antonio Carreño (1834). The voice goes on speaking about the ways to be a good hostess:

> Today, as yesterday, you have to observe a series of rules in order to be a kind, well-bred hostess. Thus, my friend, you must know how to sit at the table as this is a mirror that reflects good manners more than other settings. And never forget that eating vulgarly is a great insult to others. And eating in a hurry is bad for your health. One such mistake is to break up your bread and make little balls. But does that not deprive us of many satisfactions and true comfort which lies not in abandon, but in the enjoyment of beauty and order?[14]

Once we cut inside Rosa's bedroom, there is a change from this almost dreamlike scene to another in which an alarm clock announces the political campaign of Patricia Mercado, candidate for the Alternativa party in Ciudad Juárez, a city known for its violence against women. Rosa wakes to the ominous reality of aggression against women. The allusion to Carreño's manual refers to the gender norms expected of bourgeois Mexican women, and it is drastically cut and transitioned to the current state of gender violence. At first sight, the documentary seems to be about the violence against women inflicted by Jorge Riosse, "the killer of the Merced," who murdered sex workers and was the filmmaker's grandmother's tenant and friend. The news audio heard at the beginning of the documentary also informs the viewer of the violence suffered by women in Mexico, helping appeal to diverse audiences that all seem to agree on the topic of gender violence. However, in keeping with the fragile wealthy woman's story of cohabiting with evil, the documentary unintentionally uncovers an intimate relationship and the presence of desire in senescence.

In recent Mexican documentary films, narratives of self-reflection and self-referential proposals have begun to take on value. One of the rationales is the incentive to face a certain theme and to capture it on film. *Intimidades de Shakespeare y Víctor Hugo* offers a glimpse of a well-off, aging woman's life, showing that it is tinged with loneliness. The representation of Rosa is relatively unique among those on the silver screen. Very few films focus on elderly characters, and even fewer center characters who live mundane upper-middle-class lives. As such, her portrayal is of keen interest in any effort to chart the relationship between criminality and old age on film. More typically, the placeholder for a main character is someone with a more fascinating life. That is, someone with an intriguing story to tell; however, the director gradually presents the intimate friendship that developed between Rosa and Riosse via interviews where her

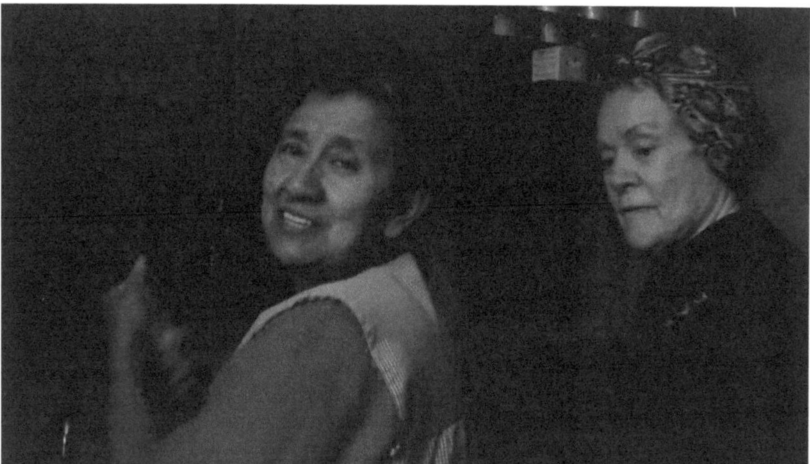

Figure 04. Rosa Carbajal and Flor, her domestic worker, remember how the rooms were arranged and the first time they met Jorge Riosse.

grandmother narrates her personal stories about Riosse, arousing interest in the viewer.

The documentary focuses on the intimate spaces and quotidian life of the Colonia Anzures house, where Flor, the housekeeper, is shown cleaning and walking up and down the stairs filling in the gaps of the stories that Rosa shares, while catching on camera the familiar scenes that the director remembers from childhood. At that time, Jorge Riosse was a man in his early twenties who was a talented poet, a skilled painter, and a virtuoso guitarist and singer, as evidenced by cassette tapes recorded by Rosa and played off-screen while Rosa is in conversation with her granddaughter. The camera reveals his work around the house, and bit by bit this ingeniously constructed documentary also brings out Riosse's darker side alongside Rosa's own constructed pathology. The documentary offers the sensuous experience of sounds and images shown by the grandmother which move the viewer, activating feelings and emotions, such as the nostalgic desires experienced by Rosa, and they also tap into values and beliefs that reprimand her for feeling such things. Further, when invoking memories of Rosa's dead brother, Flor and Olaizola are careful not to upset Rosa, equating her vulnerability with an old woman's mental and emotional fragility.

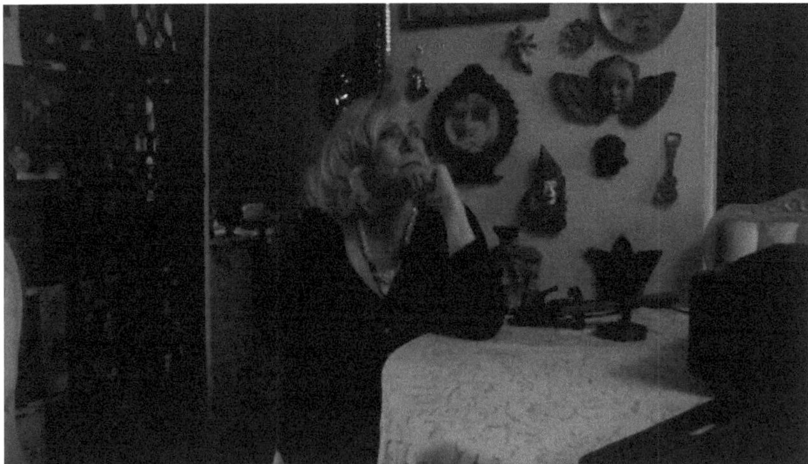

Figure 05. Rosa Carbajal listening to an old recording of Jorge Riosse singing.

Told from the perspective of the director's grandmother's memories, Olaizola's film draws on the images, objects, and confidences that Riosse left on his way through the house, combined with an investigative report of the times in which the story took place. This introspective look gives context to the intimate relationship that arose between the two. In Jorge Ayala Blanco's analysis of the film, he argues that the geriatric representation of Rosa is replete with references to illness, given that cinema has idealized the association of old age with tragedy.[15] Viewed through the lens of pathology, he describes Rosa as an accomplice to Riosse's murderous scheme: "He was seen dressed as a woman walking through Reforma at the height of the Chapultepec cinema a few blocks from the guest house…the lady used to receive as nice trophies identification cards or passports of his eventual sentimental conquests, national and American ladies who apparently occasionally flirted with him in his nocturnal wanderings."[16] Partly because of this tradition, the social perception of older women having intimate relations with a younger man is charged with perversity. And a price must always be paid for breaking age boundaries. The elder character once again gives way to death; this time, however, tragedy befalls her younger male companion's faith.

If there existed a portrayal of a malevolent older woman accomplice to the crimes against women enacted by a homophobic homosexual man, the filmmaker is sure to dispel with that representation of her grandmother. Instead, she presents her grandmother as isolated and vulnerable, subject to the whims of dangerous, unstable younger people. The documentary subtly draws a parallel between geriatric intimacy and criminality. The viewer is warned of the horrific consequences suffered by older women who continually refuse to obediently adhere to their prescribed social role. Senior intimacy, homosexuality, and serial killers all share a pathology when they resist social-cultural exigencies.

The success of this personal documentary is due to the fact that it couples its account of personal experience with larger social and historical ramifications but retains a local focus. The coupling of the personal and the social often serves to establish credibility; the mysterious past of Olaizola's grandmother's relationship with a younger alleged criminal and the concerned responses to and fear about her sexuality dominated her family. Olaizola starts from what she knows best—personal experience—and extends outward into the social taboo of May–December relationships. Through the film's voiceover narration, we come to understand that the particular concern is not Riosse's dangerousness but Rosa's late-onset sexuality. The documentary teaches us that such moments of entrance into catastrophic loss typify Mexican culture's construction of feminine aging. This, along with the dearth of other commercial cinema, may result in representations that draw more upon stereotypes or assumptions about old age than they do upon lived experiences. Furthermore, many representations of old age are located in female characters and are formally structured so as to marginalize and isolate them from their social surroundings. Rosa's assumed sexual pathology inevitably leads to social marginalization. It is promising, however, that Mexican documentarians have begun to include more representations of elderly people in their films, but the quality of those depictions deserves further scrutiny from elder audiences.

Despite the work of many documentary filmmakers, there are still many limitations to how gerontological cinema is approached. Cinema has for a long time sought the complicity of younger audiences and has almost forgotten the existence of other potential, older audiences. Undoubtedly, there are many areas that are still left to explore to better represent senior intimacy in documentary films. Certainly, cinema can provide benefits when it tells stories about elderly characters that are not marked by prejudice by offering diverse reflections on aging. The work of this chapter has been part of an endeavor to think about filmic characteristics of old age, desire, and intimacy and how these qualities are negatively activated in relation to our ideas of disability. I have sought to re-imagine intergenerational relationships and gerontological desires that are associated with pathology. This chapter has been concerned with challenging the cultural scripts that can dictate the models of normativity. Patterns of anxiety relating to old age have consistently haunted film. It is in thinking through the kinds of unsettling feelings that aging characters provoke that leads us to imagine other forms of understanding old age and relationships that are not a pathology.

Chapter 10

PeaceMaker: Simulating Settler-Colonialism and Subaltern Gaming

Meryem Kamil

> Congratulations! You and your Palestinian counterpart have won the PeaceMaker Medal for achieving a two-state solution. Jerusalem now serves as the capital of the two countries. Joint Palestinian and Israeli security forces are working together to implement the peace settlement. You are a true PeaceMaker! (*PeaceMaker: Israeli Palestinian Conflict*)

In 2005, two graduate students at Carnegie Mellon developed *PeaceMaker: Israeli Palestinian Conflict* as part of a portfolio of games that "promote deeper engagement with current events around the world" and "change the way people consume information and understand the world around them."[1] The discourse around ImpactGames, the company established by the two, explicitly endorses a blurring of game and simulation. "Imagine fantasy sports meets the evening news," reads the description of another ImpactGames project.[2] ImpactGames draws players into game worlds that are modeled from events and political structures but feature fictionalized scenarios.

PeaceMaker simulates the Israeli–Palestinian conflict and the uneven nature of sociopolitical relations. For example, its gameplay presents limitations on Palestinian agency through minimal turn options and automatically canceled player choices.[3] Despite this acknowledgment of asymmetricality, the game aesthetics and narrative fall short of contextualizing Israel as a settler-colonial state. In fact, the game often echoes colonial discourse on Palestinian violence and primitivity. As a result, the gameplay and narrative of *PeaceMaker* are at odds with one another.

Despite the internal incongruity of the game, *PeaceMaker* can be approached through "subaltern gaming" or "playing from below" to experiment with alternate political possibilities for Palestinians. I propose the concept of *subaltern gaming* as an orientation to gameplay that destabilizes common rules and goals of gaming. Subaltern gaming is an inflection of the concept of queer gaming, defined by Bo Ruberg as "a transformative practice that remakes games."[4] Queer gaming allows gamers to use play as a practice of resistance and, in doing so, allows for players to propose alternative orientations toward power. Queer play emphasizes pleasure in losing, the joy of boredom, and the freedom of transgressive gaming. Gaming from below operates in a similar orientation; rather than winning or beating a game, the player's discovery of rules and game mechanics is the primary aim for subaltern gaming.

Subaltern gaming draws from postcolonial studies' concept of the subaltern, a class of people subjected to power. The subaltern refers to those on the margins, those with limited power due to race, class, geography, sexuality, or any other identifier that is used to demarcate the ideal citizen from the Others.[5] Like postcolonial subaltern studies, subaltern gaming centers questions of authority, agency, and subjects' capacity for resisting systems of power. Subaltern gaming *imagines* and has the capacity to aid in *producing* alternative matrices of control and freedom. Subaltern gaming prevents us from accepting unequal systems and dynamics as the only possibility.

Central to subaltern gaming is the blurring of *game* and *simulation*, of game worlds and sociopolitical systems. Either through design or play, the game functions as a porous experiential space. Scholars like Espen Aarseth and Patrick Crogan argue the essence of computing is simulation, citing the historical development of computers as simulation systems for military training.[6] Indeed, simulations and games share many characteristics. Games are rule-based systems of play with quantifiable results and elements of indeterminacy. In other words, games are activities made possible by rules. Likewise, simulations are environments of experimentation. They model more complex systems and allow users to tinker with rules and behaviors. A flight simulator, for example, models the controls of a plane and allows the user to learn a flight system's behaviors. A flight simulator is not a plane, and only replicates parts of the experience of flight. Simulations are tools for understanding a larger system. Key to simulation are the possibility of contesting rules and finding unexpected behaviors in a dynamic system. Simulation experimentation and gameplay both refer to limited freedom of action within spatial and experiential boundaries. Unlike with physical games that come with rulebooks, digital games prompt users to discover rules during play. The behaviors of a system are more often discovered rather than clearly delineated. In this regard, all digital games are simulations.

This essay makes the following claims: one, *PeaceMaker* blurs the distinctions between fiction and history. This slippage between game and reality is enacted through *PeaceMaker*'s narrative, game mechanics, and goals. In particular, the game situates players as arbiters of peace in a geography characterized by violence, a narrative that elides the role of settler-colonialism and naturalizes violence. Two, *PeaceMaker* limits player control and occludes game rules to simulate the effects of unequal relations between Palestinians and Israel. Asymmetry of power is conveyed through different turn options for each player-character. Additionally, *PeaceMaker* cancels many player choices, destabilizing in-game causality and prompting the player to focus on discovering system behaviors. Game rules are briefly apparent to the user when actions do not yield expected results. This breakdown of control within a game makes apparent both the logics of gameplay *and* the logics of settler-colonialism. Three, a subaltern orientation toward *PeaceMaker* allows the player to imagine both alternative gameplay and an alternative Palestinian future. Subaltern gaming allows users to tinker in an interactive, immersive environment that can facilitate anticolonial future-building. Put simply, games can act as blueprints for change to be enacted upon real-world systems.

Method

Close reading, close play, and visual analysis are methods used in this chapter to critically examine video games. The term "play" features across fields including performance studies, cinema studies, and digital studies. Edmond Chang explains how to critically engage with video games using play as a method:

> Close playing, like close reading, requires careful and critical attention to how the game is played (or not played), to what kind of game it is, to what the game looks like or sounds like, to what the game world is like, to what

> choices are offered (or not offered) to the player, to what the goals of the game are, to how the game interacts with and addresses the player, to how the game fits into the real world, and so on...Close playing reveals the ways these elements, these spaces are also connected and dependent on the logics, narratives, and histories of the real world.[7]

An attention to game-world logics and play is what differentiates analysis of games from reading of film or video. Alexander Galloway explains that reading in-game action as a text subject to interpretation is central to game analysis: "Play is a symbolic action for larger issues in culture. It is the expression of structure...It is an aesthetic, enacted vehicle for a 'powerful rendering of life.'"[8] Therefore, the arguments presented in this essay rely on analyses of visual styles, genre, and player choice.

Game Mechanics: Portraying Uneven Power Dynamics and Foreclosing Alternative Possibilities

At the start of *PeaceMaker*, players choose between acting as the Israeli prime minister or a leadership role in the Palestinian Authority. Gameplay consists of choosing from three sets of turn options from a drop-down menu: political, security, and construction. Each of these categories contains various actions, depending on which role the player has chosen. Actions include giving speeches, closing borders, increasing military presence, asking for aid, and negotiating with other parties.

Playing as either the Palestinian or Israeli leadership allows for different types of actions to be taken. For much of the Palestinian play, actions are automatically canceled by the game. For example, if the player requests monetary aid from Jordan or Egypt, the nations' leaders explain they would invest "in the future" and the request is denied. Any declaration of an independent Palestinian state is canceled by the game. As the Israeli character, the player is offered a much wider range of actions that have immediate results. The leader can withdraw military forces, offer aid to Palestinians, free prisoners, build more settlements, and deploy troops.

PeaceMaker translates the uneven power of Palestine and Israel in its game mechanics. Palestinian sovereignty is continually eroded through (1) Israeli practices of apartheid in the differential treatment of Jewish and Arab citizens of Israel;[9] (2) Israeli settlement of Palestinian territories[10] and

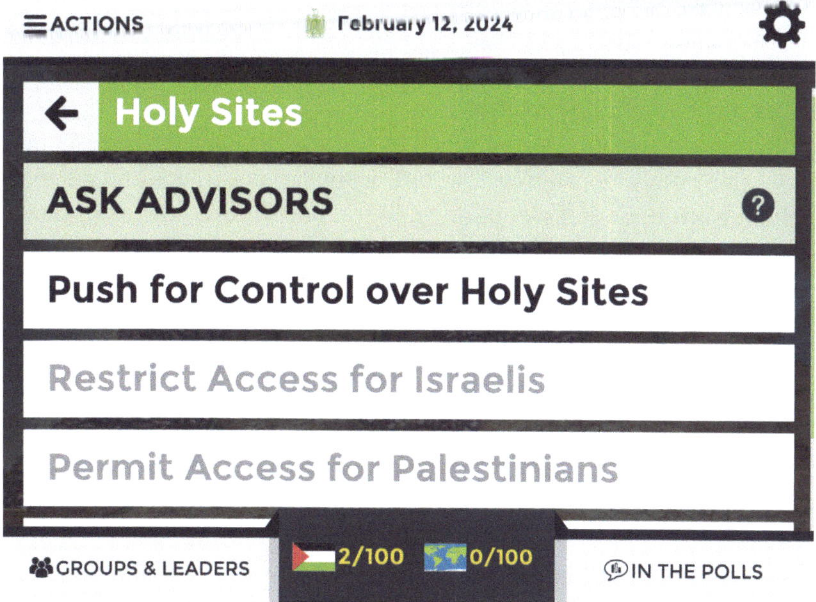

Image 01. When acting as the Palestinian leader, several actions are unavailable to the player. Here, the Palestinian leader is prevented from placing any restrictions on access to Holy Sites in Jerusalem.

the construction of the Separation Wall that snakes through Palestinian towns in the West Bank;[11] and (3) the siege and blockade of the Gaza Strip, commonly referred to as the world's largest open-air prison.[12] *PeaceMaker* disadvantages the Palestinian character in ways that reflect some of the limited sovereignty of Palestinians outside the game world. Thus, the game illustrates inequality's systemic nature, how established processes for peace, justice, and diplomacy inhibit Palestinian agency.

At the same time, positioning Palestinian and Israeli leadership as opposite equivalents obscures the colonial relationship between indigenous Palestinians and the settler state of Israel. The game occludes the split in Palestinian politics symptomatic of the partitioning of Gaza from the West Bank, and makes little mention of Palestinian citizens of Israel. The choice of player-character casts the conflict as one with comparable sides rather than the inherent unevenness of a struggle between settler and native. Additionally, the option to play as either Israeli or Palestinian political leadership imagines that significant change can only be caused by governing bodies. Such an understanding of geopolitics obscures the diversity of viewpoints in either population or the capacity of grassroots organizing for instilling change.

In *PeaceMaker*, each action taken by the player-character corresponds with game points, or "approval ratings" from various groups and factions including settler councils, opposing political parties, and doctors in Gaza. The game ends in failure if approval ratings fall low enough for the game to trigger loss of power for the player-character. The game is beaten once approval ratings from *both* Palestinian and Israeli publics reach one hundred points. Full approval rating triggers the creation of two states and the end of the game.

PeaceMaker endorses one of the two solutions that political analyses of the Palestine–Israel conflict propose: a two-state solution rather than a one-state solution.[13] A one-state solution would result in the creation of a multi-ethnic state that is not defined by religion, and would require economic and social integration of all populations. A two-state solution would establish a separate Palestinian state on some iteration of borders established since the creation of Israel in 1948.

The two-state solution takes the continuity of an Israeli settler-state as a given, and works within the parameters of European colonialism. During British rule over Palestine after the fall of the Ottoman Empire, several contradictory agreements were made to divide up the land between the Arab population and an influx of mostly European Jewish settlement, including the Sykes–Picot Agreement, the Hussein–McMahon Correspondence, and the Balfour Declaration.[14] In 1948, the United Nations adopted Resolution 181, which established Jewish and Arab states in the formerly British-occupied region.[15] The creation of Israel resulted in the ethnic cleansing of Palestine, known as the Nakba or "catastrophe."[16] In 1949, the Green Line re-wrote the borders proposed in Resolution 181 to expand Israel over 78% of historic Palestine.[17] These borders shifted in 1967 following the Six-Day War and according to the Oslo Accords brokered in the 1990s.[18] Regardless of which borders are imagined to contain future Palestinian and Israeli states, proponents of the two-state solution—including ImpactGames—elide the feasibility of accountability for the violence of settler-colonialism. The game's investment in a two-state solution dismisses any possible outcome that prioritizes repatriation of Palestinian land and life, instead treating the settler and indigenous claims as equal.[19]

Game Aesthetics: Visualizing Settler-Colonial Narratives about Palestine

In casting Israeli and Palestinian concerns about land, sovereignty, and agency as equal, the game reflects real-world anti-Palestinian discourses on modernity and violence that serve as justification for settler-colonial practices. For example, the map featured in the game's root menu depicts Israeli cities like Tel Aviv, Netanya, and Haifa with skyscrapers and sleek buildings. In contrast, Palestinian towns are identified by their English names and illustrated with stone buildings. The game's visual cues reflect discourse of European settlement of the Middle East as modernizing missions. In fact, forty years before becoming Israel's first prime minister, David Ben-Gurion penned an essay in 1915 that proclaimed, "The [Palestinian] land is waiting for a cultural, industrious people," arguing

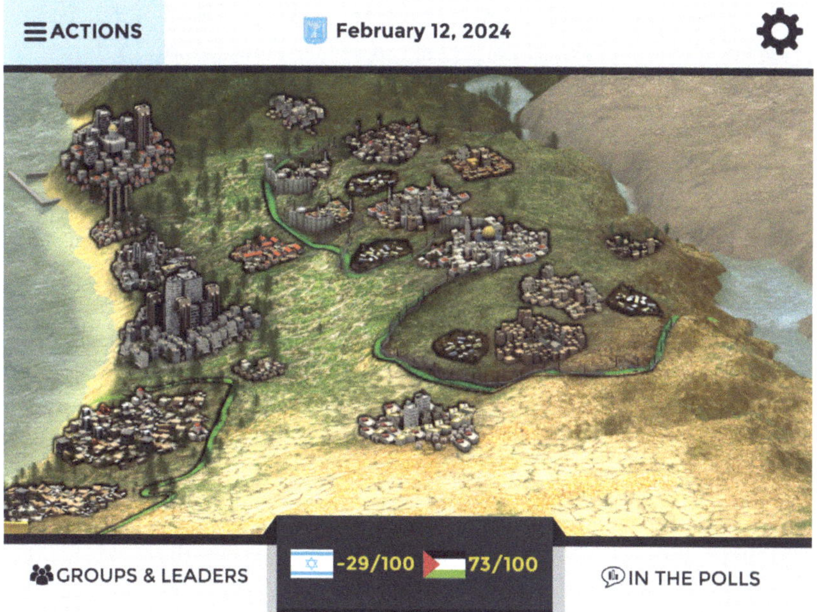

Image 02. The basemap for *PeaceMaker* depicts the Green Line and portions of the Separation Wall, and juxtaposes the high-rises of Israeli centers like Tel Aviv with Palestinian villages. Further, Israeli settlements are shown as temporary sites with portable buildings, a stark contrast to the sprawling hill-top enclaves settlements tend to be.

that settlers could "introduce to the land improved tools, updated agricultural methods and develop the land's drainage and transportation systems."[20] Similarly, *PeaceMaker*'s imagined geography reifies settler-colonial conceptions of the land, that Israel is a modern state and Palestinians are pre-civilization.

Furthermore, West Bank towns are presented alongside settlements that are signified through temporary, portable buildings that are dwarfed by the stone buildings. The images used in *PeaceMaker* imply that settlements are small outposts at the mercy of Palestinian towns. However, currently over 200 Israeli settlements house upwards of 700,000 Israelis in the occupied Palestinian Territories.[21] In 2005, when *PeaceMaker* was released, the settler population hovered around 275,000.[22] *PeaceMaker*'s illustration of settlements reflects ideological choices made by game developers that elide the extent of Israeli settlement. Further, spatial representation fails to depict settler violence, including the re-routing of natural resources to sustain these settlements.[23] Maps are subjective representations of geography. *PeaceMaker*'s map uses imagery that reflects beliefs about Israeli modernity and minimizes the impact of settler-colonialism. In doing so, the gameworld casts the two-state solution the player-character works toward as the only option for peace.

Game Narrative: Decontextualizing Sociopolitics and Blurring Fact with Fiction

Additionally, the in-game narrative presents violence as intrinsic to the land and to Palestinian people. Upon launching the game, the player views a montage of grainy videos of approaching tanks, ships on fire, planes exploding, soldiers marching, and men in keffiyehs with dates superimposed over the images. A few images were identifiable as clips from major events regarding Palestine and Israel, including footage of the Munich Olympiastadion and the 1969 plane hijacking by the Popular Front for the Liberation of Palestine. The game player is drawn into this mostly grayscale world of seemingly random, continuous violence. A news ticker displays headlines:

> Police criticized over prison policy...President cooperates with militants... Gaza approaches independence...Government supports peace plan...

> Security measures doing their job...Palestinians compatriots aid delayed... Report shows UN concern for Palestinians... Israeli prime ministers support slipping...Israel imposes curfew...Militant killed during raid

The montage and news ticker create a narrative to introduce the player into the game world. The player is positioned as a peacemaker, the sole person capable of ending the senseless violence. Appropriately, we can consider *PeaceMaker* as a "god game," a genre of video games that positions the player as leader in control of the game world. *PeaceMaker* decontextualizes Palestinian resistance from historical conditions of settler-colonialism in order to center the player as a key figure in bringing peace to a war-torn region.

PeaceMaker includes a timeline that presents players with context for this violence. It is not clear whether this timeline portrays fictionalized events or not. For example, the period of 1920–1948 is described as when "the British rule [sic] Palestine based on a mandate from the United Nations. Arabs and Jews in Palestine are in constant conflict. Each side wants its own state." However, the United Nations, the international body that facilitated the Partition Plan, was not established until 1945. Furthermore, prior to 1948 some resistance was directed at British rule, as in the Great Palestinian Revolt.[24] The events summarized on the timeline serve the game's narrative that the two-state solution is the only tenable option to ease Palestinian and Israeli tension. The start of a new game is displayed as the next date on the timeline, linking the game's political narrative with the user's play.

In-game alerts also provide a narrative of ahistorical, decontextualized events. Play is interrupted occasionally by notifications of settler protests, Palestinian suicide bombings, and anti-government rallies that then affect the polling numbers. In particular, the suicide bombing alert is ahistorical, considering Hamas denounced suicide bombings following the Second Intifada in the early 2000s. Another alert reported that eighteen Palestinians were killed and forty wounded by tank fire. When I searched for these statistics, I could not find anything that matched those specific numbers. These semi-real stories are accompanied by images of wailing Palestinian women. Though the developers claim that events within the game are "based on real events," this statement acts as both a disclaimer and a deliberate blurring of the game narrative against real events. The statistics, images, and alerts in *PeaceMaker* seem real because of the aesthetics used in the game. Grainy footage and arbitrary statistics provide an aura of realism within the game world.

The ripped-from-the-headlines places and events referenced in *PeaceMaker* are meant to influence player perspectives on sociopolitical events. In a quantitative analysis of Jewish, Palestinian, Turkish, and American undergraduate focus groups playing *PeaceMaker*, Ronit Kampf and Nathan Stolero found that Turkish and American players felt they gained knowledge regarding the conflict after playing the game, acquiring "a more neutral perspective" of the geopolitics of Palestine.[25] While *PeaceMaker* is marketed as an educational game, it functions along the same lines as misinformation by presenting game narratives as historical fact.

By blurring game narrative with sociopolitics, *PeaceMaker* forecloses alternative forms of engagement with the settler structures it simulates. Within game studies, scholars argue whether games are ideological or mechanical. For example, a game about looting does not teach players how to steal cars, but how to beat a game. The narrative is not central to a game. Instead, it serves as a backdrop to interpellate players, to draw them into the game world. Similarly, I do not claim that *PeaceMaker* play translates to political action outside the game world. However, because developers position *PeaceMaker* as a pedagogical tool, I take seriously the ways this game *trains players to think* about Israeli settler-colonialism in particular ways. *PeaceMaker* presents players with limited options for Palestinian and Israeli futures. Sovereignty is based on normalizing tactics that position Palestinians and Israelis as equal parties, both to blame for decades of violence. In-game actions are possible through the lens of diplomacy, from building infrastructure to delivering speeches. As Nick Irving posits, simulation games risk "narrowing the political imaginaries of players."[26] By presenting two incompatible populations that need to be guided by the player toward peace, *PeaceMaker* makes invisible the tangible ways Palestinians and their Israeli allies continually resist Israeli occupation.

In addition, we can read the possible outcomes of the game as reinforcing Israeli narratives of what conflict and peace look like. The player is only successful once a two-state resolution is achieved. The two-state solution proposes separate Palestinian and Israeli nations. As critics have noted, the two-state solution runs up against similar issues as the histories of segregation and Native American removal in the United States: separate is unequal, the ghettoization of Palestinians furthers indigenous removal and erasure, and asymmetrical power relations would persist because one nation has historically benefited from exploitation of natural resources while the other has not.[27]

Failure to win the game also triggers actions within *PeaceMaker* that reflect settler-colonial imaginaries. For the Israeli player-character, failure to achieve the two-state solution results in impeachment, a peaceful political removal of the leader. For the Palestinian player-character, however, failure to achieve the two-state solution results in insurrection. The game calls this insurgency Intifada, a reference to two periods of both violent and non-violent resistance in the late 1980s and early 2000s.[28] Despite several certified Palestinian elections across the West Bank and Gaza, political upheaval from Palestinians is imagined as inherently violent in *PeaceMaker.*

Game Alternatives: Subaltern Gaming and Possible Futures

Despite *PeaceMaker* being billed as an avenue for understanding a real-world conflict, the game's narrative reflects and endorses political ideologies more consistent with settler-colonial narratives. Players are positioned as pro-peace only if they accept settler-colonial myths that Palestinians are inherently violent (as seen in game narratives of violence), that Palestinians are premodern (as depicted through contrasting buildings on the game map), and that the problem of Palestine is that of incurable hatred rather than a history of settler-colonialism and asymmetric power relations (as conveyed through advocating of the two-state solution).

However, just as Ruberg explains that all games can be queered through play, I posit that *PeaceMaker* can be experienced through *subaltern gaming*, an alternative orientation that aims to destabilize the logics of gameplay. I enjoyed acting as the Israeli player-character and making decisions that benefited Palestinians. Though the game penalizes partisan play through the public opinion polls, I leveraged my position as prime minister to withdraw troops and settlements from Palestinian lands. Despite my plummeting approval ratings, I unconditionally funded Palestinian education, provided reconstruction aid, and increased work permits. However, my power as Israeli prime minister was sometimes thwarted by the legislature that prevented the dismantling of the Security Wall or stalled any initiative related to refugee return or compensation.

Inevitably, my player-character faced impeachment and I failed to beat *PeaceMaker.* However, my gameplay choices raised important questions: What other avenues for peace are there for Palestinians outside of the diplomatic processes presented in the game? How can possible ranges of action be opened up so that the player is not forced to consider their own political power as the primary metric for success? What does productive, generous play look like, and can that be translated to political action outside the game? By framing peace as the only way to guarantee the longevity of Israeli and Palestinian societies, and understanding the two-state solution as the only way toward that peace, *PeaceMaker* models only one possible orientation toward settler-colonialism.

Games are bounded spaces where players are invited to intervene and thus re-shape the game world. As a game that features the conflict in Palestine, *PeaceMaker*'s game world serves as a micro-representation of sociopolitical relations. *PeaceMaker* leverages game narrative and mechanics to model forms of Palestinian sovereignty, or lack thereof. The limitations placed on players create an emotional, affective link between the represented characters and the users, punctuated by feelings of frustration directed at game mechanics and, by extension, settler-colonial logics.

Unlike with other virtual environments, the game world prompts the player to actively test the parameters established by the game developers. This experimentation impacts the game results. Games are a vehicle for experimenting with rules and control. Indeed, game studies scholars define games as activities made possible by rules, or rule-based systems of play. Play, freedom of movement or action, can only exist within spatial and experiential boundaries and controls. The rules of play outline the conditions of possibility for action. However, the game worlds are not one-to-one translations of "the real," even as they portray historical events. Rather than take games as complete representations of political systems, we can instead see the affordances of creating game worlds to imagine and troubleshoot alternative formulations of sovereignty and agency. Therefore, games that disrupt player expectations of cause and effect, of player agency, gesture to a formulation of settler colonialism not as an inevitable and impermeable process, but as a set of logics and rules that can be modified or subverted. This orientation toward gameplay is what this chapter formulates as gaming from below, or subaltern gaming.

Chapter 11

Heritage Minutes: A Decolonial Feminist Reading of *Peacemaker*

Anna Shah Hoque

Misrepresentation in mainstream North American media distorts our understanding of Indigeneity, perpetuating discursive harms that extend to the dislocation of Indigenous contributions in film, cinema, and visual archival spaces.[1] Representations of Indigeneity often lean on visual conventions imbued with negative stereotypes and deficit-based logic. As Eve Tuck[2] explains, a deficit-based lens shapes an understanding of Indigeneity through a pathologizing or victimizing narrative, marginalizing or excluding Indigenous ways of knowing and being. This seldom allows for a nuanced, complex representation of Indigenous peoples in settler national mediascapes. When I employ the language of settler or settler colonial nationalism, I am referring to Canada's unequivocal claim through nationalism of naturalizing white settlers' claims to Indigenous lands. This process of settler occupation has involved self-appointing themselves as administrators through the language of the Crown and God, thereby usurping Indigenous sovereignties.[3] Dominant forms of media have employed harmful discursive and visual cues to legitimize settler claims, suppressing a meaningful engagement with Indigenous perspectives.[4] Stereotypes and homogenized narratives are weaponized to craft simplistic portrayals of Indigenous peoples aligning with settler understandings of Indigeneity.

Recognizing the prevalent framing practices inherent in predominant depictions of Indigeneity, in this chapter I analyze *Peacemaker*, the inaugural Indigenous-themed *Heritage Minutes* released on June 28, 1992, through a decolonial feminist framework (see Figure 1). I argue

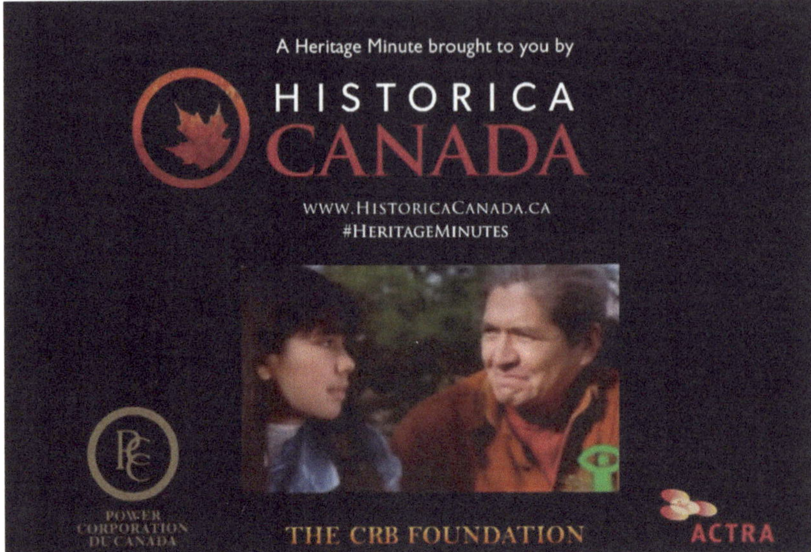

Figure 01. Closing visual of *Peacemaker*, the inaugural Indigenous-themed *Heritage Minutes* released on June 28, 1992. Courtesy of Historica Canada.

that *Peacemaker*, as an Indigenous-led and place-based visual storytelling media text, is a pivotal catalyst for cultivating a decolonial approach to the archival potential within the *Heritage Minutes* project. My analysis aims to strategically intervene by challenging the entrenched perception of the *Heritage Minutes* as a cultural artifact solely tethered to a monolithic "Canadian" identity.

What happens when a Kanien'kehá:ka (Mohawk) filmmaker works with a settler colonial cultural institution to share a story of Indigenous governance and intergenerational storying, emphasizing the richness at the "peripheries"? How does this shift the audiences' attention to witnessing alternate expressions of Indigenous nationhood and history? This chapter draws on a visual analysis of *Peacemaker* and a video interview via Skype with Kanien'kehá:ka filmmaker, writer, and co-producer T'hohahoken Michael Doxtater, to explore how Doxtater uses *Heritage Minutes* to convey an Indigenous-centric narrative about nation-making through humor and subversion.

While significant scholarship has looked at representations of Indigeneity and resistance to colonial narratives, much of the critiques raised address cultural industries in the "United States,"[5] inadvertently overlooking the contributions of Indigenous cultural producers in settler colonial Canada. I bring attention to *Peacemaker* as a short film that embodies Indigenous acts of insurgency, broadening the scope of *Heritage Minutes* beyond its traditional confines within a "Canadian" archive. This approach redirects the viewer's focus to what I call the "peripheries of the archives." In other words, I propose that these "peripheries," influenced by Indigenous interventions in *Heritage Minutes*, prompt a reorientation toward an alternate epicenter. This shift deliberately embraces the margins of dominant cultural spaces, emphasizing alterations to media texts by Indigenous filmmakers and creatives who operate at these edges—engaging in reinterpretations and new forms of relationalities. This space of the "peripheries" fundamentally serves as a locus of critique and reception to foster decolonial perspectives.

Jolene Rickard uses the term visual sovereignty to address the importance of Indigenous visual traditions that play a part in more significant conversations about Indigenous sovereignty.[6] The familiar and recognizable aesthetics and platform of *Heritage Minutes* offer a chance to exercise what Michelle Raheja suggests is "...a way of reimaging Native-centered articulations of self-representation and autonomy that engage the powerful ideologies of mass media but do not rely solely on the texts and contexts of Western jurisprudence."[7] Indigenous and decolonial scholarship recognizes Indigenous storytelling and visual arts as crucial in interrupting colonial and settler colonial representations of Indigenous identities to encourage complex modalities of remembering, re-imagining, and refuting.[8] Jarrett Martineau and Eric Ritskes explain that "...despite sustained attempts at its eradication; [I]ndigeneity is the presence of resistance and disruption, an existence in resistance to settler colonial genocidal replacement...represencing helps Indigenous peoples 'make sense' of the chaos imposed by ongoing settler colonialism...'speak back' to create new ways of knowing/being/doing outside of settler logic."[9]

In the following sections, I (1) introduce Historica Canada and *Heritage Minutes*, (2) explore scholarly works concerning *Heritage Minutes*, (3) propose turning to visual sovereignty within a desire-based framework, and (4) offer a decolonial feminist analysis of Doxtater's *Peacemaker*, with a subtle nod to an alternate epicenter. My intention is not to produce a grand theory between film and decolonization but to reflect on this one-minute short film as a portal to highlight a broader understanding of the decolonial efforts of Indigenous media practitioners who continue to generate a visible Indigenous presence in "Canadian" mainstream media. A decolonial feminist analysis of *Peacemaker* reflects on its covert hijacking of a settler media text and situates its critical intervention in conjunction with the timing of its release in 1992. Margaret Kovach explains, "the purpose of decolonization is to create space in everyday life, research, academia and society for an Indigenous perspective without it being neglected, shunted aside, mocked or dismissed."[10] I suggest that Indigenous creatives defy settler colonial logics through visual storytelling. In *Peacemaker*, Doxtater reclaims and reinterprets a Canadian cultural text, persuading viewers to see it through a decolonial lens[11] as an Indigenous media text rather than solely a "Canadian" one.

In the Backdrop of Settler Nation-Making

The sophistication of settler colonialism lies in its ability to place Indigeneity out of context, in both time and space and in the backdrop of legitimizing settler colonial claims to both. As Maile Arvin, Eve Tuck, and Angie Morrill explain, "Settler colonialism is a persistent social and political formation in which newcomers/colonizers/settlers come to a place, claim it as their own, and do whatever it takes to disappear the Indigenous peoples that are there."[12] In other words, settler colonialism neutralizes and masks everyday violence, political, legal, visceral, administrative, systemic, and discursive, by usurping Indigenous claims to territory and normalizing settler occupation. Settler coloniality weaponizes nationalism, coupling it with white supremacist ideologies to naturalize non-Indigenous claims of Indigenous territories. Political and religious doctrines, like the Doctrine of Discovery and terra nullius, have been employed to legitimize claims to Indigenous territories in the United States and Canada. Additionally, colonial and settler colonial visual and literary traditions have been instrumental in shaping mainstream narratives that normalize the act of occupation while devaluing Indigenous cosmologies, knowledge systems, governance structures, and histories.

Colonial tropes and negative stereotypes of Indigenous peoples in dominant cultural productions have conveyed the impression that Indigenous peoples are not an active part of media and cinematic history. These colonial tropes have morphed and mutated to encompass a persistent dehumanizing and damaging framing of Indigeneity.[13] Visual scholars Michelle Raheja, Wendy Gay Pearson, and Susan Knabe explored the complex realm of Indigenous participants in settler media, navigating spaces often laden with misconceptions and stereotypes.[14] They illustrated how Indigenous actors used these platforms to challenge prevailing narratives and produced more nuanced portrayals of Indigenous cultures. Furthermore, they noted that Indigenous participation in settler cultural industries is intricately linked to the broader sociopolitical climate in the United States and Canada, historically marked by efforts to restrict Indigenous access to territories, languages, and cultural practices. Raheja explicitly addressed the contributions of Indigenous actors and producers in Hollywood during the early 1900s, when there was strict policing of Indigenous customs and rituals by the settler nation-states of the United States and Canada (e.g. potlatch ban). Gerald Robert Vizenor has argued that Indigenous participation in mainstream media and film renders Indigenous identity legible to the settler polity and establishes a visual legacy of Indigenous presence amid the concurrent myth of impending disappearance.[15] The film industry functioned as a platform for subversive strategies. Firstly, it provided a means to create a visual archival legacy countering settler rhetoric perpetuating the myth of extinction. Secondly, it became a platform for practicing language and connecting with other Indigenous nations, allowing the continuation of rituals often prohibited by law beyond the confines of the studio or film set. And lastly, participating in mainstream cinematic culture afforded access to the greater public, enabling Indigenous actors and creatives to leverage their notoriety to educate non-Indigenous audiences about Indigenous realities.

Historica Canada's *Heritage Minutes*: A Settler Colonial Archival Project

Heritage Minutes emerged in response to concerns about the erosion of Canadian culture in the 1970s and 1980s, fueled by fears of American cultural dominance. In 1986, Charles Bronfman, a billionaire philanthropist and an Order of Canada recipient, launched The Heritage Project through the Charles R. Bronfman (CRB) Foundation (now Historica Canada)—the initiative aimed to educate Canadians about their heritage.

Guided principally by the moral imperative of generating and preserving "Canadian" heritage, the CRB Foundation developed the building blocks of media, Canada, and archives beyond traditional news resources. *Heritage Minutes*, the flagship product, began in 1991, presenting one-minute short films of "dramatic interpretations of pivotal events in Canada's history...60-second vignettes [to] commemorate notable Canadians, achievements in innovation, and instances of perseverance and bravery...intended to entertain, educate and encourage further research into our nation's past." Initially prolific in the 1990s and revitalized in 2012, the collection now includes nine shorts directly addressing Indigenous themes.

The *Minutes* were designed to capture key moments in Canadian history, a blend of education and entertainment, emblematic of Canadian media culture, a form of "edutainment."[16] Scholars have explored the relationship between the *Minutes* and public education, with early speculation suggesting they could serve as a tool of propaganda to maintain Canadian cultural hegemony. In 2002, Normand Lester, a Francophone journalist with Radio-Canada, published *Le Livre noir du Canada Anglais/ The Black Book of English Canada*, exposing a Canadian media landscape that was far from egalitarian, highlighting state and market collusion between fundamental placeholders within the organization, telecommunication industries, and government endorsements. Lester's work signaled to the *Minutes* as nationalistic propaganda driven by elite Anglo ideologies that obscured or sidelined other narratives.[17] Peter Hodgins mapped out how nostalgia and propaganda in the *Minutes* functioned to cultivate and maintain metanarratives or mythologies about the Canadian nation-state to foster a collective Canadian identity.[18] Katarzyna Rukszto examined parodies made in response to *Heritage Minutes*, seeking to understand notions of national collectivity that emerged through audience reception and the production of unauthorized parodies that would poke fun at the aesthetics and delivery of the official *Minutes*.[19] Historically, Historica Canada's response to the parodies has been overwhelmingly positive, listing them on the official website.[20] The parody videos are no longer listed on the website, and accessing the *Heritage Minutes* now requires using the search function to locate them. Yet the brief incorporation of parodies on Historica Canada's website implied an unspoken endorsement signaling the organization's adaptability and adoption of these unofficial media texts to celebrate audience engagement with the texts. The parodies testify to the cultural saliency and impact of the *Minutes*. However, in its history, Historica has never included unofficial Indigenous responses to the *Minutes* on its website. For example, *Heritage Mythologies – O Kanata Day*, part of Kanien'kehá:ka (Mohawk) artist-scholar Jackson 2bears's "Iron Tomahawks" Live Cinema/Scratch Video performance series, which draws on the aesthetics of *Heritage Minutes*, and incorporates splices of scenes from existing *Heritage Minutes*, remains uncited and unlisted by Historica Canada.

The omission of Indigenous perspectives and experiences and the exploration of alternative narratives also extend into academic examinations of *Heritage Minutes*. In each of the existing critiques, the *Minutes* are identified in their role as a hegemonic "Canadian" text, naturalizing the settler nation-state as ever-present, obscuring its continuing occupation of Indigenous territories, constraining Indigenous self-governance, and enveloping Indigeneity into "Canadian" identity. For instance, Ruksztо's examination of parodies explores the "Canadian" public's fascination with the *Minutes*, showing how audience members produce new interpretations of favored *Minutes*. In her examination, "Canadian" operates as a blanket category and is reproduced with a predisposition and an investment in the existing nation-state. Similarly, Hodgins argues that *Peacemaker* is a short film that categorically represents the interests of the Canadian elite but disguised as Indigenous lore. His reading of the media text dismisses various Indigenous teleological tactics to share alternate cosmologies and governances. Hodgins's examination of the media text ignores Indigenous storytelling practices that center alternate epistemological and ontological associations with time and space to upend colonial understandings of temporality and spatiality. In short, while analyses have provided critique on the function of *Heritage Minutes* in contributing to and upholding prescribed values about Canadian identity, scholarly examinations of the short films have not meaningfully accounted for Indigenous contributions to *Heritage Minutes*.

Desire and Visual Sovereignty: A Decolonial Feminist Reading of the Peripheries of Settler Colonial Archives

Existing as the target of what Raheja calls "discursive genocide"[21] is a reality that informs much of the representations of Indigeneity depicted through settler imaginary. Debates about the politics of recognition and

Indigeneity signal how easily Indigenous visualities are dismissed of their political significance.[22] What forms of community configurations emerge when grounded in "desire"? As Tuck explains, "Desire-based research frameworks are concerned with understanding complexity, contradiction, and the self-determination of lived lives."[23] To this end, I turn to visual sovereignty as an analytic to argue its place as an invaluable lens to read visual forms of archival disruption and resistance. Interpreting *Heritage Minutes* exclusively as "Canadian" places Canada at the center, thereby sidelining Indigenous nation-building efforts in the peripheries. I advocate for a reorientation toward the "peripheries" as an act of decolonization. This shift aims to attend to the agitations produced on the edges of officiated settler archives, emphasizing Indigenous visual interventions. Visual sovereignty amplifies Indigenous presence in settler culture industries as actors, filmmakers, producers, writers, and creatives. As an analytical tool, it is productive in countering the genocidal discourse present in colonial and settler colonial representations of Indigeneity. Visual sovereignty shifts the focus to Indigenous-led and -produced content, offering a nuanced and complex understanding of Indigenous cultural productions and drawing attention to the rich genealogy of Indigenous visual strategies of resistance and resurgence.

Visual sovereignty, placed in a desire-based framework, contributes to a decolonial feminist analytic in three key ways: (1) by articulating the presence and the (re)presencing of Indigeneity within contemporary and historical archival spaces, (2) by disrupting colonial narratives that perpetuate the framing of Indigeneity as confined to the past, and (3) by highlighting the intricate and contradictory relationship between cultural productions and Indigenous participation. Raheja explains that visual sovereignty "...simultaneously addresses the settler population by creating self-representations that interact with older stereotypes but also, more importantly, connects film production to larger aesthetic practices that work toward strengthening treaty claims and more traditional (although by no means static) modes of cultural understanding."[24] It provides a framework grounded in decoloniality and feminist critiques as a template for conversations outside the settler nation-state's trappings while making legible Indigenous identities in dialogue within or repudiating settler-led narratives. A decolonial feminist analysis centers on Indigenous contributions to address the complex intersections of Indigeneity, visualities, nation-making, and settler colonial formations.[25] It encourages looking beyond the surface of media texts to reveal the contradictions inherent in visual creations linked to ongoing occupation projects. Using visual media to reject colonial falsehoods through storytelling, this form of decolonial intervention aids in mobilizing Indigenous political and cultural resurgence and re-presenting their individual and nations' identities.

Toward a New Epicenter: Analyzing *Peacemaker* in the Peripheries of Settler Colonial Archives

> If you go back to 1992, google the mainstream films that came out that year. You'll see that there's a whole bunch of them. They're all around the idea of 1992, the Columbus discovery. And nobody knows me. I know the story. It's my joke on the media industry. Hahaha, there was only 1 minute, $350,000 produced in Canada...called Peacemaker. It was the only [one]—shame on you all for ignoring and excluding the Native voice, shame on you, right?...The idea...[that while] hundreds of minutes of film commemorating 1992 [were made]...[This] was the only [Indigenous] minute out there.[26]

1992 was a big year for Canada and North America. It was the 125th anniversary of the Confederation of Canada and the 500th celebration in the United States, the Columbus Quincentennial. Amid all the celebrations lay fresh the lingering ghosts of the events of Kanehsatake that took place in 1990. In the wake of Kanehsatake, CRB Foundation's Creative Director Patrick Watson approached T'hohahoken Michael Doxtater to take over the late Robert Markle's work of producing the first Indigenous-themed *Heritage Minute*. Doxtater is a Kanien'kehá:ka (Mohawk) scholar and filmmaker from the Six Nations of the Grand River territories. *Peacemaker* is a one-minute short film that depicts a conversation between an older Indigenous man and a young person as they plant a tree, which the man says represents their people and is a "tree of Great Peace." The audience, alongside the young person, is drawn into hearing about the Great Law of Peace, which narrates the birth of the Haudenosaunee Confederacy through the referent of the tree. The Confederacy is an Indigenous governance structure and a set of alliances predating the colonial occupation of Indigenous territories of North America and continues to inform formations of Indigenous nationhood. The film begins and ends with an interaction between two people, an Indigenous elder and a youth. I reflect on the sentence asked by the young person to their elder as they plant a tree of Great Peace, "Does the Great Peace [referring to the desires and doctrines attached to this law] still have power?" [elder figure responds] "Well, you're here, aren't ya?" as the short concludes. The words shared by the elder place Kanien'kehá:ka peoples in their homelands. The interaction of planting while explaining the relevance of this act (see Figure 2) signals to Indigenous acts of storying the land, locating Indigenous peoples' survivance,[27] and practicing intergenerational knowledge transmissions through place-based actions.

What happens when we interact with a media text from the point of view that dislocates the colonial archive as the epicenter? In this section, I apply the concept of visual sovereignty through a desire-based framework[28] to produce a decolonial feminist analysis. I argue that *Peacemaker* operates in the "peripheries," a liminal space that invites critique and reception to generate a different relationship to the borders and boundaries of settler colonial archival projects. What unfolds when we delve beneath the surface of a *Heritage Minute* to immerse ourselves in Indigenous-led stories?

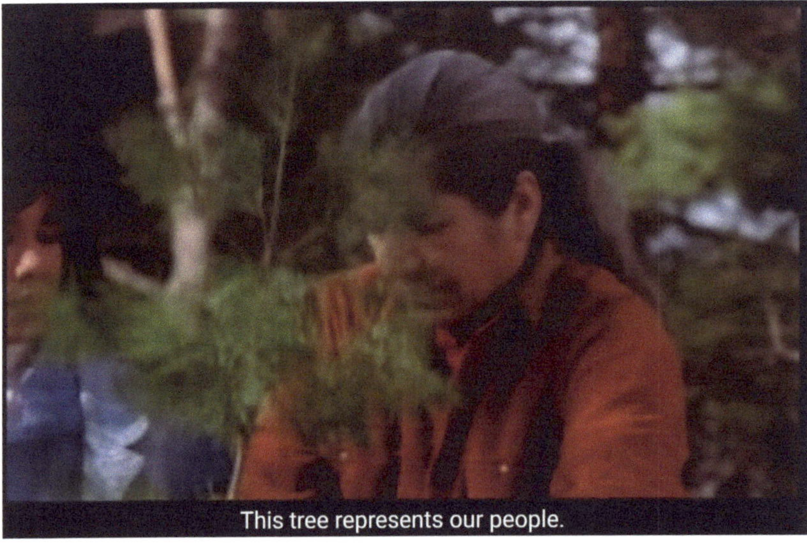

Figure 02. Indigenous elder telling the Indigenous young person about the "Great Law of Peace" and the Tree of Great Peace, *Peacemaker, Heritage Minutes*, 1992. Courtesy of Historica Canada.

Peacemaker highlights the contradictory nature of Indigenous cultural producers working with or within settler cultural texts. On the one hand, it potentially risks reproducing colonial understandings of Indigeneity; for example, linguistically, "Iroquois" does not address how the Kanien'kehá:ka nation identifies itself. Conversely, an Indigenous-produced media text invites a deeper level of analysis to grasp its archival interventions. The short film showcases Indigenous territory, governance structures, and assertions of sovereignty. For instance, the planting of the white pine tree in *Peacemaker* and the re-enactment of the founding of the Confederacy were filmed in Kanehsatake. Doxtater's decision to visually incorporate Kanehsatake is relevant as it is a location that politically signifies the importance of militant resistance. More commonly remembered as the "Oka Crisis," Kanehsatake is the place of the stand-off in the township of Oka, Quebec, between Kanien'kehá:ka community members, Sûreté du Québec, and the Canadian Army in 1990. The decision to highlight this landmark location, which had brought unfavorable international media attention to settler colonial Canada's continual overriding of Indigenous rights to territory, is crucial in the continuous presencing of Indigenous claims to their territories. As Doxtater explained, "Indigeneity is a particular place."[29] Kiera Ladner and Leanne Simpson credit Kanehsatake as a significant event that reinvigorated Indigenous acts of assertion to territories, fostered global Indigenous organizing and called for accountability and recognition of rights of self-determination.[30] Within the ecosystem of a "Canadian" cultural text, visual inclusions of contested territories in *Peacemaker*, with Indigenous actors taking up the screen, telling a story that couples the past to the present, and centering a kin-based intergenerational story practice, audiences are invited albeit briefly to develop an alternate set of spatial and temporal relations with Indigenous stories.

Alongside place-based visuals, Doxtater's hiring decisions for the short film cast employ subversion strategies and his activation of the politics of Indigenous humor opens up the pathway to generate oppositional and alternate readings. Citing Paula Gunn Allen, Drew Hayden Taylor in Lischke shares, "[Indigenous humor is widely used by [Indigenous peoples] to deal with life. [Indigenous] gatherings are marked by laughter and jokes, many directed at the horrors of history, and at the continuing impact of colonization, and at the biting knowledge that living as an exile in one's own land necessitates."[31] This perceptive device of humor enables Indigenous culture producers to build in nuanced readings that draw on insider knowledge to

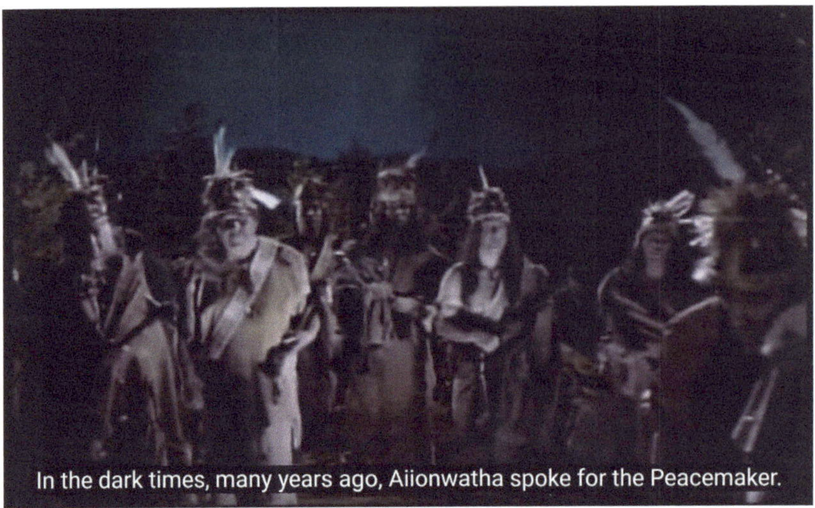

Figure 03. Re-enactment of Hiawatha gathering with Indigenous leaders, *Peacemaker, Heritage Minutes*, 1992. Courtesy of Historica Canada.

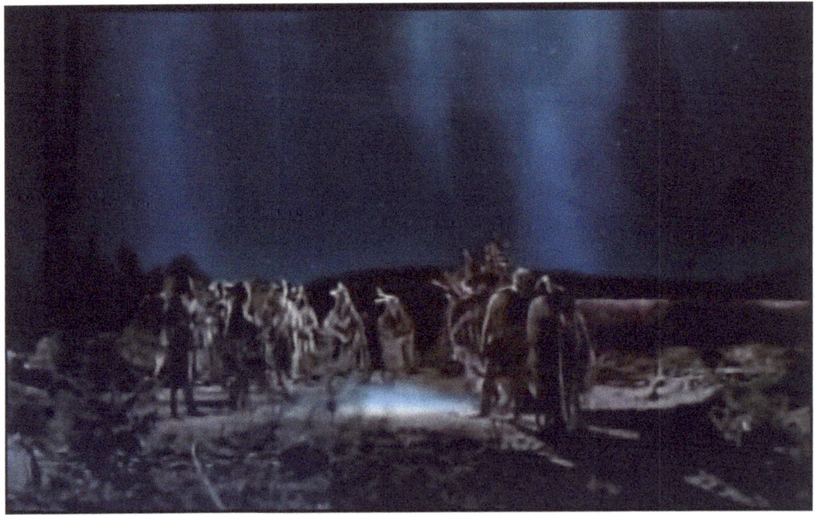

Figure 04. Re-enactment of the origin story of the Haudenosaunee Confederacy, *Peacemaker, Heritage Minutes*, 1992. Courtesy of Historica Canada.

gain meaning and understanding that may be missed or overlooked by the general audience. For example, in *Peacemaker*, Doxtater's hiring decision draws on insider humor to poke back at the settler state as viewers witness the birthing of the Confederacy, carried out by actors who were members of the Warrior Society in real life.

At the time of the filming, many of the actors who made an appearance in the short film (see Figures 3 and 4) were on the United States of America's watchlist, viewed as dangerous individuals and a threat to national security due to their involvement in the American Indian Movement (AIM) or, as Vine Deloria Jr. coined, the Red Power Movement.[32] "Jon Philips...Mark Maracle is the guy playing Hiawatha. They were the gun-toting AK47 guys down in New York State...These Warrior Society guys are in the film."[33] The Warriors, attired in regalia provided by the film production company, play an essential role in occupying the screen through the visual landscape. As Raheja points out, these acts of "playing Indian" in media production serve as essential visual signifiers of Indigeneity (see Figure 5). Despite their inaccuracy, for example, the homogenized attire that is not representative of each nation, they offer a direct and vivid challenge to the settler state by occupying the dominant visual landscape with Indigenous

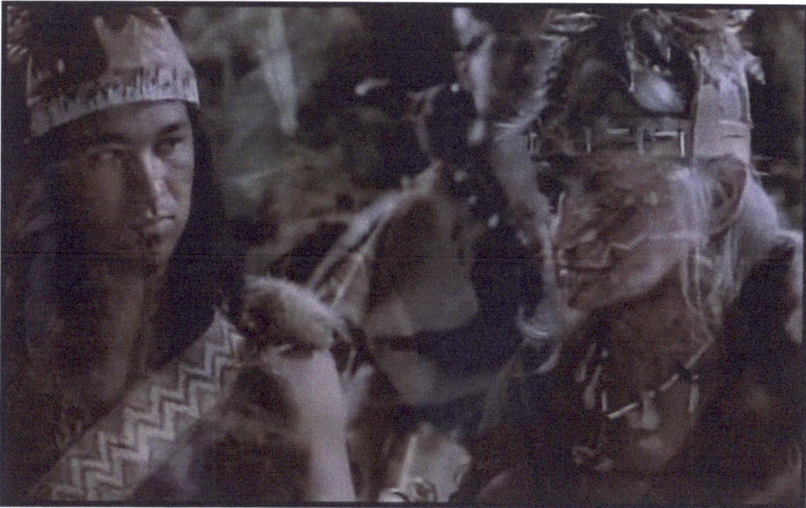

Figure 05. Close-up of key figures in the re-enactment of the origin story of the Haudenosaunee Confederacy, *Peacemaker, Heritage Minutes*, 1992. Courtesy of Historica Canada.

bodies. There is subtle laughing at the settler audience in how the settlers perceive this attire as authentically "Indigenous," attached to a distant past. At the same time, the members of the Warrior Society playing in the film are contemporary participants, seen as active threats to settler nation-making. Indigenous insiders would understand this act of poking back at the nation-state with the visual occupation of Warriors who were marked as both "dangerous" and "terrorist" by settler entities. The re-enactment is a recommitment of Indigenous solidarity and militant resistance on screen, performing a hijacking to reassert Indigenous place-making and rejecting the media text as one attached to "Canadian" values.

Doxtater "flips the script" on the original intention of the *Heritage Minute* by re-appropriating the settler platform. Non-Indigenous viewers, while left out of this complex interpretation, learn of governance structures that existed before pre-contact. The short film detaches *Heritage Minutes* from its original purpose of presenting "Canadian" historical moments that overshadow Indigeneity. Instead, it centers Indigenous peoples and territories, both past and present, to emphasize the ongoing Indigenous presence and resistance beyond the colonial imagination. Notably, this short film strives to create a narrative that deliberately avoids any engagement with coloniality, effectively dismissing its intersections.

A decolonial feminist analysis of *Peacemaker* thus questions Peter Hodgins's interpretation, which undervalues the significance of Indigenous origin stories and themes of intergenerational resistance and solidarity. Focusing on Indigenous erasure or assimilation to "Canadian" nationalism from a deficit-based perspective does not capture the broader intentions of the cultural producer that is embedded with the media text. *Peacemaker* highlights the importance of relational connections across time and space among Indigenous generations, resisting settler colonial narratives that oversimplify Indigenous contributions. It subverts the notion of settler cultural text as definitive, showcasing vibrant Indigenous youth eager to learn from their elders through land-based and ancestral teachings.

Conclusion

Peacemaker offers a new perspective on *Heritage Minutes* and visual archives by focusing on an Indigenous-led narrative, challenging a cultural text often seen as a symbol of Canadian culture. Through a decolonial feminist lens, this chapter advocates moving away from settler-centric celebrations of "Canadian" achievements, urging a reorientation toward narratives frequently marginalized and undervalued in the "peripheries." In other words, *Peacemaker* offers a pathway to redefine our relationship with archives, diverging from the colonial perspective. Using a desire-based framework, I examine how this short film effectively subverts this settler nationalistic text to recount an Indigenous origin story. This challenges the notion of a fixed "true" archive exclusively linked to a "Canadian" identity. Amid ongoing efforts to construct a settler colonial archive, *Peacemaker*, as the inaugural Indigenous-produced *Heritage Minutes*, focuses on the Haudenosaunee Confederacy during Canada's 125th year of settler occupation. It disrupts the settler narratives to assert Indigenous governance, prompting viewers to momentarily reconsider their ties to the settler nation-state. By prominently featuring Indigenous elders and youth who share origin stories rooted in Indigenous knowledge and sovereignty, the film redirects attention to Indigenous nationhood, where colonization is not the central narrative, offering an alternative historical perspective.

Notes

Introduction

1. Although the initial inspiration for *Media Travels* came from discussions about issues related to teaching global media, this collection is foremost a work of research and scholarship, albeit one where the chapters are written with a consideration of their inclusion in a variety of media curricula. For more detailed discussions on the philosophical and practical dimensions of teaching global media, see the essays collected in Juan Llamas-Rodriguez, "Teaching 'the Global' in Media Studies," *Journal of Cinema and Media Studies* 61, no. 6 (2022), https://quod.lib.umich.edu/j/jcms/18261332.0061.6*. Nonetheless, those of us who research *and* teach global media understand that the two are often closely intertwined.

2. Joshua Neves and Bhaskar Sarkar, "Introduction," in *Asian Video Cultures: In the Penumbra of the Global*, ed. Joshua Neves and Bhaskar Sarkar (Durham, NC: Duke University Press, 2017), 21.

3. Consider, for instance, the enduring connections between visual culture and geography explored in Irit Rogoff, *Terra Infirma* (New York: Routledge, 2000), or the study of how networked technologies sense the world in Jennifer Gabrys, *Program Earth: Environmental Sensing Technology and the Making of a Computational Planet* (Minneapolis: University of Minnesota Press, 2016).

4. Umberto Eco, "On the Impossibility of Drawing a Map of the Empire on a Scale of 1 to 1," in *How to Travel with a Salmon & Other Essays*, trans. William Weaver (New York: Harcourt Brace, 1994), 106.

5. Joshua Foer, Ella Morton, and Dylan Thuras, *Atlas Obscura: An Explorer's Guide to the World's Hidden Wonders* (New York: Workman, 2019). See also https://www.atlasobscura.com/about.

6. See, for instance, Dipesh Chakrabarty, "Provincializing Europe: Postcoloniality and the Critique of History," *Cultural Studies* 6, no. 3 (1992): 337–57; and Malini Guha, "World Cinema 3.0? The 'World as Backdrop' for a Multimedial Age," *Canadian Journal of Film Studies* 29, no. 2 (2020): 37–51.

7. On the colonizing work of maps, see James R. Akerman, ed., *The Imperial Map: Cartography and the Mastery of Empire* (Chicago: University of Chicago Press, 2009).

8. For a recent attempt at this approach to global media, see Benjamin Birkinbine, Janet Wasko, and Rodrigo Gomez, eds., *Global Media Giants* (New York: Routledge, 2016).

9. Mark Balnaves, James Donald, and Stephanie Donald, *The Global Media Atlas* (London: BFI Institute, 2001).

10. See, for instance, Catherine Grant's notion of "material thinking" in Catherine Grant, "Dissolves of Passion: Materially Thinking through Editing in Videographic Compilation," in *The Videographic Essay: Criticism in Sound & Image*, ed. Christian Keathley and Jason Mittel (Montreal: caboose, 2016), 37–53.

11. Michael Curtin, "Post Americana: Twenty-First Century Media Globalization," *Media Industries* 71 (2020), https://doi.org/10.3998/mij.15031809.0007.106.

12. William Mazzarella, "Culture, Globalization, Mediation," *Annual Review of Anthropology* 33 (2004): 345–67, 350.

Chapter One

1. I am very grateful to Dr. Iuliia Glushneva for her assistance in the research process for this chapter.

2. Kevin O'Flynn, "Meet the Russian Kids Who Take the World's Riskiest Photos," *Rolling Stone*, May 6, 2014, https://www.rollingstone.com/culture/culture-news/high-times-meet-the-russian-kids-who-take-the-worlds-riskiest-photos-100170/.

3. On the Roofs, "Shanghai Tower (650 Meters)," February 12, 2014, YouTube, 5:19, https://www.youtube.com/watch?v=gLDYtH1RH-U.

4. Masha Gessen, "When Painting a Ukrainian Flag Is a Hate Crime in Moscow," *The New Yorker*, September 15, 2015, http://www.newyorker.com/news/news-desk/when-painting-a-ukrainian-flag-is-a-hate-crime-in-moscow.

5. Jeremy Hicks, *The Victory Banner over the Reichstag: Film, Document, and Ritual in Russia's Contested Memory of World War II*, Russian and East European Studies (Pittsburgh: University of Pittsburgh Press, 2020).

6. Hicks, *The Victory Banner*, 6.

7. Hicks, *The Victory Banner*, 5.

8. Katherine Zubovich, *Moscow Monumental: Soviet Skyscrapers and Urban Life in Stalin's Capital* (Princeton, NJ: Princeton University Press, 2020), http://muse.jhu.edu/book/78749.

9. Zubovich, *Moscow Monumental*, 139.

10. Zubovich, *Moscow Monumental*, 157.

11. Zubovich, *Moscow Monumental*, 164.

12. Zubovich, *Moscow Monumental*, 140.

13. Zubovich, *Moscow Monumental*, 3.

14. Zubovich, *Moscow Monumental*, 3.

15. Steven Jacobs, "Slapstick Skyscrapers: An Architecture of Attractions," in *Slapstick Comedy*, ed. Tom Paulus and Rob King (New York: Routledge, 2010), 153. doi: 10.4324/9780203876763-17.

16. Jacobs, "Slapstick Skyscrapers," 155.

17. Jacobs, "Slapstick Skyscrapers," 159.

18. Jacob Smith, *The Thrill Makers: Celebrity, Masculinity, and Stunt Performance*, 1st ed. (Berkeley: University of California Press, 2012), 50.

19. Jacobs, "Slapstick Skyscrapers," 153.

20. Phil Cavendish, "From 'Lost' to 'Found': The 'Rediscovery' of Sergei Eisenstein's *Glumov's Diary* and its avant-garde context." *Kinokultura* 41 (2013), http://www.kinokultura.com/2013/41-cavendish.shtml.

21. Yuri Tynianov, "On FEKS", in *The Film Factory: Russian and Soviet Cinema in Documents, 1896–1939*, ed. Richard Taylor and Ian Christie (London: Routledge, 1988), 257.

22. Alfonso Puyal, "In the City of the Eccentrics: Glumov, Mr West and Oktiabrina," *Russian Journal of Communication* 13, no. 2 (May 2021): 163–82, doi: 10.1080/19409419.2021.1934895.

23. Sergei Eisenstein, "The Montage of Attractions," in *Sergei Eisenstein, Selected Works*, ed. Richard Taylor (London; New York: I. B. Tauris, 2010), 33.

24. Eisenstein, "The Montage of Attractions."

25. Grigori Kozintsev, Leonid Trauberg, Sergei Yutkevich, and Georgi Kryzhitsky, "Eccentrism," in *The Film Factory: Russian and Soviet Cinema in Documents, 1896–1939*, ed. Richard Taylor and Ian Christie (London: Routledge, 1988), 58–59.

26. Malcolm Turvey, "Comedic Modernism," *October* 160 (June 2017): 5–29, doi: 10.1162/OCTO_a_00289. Turvey distinguishes his term, comedic modernism, from William Solomon's use of slapstick modernism in *Slapstick Modernism: Chaplin to Kerouac to Iggy Pop* (Urbana: University of Illinois Press, 2016).

27. Puyal, "In the City of the Eccentrics," 163.

28. Eisenstein, "The Montage of Attractions," 34.

29. Cavendish, "From 'Lost' to 'Found'."

30. Tom Gunning, "Modernity and Cinema: A Culture of Shocks and Flows," in *Cinema and Modernity*, ed. Murray Pomerance (New Brunswick, NJ: Rutgers University Press, 2006), 306.

31. Maria Belodubrovskaya, "The Cine-Fist: Eisenstein's Attractions, Mirror Neurons, and Contemporary Action Cinema," *Projections* 12, no. 1 (June 22, 2018): 1–19.

32. Smith, *The Thrill Makers*, 3.

33. Isher-Paul Sahni, "More Than Horseplay: 'Jackass', Performativity, and the MoMA," *Studies in Popular Culture* 35, no. 2 (2013): 69–94.

34. *URBEX: Enter at Your Own Risk*, season 1, episode 1, "Unstoppable," directed by Darren Lovell and Gavin Searle, aired August 1, 2016, on Red Bull TV.

35. V. N. Volosinov, as quoted in Smith, 3.

Chapter Two

1. Susan Douglas, *Listening In: Radio and the American Imagination* (Minneapolis: University of Minnesota Press, 1999), 57.

2. Douglas, *Listening In*, 57, 73.

3. Archivo Histórico de la Secretaría de Educación Pública (hereafter, AH-SEP) Sección Dirección de Extensión Educativa por Radio, Expediente A-4/235.3(S-3)/-1.

4. AH-SEP, Sección Dirección de Extensión Educativa por Radio, Expediente A-4/235.3(S-3)/-1.

5. Pablo Palomino, *The Invention of Latin American Music: A Transnational History* (New York: Oxford University Press, 2020).

6. For a brief and comprehensive overview of music in Mexico see Alejandro Luis Madrid, *Music in Mexico: Experiencing Music, Expressing Culture* (New York: Oxford University Press, 2013). For the influence of African melodies and practices in Mexican music see Theodore Cohen, *Finding Afro-Mexico: Race and Nation after the Revolution* (Cambridge: Cambridge University Press, 2019), especially chapter 5, "Africanizing 'La Bamba'," 154–90. Pablo Palomino questions the role of music in the imagining of Latin America, not just Mexico, and claims that music served a national role. Pablo Palomino, *The Invention of Latin American Music*, 2.

7. Ricardo Pérez Montfort, "La expresión musical popular mexicana del Porfiriato a la Revolución. De la pieza académica a la canción revolucionaria," in *Estampas de nacionalismo popular mexicano. Diez ensayos sobre cultura popular y nacionalismo* (México: Centro de Investigaciones y Estudios Superiores en Antropología Social, 2003), 97–120.

8. This is the subject of much of Ricardo Pérez Montfort's work and involves other forms of media—film, radio, theater, etc. See *Estampas de nacionalismo popular mexicano.*

9. Claes af Geijerstam, *Popular Music in Mexico* (Albuquerque: University of New Mexico Press, 1976), 131.

10. Yolanda Moreno Rivas, *Historia de la música popular Mexicana* (Mexico City: Editorial Océano, 2008), 16.

11. Moreno Rivas, *Historia de la música popular Mexicana*, 19.

12. Robert Stevenson, *Music in Mexico: A Historical Survey* (New York: Thomas Y. Crowell, 1952), 218.

13. Mark Pedelty, *Musical Ritual in Mexico City: From the Aztec to NAFTA* (Austin: University of Texas Press, 2004), 102.

14. Moreno Rivas, *Historia de la música popular Mexicana*, 21–23.

15. For more on the Mexican-American War (1846–1848), see "A Continent Divided: The U.S.-Mexico War," University of Texas at Arlington, https://library.uta.edu/usmexicowar/index.php.

16. Pedelty, *Musical Ritual*, 104–5.

17. Pérez Montfort, "La expresión musical popular mexicana," 106–7.

18. For more on this time period, see "Porfirio Díaz," New World Encyclopedia, https://www.newworldencyclopedia.org/entry/Porfirio_D%C3%ADaz.

19. Stevenson, *Music in Mexico*, 219.

20. Af Geijerstam, *Popular Music in Mexico*, 94.

21. Stevenson, *Music in Mexico*, 208.

22. Pérez Montfort, "La expresión musical popular mexicana," 106–7.

23. Ricardo Pérez Montfort, "Una region inventada desde el centro. La consolidación del cuadro estereotípico nacional, 1921–1937," in *Estampas de nacionalismo popular mexicano*, 124–27.

24. Moreno Rivas, *Historia de la música popular Mexicana*, 19–20.

25. Robert Stevenson, *Music in Mexico*, 219.

26. Stevenson, *Music in Mexico*, 219.

27. Pérez Montfort, "La expresión musical popular mexicana," 98–100.

28. Af Geijerstam, *Popular Music in Mexico*, 93.

29. Both Claes af Geijerstam (pp. 93–94) and Robert Stevenson profile Juventino Rosas in their monographs on the history of music in Mexico. Stevenson (p. 207) highlights his indigenous (Otomí) background, but I have not read any other sources that mention that.

30. There are a number of examples. See Ricardo Pérez Montfort, "Del rancho a la capital. Notas sobre 'lo popular' en el studio del cancionero mexicano y su relación con los inicios del bolero ranchero," in *Expresiones populares y estereotipos culturales en México. Siglos XIX y XX. Diez ensayos* (Mexico City: CIESAS, 2007), 95–118.

31. Af Geijerstam, *Popular Music in Mexico*, 94.

32. Stevenson, *Music in Mexico*, 205.

33. Stevenson, *Music in Mexico*, 208.

34. Stevenson, *Music in Mexico*, 218.

35. Af Geijerstam, *Popular Music in Mexico*, 94.

36. "Over the Waves Waltzes (Sobre las Olas)," Juventino Rosas, sheet music published on October 9, 1895, Ball State University, https://dmr.bsu.edu/digital/collection/ShtMus/id/240.

37. Af Geijerstam, *Popular Music in Mexico*, 94.

38. For a general overview of radio development and early radio technology see Bill Kovarik, "The New World of Radio," in *Revolutions in Communication: Media History from Gutenberg to the Digital Age* (New York; London: Bloomsbury Academic, 2011), 275–308.

39. Rubén Gallo, *Mexican Modernity: The Avant-Garde and the Technological Revolution* (Cambridge, MA: MIT Press, 2005), 117–67.

40. Douglas, *Listening In*, 51.

41. Gallo, *Mexican Modernity*, 120.

42. Douglas, *Listening In*, 28.

43. Douglas, *Listening In*, 58.

44. Kristen Haring, *Ham Radio's Technical Culture* (Cambridge, MA: MIT Press, 2008).

45. Sonia Robles, "'Good Luck and Buenos Notches': Early Amateur Interactions with Mexican Radio," *Technology Stories* 8, no. 2 (2020), https://doi.org/10.15763/jou.ts.2020.09.28.08.

46. Pablo Palomino, *The Invention of Latin American Music: A Transnational History* (New York: Oxford University Press, 2020), 84.

47. Jason Loviglio and Michele Hilmes, "Introduction: Making Radio Strange," in *Radio's New Wave: Global Sound in the Digital Era*, ed. Jason Loviglio and Michele Hilmes (New York: Routledge, 2013), 1–7.

Chapter Three

1. For more discussion of these theoretical concepts, see Joseph Straubhaar, "Beyond Media Imperialism: Asymmetrical Interdependence and Cultural Proximity," *Critical Studies in Mass Communication* 8 (1991): 39–59, and Dal Yong Jin, "Transnational Proximity and Universality in Korean Culture: Analysis of *Squid Game* and BTS," *Seoul Journal of Korean Studies* 35, no. 1 (2022): 5–28, doi: 10.1353/seo.2022.000.

2. Since the mid-2000s, a growing number of Korean TV dramas have experimented with new genres and narrative strategies that deviate from the more conventional Korean TV dramas produced in the 1990s by the terrestrial networks. Additionally, the emergence of specialized TV drama production companies such as Hwa & Dam Pictures, Studio Dragon, and Samhwa Networks has led to the production of higher quality Korean TV dramas. Amid these changes in the Korean television industry, there has been a growing presence of fantastic Korean TV dramas that address the themes of social class struggles and traumatic pasts. More importantly, these Korean TV dramas were written by women who have emerged as star writers, especially Kim Eun-sook and Park-Jieun. Kim wrote such hits as *Secret Garden* (SBS, 2010–2011), *Inheritors* (SBS, 2013), *Descendants of the Sun* (KBS, 2016), *Guardian: The Lonely and Great God* (tvN, 2016–2017), *Mr. Sunshine* (tvN, 2018), and *The King: Eternal Monarch* (SBS, 2020). Park Ji-eun wrote hit Korean TV dramas, including *My Love from the Star* (SBS, 2013–2014), *The Legend of the Blue Sea* (SBS, 2016–2017), and *Crash Landing on You* (tvN, 2019 2020).

3. Ella Shohat and Evelyn Alsultany, "The Cultural Politics of 'the Middle East' in the Americas: An Introduction," in *Between the Middle East and the Americas: The Cultural Politics of Diaspora*, ed. Evelyn Alsultany and Ella Shohat (Ann Arbor: University of Michigan Press, 2013), 3–41.

4. Cynthia Duncan, *Unraveling the Real: The Fantastic in Spanish-American Ficciones* (Philadelphia: Temple University Press, 2010), 2.

5. Bliss Cua Lim, *Translating Time: Cinema, the Fantastic, and Temporal Critique* (Durham, NC: Duke University Press, 2009), 101.

6. Lim, *Translating Time*, 135.

7. Tzvetan Todorov, *The Fantastic: A Structural Approach to a Literary Genre*, trans. Richard Howard (Ithaca, NY: Cornell University Press, 1975), 8.

8. Joshua Landy and Michael T. Saler, "Introduction: The Varieties of Modern Enchantment," in *The Re-Enchantment of the World: Secular Magic in a Rational Age*, ed. Joshua Landy and Michael Saler (Stanford, CA: Stanford University Press, 2009), 2.

9. Landy and Saler, "Introduction: The Varieties of Modern Enchantment," 6.

10. Jie Lu, "Representing History, Trauma, and Marginality in Chinese Magical Realist Films," in *Transpacific Literary and Cultural Connections: Latin American Influence in Asia*, ed. Jie Lu and Martín Camps (Cham, Switzerland: Palgrave Macmillan, 2020), 210.

11. Kim Ki-young's film *Insect Woman* (*Chungynyeon*, 1972), for instance, represents the fantastic cinema in the 1970s: Korean Classic Film, "(1972) / *Insect Woman* (*Chungnyeo*)," December 3, 2015, YouTube, 1:55:38, https://www.youtube.com/watch?v=Mwh2Z1Q8q9o.

12. Soyoung Kim and Chris Berry, '"Suri Suri Masuri': The Magic of the Korean Horror Film: A Conversation," *Postcolonial Studies* 3, no. 1 (2000): 53.

13. Kim and Berry, "Suri Suri Masuri," 54–55.

14. Mariano Siskind, *Cosmopolitan Desires: Global Modernity and World Literature in Latin America* (Evanston, IL: Northwestern University Press, 2014), 81.

15. Siskind, *Cosmopolitan Desires*, 81.

16. Homi K. Bhabha, "Introduction," in *Nation and Narration*, ed. Homi K. Bhabha (London; New York: Routledge, 1990), 7.

17. Fernando Sdrigotti, "What We Talk About When We Talk About Magical Realism," Los Angeles Review of Books, October 2, 2020, https://lareviewofbooks.org/article/what-we-talk-about-when-we-talk-about-magical-realism/.

18. Sdrigotti, "What We Talk."

19. Sylvia Molloy, "Latin America in the U.S. Imaginary: Postcolonialism, Translation, and the Magic Realist Imperative," in *Ideologies of Hispanism*, ed. Mabel Moraña (Nashville: Vanderbilt University Press, 2005), 191.

20. Siskind, *Cosmopolitan Desires*, 60.

21. Chungmoo Choi, "Decolonization and Popular Memory: South Korea," *positions: East Asia Cultures Critique* 1, no. 1 (Spring 1993): 95.

22. Ben Holgate, "East Asian Magical Realism," in *Magical Realism and Literature*, ed. Christopher Warnes and Kim Anderson Sasser (Cambridge: Cambridge University Press, 2020), 182–97.

23. Soo-Hyun Hwang, "Recepción e influencia de la literatura hispanoamericana en Corea," *Anales de Literatura Hispanoamericana* 44 (2015): 333–52.

24. Holgate, "East Asian Magical Realism," 182.

25. Yu-jin Lee, "Romaentik Deurama Hiteu Jejogi! Kim Eun-sook Jakgaui Insaeng Yeokjeon," *The Kyunghyang Shinmun*, January 31, 2011, http://news.khan.co.kr/kh_news/art_print.html?med_id=lady&artid=201101311413111.

26. Martín Camps, "The Plague of Modernity: Macondo, Inc. and the Branding of 'Magical' Latin America," in *Critical Insights: Magical Realism*, ed. Ignacio López-Calvo (Ipswich, MA: Salem Press, 2014), 84.

27. Landy and Saler, *The Re-Enchantment of the World*, 6.

28. Duncan, *Unraveling the Real*, 34.

29. Carla Marcantonio, *Global Melodrama: Nation, Body, and History in Contemporary Film* (New York: Palgrave Macmillan, 2015), 7.

30. Duncan, *Unraveling the Real*, 16–17.

31. *Chaebol* is a Korean term used to describe family-controlled conglomerates that dominate the nation's economy.

32. Landy and Saler, *The Re-Enchantment of the World*, 12.

33. Steve Choe, "Melos in the World of K-Drama," *Korea Europe Review: An Interdisciplinary Journal of Politics, Society, and Economics*, no. 3 (12/27 2022): 1–18.

34. Choe, "Melos in the World of K-Drama," 1–18.

35. For example, in a brief scene, Joo-won is reading the book *Cheonjaettogi Chasangmun* (Gim Nam-il, 2010), which tells a story about a woman working as a teacher in a rural area in the 1950s who gives birth to a primate rabbit. Later, in episode ten, Ra-im receives a package in the mail containing books that she has purchased. Among them is Lewis Carroll's widely popular fantasy novel *Alice's Adventures in Wonderland* (1865), which is an important reference point throughout the drama. The fantasy novel allows both protagonists to develop a more intimate emotional connection with one another.

36. Kenneth Chan, *Sino-Enchantment: The Fantastic in Contemporary Chinese Cinemas* (Edinburgh: Edinburgh University Press, 2021), 15.

37. Ella Shohat and Evelyn Alsultany, "The Cultural Politics of 'the Middle East' in the Americas: An Introduction," 21.

38. Ella Shohat and Evelyn Alsultany, "The Cultural Politics of 'the Middle East' in the Americas: An Introduction," 13.

Chapter Four

1. Andrew Higson, "The Concept of National Cinema," *Screen* 30, no. 4 (October 1, 1989): 36–47, https://doi.org/10.1093/screen/30.4.36.

2. Mark J. P. Wolf, ed., *Video Games around the World* (Cambridge, MA: The MIT Press, 2015).

3. Sebastián Baeza-González, "Video Games Development in the Periphery: Cultural Dependency?," *Geografiska Annaler: Series B, Human Geography* 103, no. 1 (January 2, 2021): 39–54, https://doi.org/10.1080/04353684.2021.1894077; Mia Consalvo, "Console Video Games and Global Corporations: Creating a Hybrid Culture," *New Media & Society* 8, no. 1 (February 1, 2006): 117–37, https://doi.org/10.1177/1461444806059921; Vit Sisler, Jaroslav Svelch, and Josef Slerka, "Video Games and the Asymmetry of Global Cultural Flows: The Game Industry and Game Culture in Iran and the Czech Republic," *International Journal of Communication (Online)* (September 1, 2017): 3857–80.

4. Rachel Lara van der Merwe, "From Global to National: Mapping the Trajectory of the South African Video Game Industry," in *Re-Imagining Communication in Africa and the Caribbean: Global South Issues in Media, Culture and Technology*, ed. Hopeton S. Dunn et al. (Switzerland: Palgrave Macmillan, 2021), 137–56, https://doi.org/10.1007/978-3-030-54169-9.

5. Felan Parker and Jennifer Jenson, "Canadian Indie Games between the Global and the Local," *Canadian Journal of Communication* 42, no. 5

(2017): 867–91; John Vanderhoof, "Indie Games of No Nation: The Transnational Indie Imaginary and the Occlusion of National Markers," in *Game History and the Local*, ed. Melanie Swalwell (Cham, Switzerland: Springer, 2021), 159–76, https://doi.org/10.1007/978-3-030-66422-0_9.http://dx.doi.org/10.22230/cjc.2017v42n5a3229.

6. Metacritic, "Beautiful Desolation for PC Game Reviews," 2020, https://www.metacritic.com/game/pc/beautiful-desolation; Metacritic, "Beautiful Desolation for PlayStation 4 Game Reviews," 2021, https://www.metacritic.com/game/playstation-4/beautiful-desolation; Metacritic, "Beautiful Desolation for Switch Game Reviews," 2021, https://www.metacritic.com/game/switch/beautiful-desolation; Steam, "BEAUTIFUL DESOLATION on Steam," 2020, https://store.steampowered.com/app/912570/BEAUTIFUL_DESOLATION/.

7. The term triple-A is an informal industry term referring to games produced and distributed by a mid- to major-size game publisher; i.e. these are the games with the broadest audiences and with the largest global cultural impact.

8. Benedict Anderson, *Imagined Communities: Reflections on the Origin and Spread of Nationalism* (London: Verso, 2006), 6.

9. Edward W. Said, *Culture and Imperialism* (New York: Vintage, 1993); Timothy Brennan, "The National Longing for Form," in *Nation and Narration*, ed. Homi K. Bhabha (London; New York: Routledge, 1990), 44–70.

10. Higson, "The Concept of National Cinema"; Mette Hjort and Scott Mackenzie, eds., *Cinema and Nation* (London; New York: Routledge, 2000).

11. Ziad Fahmy, *Ordinary Egyptians: Creating the Modern Nation through Popular Culture* (Stanford, CA: Stanford University Press, 2011), 15.

12. Higson, "The Concept of National Cinema."

13. Martin Hand and Karenza Moore, "Community, Identity and Digital Games," in *Understanding Digital Games*, ed. Jason Rutter and Jo Bryce (London: SAGE, 2006), 166–82; Adrienne Shaw, "What Is Video Game Culture? Cultural Studies and Game Studies," *Games and Culture* 5, no. 4 (October 1, 2010): 403–24, https://doi.org/10.1177/1555412009360414.

14. Paula Callus and Cher Potter, "Michezo Video: Nairobi's Gamers and the Developers Who Are Promoting Local Content," *Critical African Studies* 9, no. 3 (September 2, 2017): 302–26, https://doi.org/10.1080/21681392.2017.1371620; Parker and Jenson, "Canadian Indie Games between the Global and the Local"; Vit Sisler, "Video Game Development in the Middle East: Iran, the Arab World, and Beyond," in *Gaming Globally: Production, Play, and Place*, ed. Nina B. Huntemann and Ben Aslinger (New York: Palgrave Macmillan, 2016), 251–71, http://ebookcentral.proquest.com/lib/ucb/detail.action?docID=1138384; Iskandar Zulkarnain, "'Playable' Nationalism: 'Nusantara Online' and the 'Gamic' Reconstructions of National History," *Sojourn: Journal of Social Issues in Southeast Asia* 29, no. 1 (2014): 31–62.

15. Nick Webber, "The Britishness of 'British Video Games'," *International Journal of Cultural Policy* 26, no. 2 (February 23, 2020): 135–49, https://doi.org/10.1080/10286632.2018.1448804, 136.

16. Webber, "The Britishness of 'British Video Games'," 142.

17. Higson, "The Concept of National Cinema," 137.

18. Consalvo, "Console Video Games and Global Corporations"; Sisler, Svelch, and Slerka, "Video Games and the Asymmetry of Global Cultural Flows"; Baeza-González, "Video Games Development in the Periphery."

19. Wolf, *Video Games around the World*, 4.

20. Wolf, *Video Games around the World*, 5.

21. Amelia Zollner, "Major Publishers Report AAA Franchises Can Cost over a Billion to Make," IGN, April 28, 2023, https://www.ign.com/articles/major-publishers-report-aaa-franchises-can-cost-over-a-billion-to-make.

This has increased significantly since 2016, when triple A games typically cost around US$100 million; see: Aphra Kerr, *Global Games: Production, Circulation and Policy in the Networked Era* (New York: Routledge, 2016), 87, https://doi.org/10.4324/9780203704028.

22. More affordable doesn't mean cheap; for instance, a successful mobile game in 2016 still cost at least US$100,000 to develop at the outset; see Kerr, *Global Games*, 93. For a deeper understanding of the many variable costs involved in game development and distribution, see in its entirety Kerr, *Global Games*.

23. Chris Young, "Unity Production: Capturing the Everyday Game Maker Market," in *Game Production Studies*, ed. Olli Sotamaa and Jan Svelch, Games and Play 5 (Amsterdam: Amsterdam University Press, 2021), 141–58, https://doi.org/10.1515/9789048551736-009.

24. Jennifer R. Whitson, "The New Spirit of Capitalism in the Game Industry," *Television & New Media* 20, no. 8 (December 1, 2019): 790, https://doi.org/10.1177/1527476419851086.

25. Whitson, "The New Spirit of Capitalism in the Game Industry," 790.

26. Whitson, "The New Spirit of Capitalism in the Game Industry"; David Nieborg, "How to Study Game Publishers: Activision Blizzard's Corporate History," in Sotamaa and Svelch, *Game Production Studies*, 179–96, https://doi.org/10.1515/9789048551736-011.

27. Whitson, "The New Spirit of Capitalism in the Game Industry."

28. Maxwell Foxman, "United We Stand: Platforms, Tools and Innovation with the Unity Game Engine," *Social Media + Society* 5, no. 4 (October 1, 2019): 1, https://doi.org/10.1177/2056305119880177.

29. Young, "Unity Production," 146.

30. Young, "Unity Production," 153.

31. John Banks and Brendan Keogh, "More Than One Flop from Bankruptcy: Rethinking Sustainable Independent Game Development," in Sotamaa and Svelch, *Game Production Studies*, 161, https://doi.org/10.1515/9789048551736-010. Also see Whitson, "The New Spirit of Capitalism in the Game Industry"; Parker and Jenson, "Canadian Indie Games between the Global and the Local."

32. Marcus Toftedahl et al., "Global Influences on Regional Industries: Game Development in Nordic Countries, China and India" (The 3rd Annual Chinese

DiGRA Conference, Taichung City, Taiwan, July 1–2, 2016, Digital Games Research Association (DiGRA), 2016), http://urn.kb.se/resolve?urn=urn:nbn:se:his:diva-13427; Sisler, Svelch, and Slerka, "Video Games and the Asymmetry of Global Cultural Flows"; Baeza-González, "Video Games Development in the Periphery."

33. Kerr, *Global Games*, 146.

34. Baeza-González, "Video Games Development in the Periphery."

35. Vanderhoef, "Indie Games of No Nation", 161.

36. Vanderhoef, "Indie Games of No Nation", 175.

37. Van der Merwe, "From Global to National: Mapping the Trajectory of the South African Video Game Industry."

38. Rachel Lara van der Merwe, "Imperial Play," *Communication, Culture and Critique* 14, no. 1 (March 1, 2021): 37–51, 43, https://doi.org/10.1093/ccc/tcaa012.

39. I capitalize White in recognition that Whiteness is neither neutral nor "normal" but is a historically created racial identity. See Kwame Anthony Appiah's argument in *The Atlantic* for further explanation. Kwame Anthony Appiah, "The Case for Capitalizing the *B* in Black," *The Atlantic*, June 18, 2020, https://www.theatlantic.com/ideas/archive/2020/06/time-to-capitalize-blackand-white/613159/

40. Marc James Carpenter, "Replaying Colonialism: Indigenous National Sovereignty and Its Limits in Strategic Videogames," *The American Indian Quarterly* 45, no. 1 (2021): 43.

41. Souvik Mukherjee, "The Playing Fields of Empire: Empire and Spatiality in Video Games," *Journal of Gaming & Virtual Worlds* 7, no. 3 (Intellect, 2015), https://doi.org/10.1386/jgvw.7.3.299_1. See also for similar arguments about the significance of colonial gamescapes: Sybille Lammes, "Postcolonial Playgrounds: Games and Postcolonial Culture," *Eludamos. Journal for Computer Game Culture* 4, no. 1 (April 26, 2010): 1–6; Shoshana Magnet, "Playing at Colonization: Interpreting Imaginary Landscapes in the Video Game Tropico," *Journal of Communication Inquiry* 30, no. 2 (April 1, 2006): 142–62, https://doi.org/10.1177/0196859905285320.

42. Ian Bogost, "The Rhetoric of Video Games," in *The Ecology of Games: Connecting Youth, Games, and Learning*, ed. Katie Salen, The John D. and Catherine T. MacArthur Foundation Series on Digital Media and Learning (Cambridge, MA: The MIT Press, 2008), 117–40, doi: 10.1162/dmal.9780262693646.117.

43. Alexander R. Galloway, *Gaming: Essays on Algorithmic Culture* (Minneapolis: University of Minnesota Press, 2006).

44. Geoff King, "Die Hard/Try Harder: Narrative, Spectacle and Beyond, from Hollywood to Videogame," in *ScreenPlay*, ed. Geoff King and Tanya Krzywinska (London: Wallflower Press, 2002), 50–65.

45. Souvik Mukherjee, "Playing Subaltern: Video Games and Postcolonialism," *Games and Culture* 13, no. 5 (February 9, 2016): 2, https://doi.org/10.1177/1555412015627258.

46. Christopher A. Paul, *The Toxic Meritocracy of Video Games: Why Gaming Culture Is the Worst* (Minneapolis: University of Minnesota Press, 2018).

47. Rachel Lara van der Merwe, "We Are Not South African: Decolonizing National Identity in a Post-Apartheid State" (PhD diss., University of Colorado at Boulder, 2020), https://www.proquest.com/docview/2474895609/abstract/3A68FE7C362D46B6PQ/1.

48. Ian Bogost, *Persuasive Games: The Expressive Power of Videogames* (Cambridge, MA: MIT Press, 2010), 3.

49. Anna Anthropy, *Rise of the Videogame Zinesters: How Freaks, Normals, Amateurs, Artists, Dreamers, Drop-Outs, Queers, Housewives, and People Like You Are Taking Back an Art Form*, illustrated ed. (New York: Seven Stories Press, 2012), 67.

50. Teun A. van Dijk, "Principles of Critical Discourse Analysis," *Discourse & Society* 4, no. 2 (April 1, 1993): 249–83, https://doi.org/10.1177/0957926593004002006.

51. The Brotherhood Games, "Beautiful Desolation—Kickstarter Video," January 24, 2017, YouTube, 3:57, https://www.youtube.com/watch?v=0f5RFXfLSZ8.

52. Matthew Hughey, *The White Savior Film: Content, Critics, and Consumption* (Philadelphia: Temple University Press, 2014), http://ebookcentral.proquest.com/lib/ucb/detail.action?docID=1639075.

Chapter Five

1. Joe Parkinson and Drew Hinshaw, *Bring Back Our Girls: The Astonishing Survival and Rescue of Nigeria's Missing Schoolgirls* (London: Swift Press, 2021), 22.

2. Zulumoke Oyibo, "Making Nigeria's Biggest Scale Film: Producer Zulumoke Oyibo Reflects on Up North," *The Guardian*, December 27, 2018, https://guardian.ng/art/making-nigerias-biggest-scale-film-producer-zulumoke-oyibo-reflects-on-up-north/

3. Chris Atton, *Alternative Media* (London: SAGE, 2002), 4.

4. Mitzi Waltz, *Alternative and Activist Media* (Edinburgh: Edinburgh University Press, 2005), 2.

5. Antonio Gramsci, *Selections from the Prison Notebooks*, trans. Quintin Hoare and Geoffrey Nowell-Smith (London: Lawrence and Wishart, 1971).

6. Jonathan Haynes, *Nollywood: The Creation of Nigerian Film Genres* (Ibadan, Nigeria: Bookcraft, 2017).

7. Haynes, *Nollywood*, 53.

8. Jonathan Haynes, "Political Critique in Nigerian Video Films," *African Affairs* 105, no. 421 (2006): 511–33.

9. Añulika Agina, "NFVCB's Ban of Fuelling Poverty: Political Move or National Security?," in *African Film Cultures*, ed. Winston Mano, Barbara Knorpp, and Añulika Agina (Newcastle upon Tyne, UK: Cambridge Scholars Publishing, 2017), 223–40.

10. Atton, *Alternative Media*.

11. Tony Harcup, "Alternative Journalism," *Oxford Research Encyclopedias* (2019), doi:10.1093/acrefore/9780190228613.013.780.

12. Charles Willet, "The State of Alternative Publishing in America: Issues and Implications for Libraries," *Counterpoise* 3, no. 1 (1999): 14.

13. Alexandra Juhasz, *AIDS TV: Identity, Community and Alternative Video* (Durham, NC: Duke University Press, 1995).

14. Andrew Higson, "The Limiting Imagination of National Cinema," in *Cinema and Nation*, ed. Mette Hjort and Scott Mackenzie (London: Routledge, 2000), 63–74.

15. Susan Hayward, "Framing National Cinemas," in *Cinema and Nation*, 88–102; Stephen Crofts, "Reconceptualising National Cinema/s," in *Theorising National Cinema*, ed. Valentina Vitali and Paul Willemen (London: BFI, 2006), 44–57.

16. Crofts, "Reconceptualising National Cinema/s," 55.

17. Nancy Kranich, "A Question of Balance: The Role of Libraries in Providing Alternatives to the Mainstream Media," *Collection Building* 19, no. 3 (2000): 85–90.

18. For detailed accounts of the history, operations, impact of, and global reactions to Boko Haram, see Alexander Thurston's (2017) book *Boko Haram: The History of an African Jihadist Movement* (Princeton, NJ: Princeton University Press), https://press.princeton.edu/books/hardcover/9780691172248/boko-haram, Virginia Comolli's (2015) *Boko Haram: Nigeria's Islamist Insurgency* (London: Hurst), https://www.hurstpublishers.com/book/boko-haram/, Joe Parkinson and Drew Hinshaw's (2021) *Bring Back Our Girls* (London: Swift Press), https://swiftpress.com/book/bring-back-our-girls/ and UNICEF's 2017 report: https://www.un.org/en/academic-impact/over-half-schools-remain-closed-epicentre-boko-haram-crisis-nigeria-%E2%80%93-unicef.

19. Atta Barkindo, *How Boko Haram Exploits History and Memory*, Counterpoints (London: Africa Research Institute, 2016), 1.

20. Barkindo, *How Boko Haram Exploits History and Memory*.

21. "About the Scheme," para. 1, National Youth Service Corps (NYSC), https://www.nysc.gov.ng/aboutscheme.html.

22. Tom Gunning, "The Cinema of Attraction: Early Film, Its Spectator and the Avant-Garde," in *Early Cinema: Space, Frame, Narrative*, ed. Thomas Elsaesser (London: British Film Institute, 1990), 64.

23. Steve Neale, "Art Cinema as Institution," *Screen* 22, no. 1 (1981): 36.

24. Parkinson and Hinshaw, *Bring Back Our Girls*.

25. Jude Akudinobi, "Nollywood: Prisms and Paradigms," *Cinema Journal* 54, no. 2 (2015): 134.

Chapter Six

1. Neda Atanasoski and Kalindi Vora, "Postsocialist Politics and the Ends of Revolution," *Social Identities* 242, no. 2 (2018): 141.

2. Bodgan Popa, "Trans* and Legacies of Socialism: Reading Queer Postsocialism in *Tangerine*," *The Undecidable Unconscious* 5 (2018): 34.

3. A full copy of Law 373 can be found by clicking the following link: https://www.gacetaoficial.gob.cu/sites/default/files/goc-2019-o43.pdf.

4. Independent magazine HyperMedia has fleshed out the legal implications affecting independent filmmakers in Cuba, as well as made allusion to important groups of film and audiovisual creators that have emerged from the public sphere, such as the G-20 group, who has responded to the government's initiatives constraining their production and creative rights: https://www.hypermediamagazine.com/sociedad/decreto-373/.

5. "Decreto Ley no. 373" (Gaceta Oficial de la República de Cuba June 27, 2019), 701, https://www.gacetaoficial.gob.cu/sites/default/files/goc-2019-o43.pdf [Author translation].

6. Michaelanne Dye et al., "The Human Infrastructure of El Paquete, Cuba's Offline Internet," *Interactions* (January–February 2019): 58–62; Steffen Köhn, "Unpacking El Paquete: The Poetics and Politics of Cuba's Offline Data-Sharing Network," *Digital Culture and Society* 5, no. 1 (2019): 105–24; Jennifer Cearns, "Introduction to el Paquete," *Cuban Studies* 50 (2020): 99–110; Michelle Leigh Farrell, "Disrupting the Algorithm: The Streaming Platforms in the Cuban Audiovisual Landscape: El paquete semanal, Netflix, and Mi Mochila," *Cuban Studies* 50 (2021): 186–204.

7. Dye et al., "The Human Infrastructure of El Paquete," 60.

8. Ted Henken, "The Opium of the Paquete," *Cuban Studies* 50 (2020): 111–38.

9. Luz Escobar, "Las tarifas de la energía eléctrica subirán un 500% el próximo 1 de enero," *14ymedio*, December 12, 2020, https://www.14ymedio.com/cuba/tarifas-luz-subiran-proximo-enero_0_3002099764.html.

10. Jorge I. Dominguez, "What You Might Not Know About the Cuban Economy," *Harvard Business Review*, August 17, 2015, https://hbr.org/2015/08/what-you-might-not-know-about-the-cuban-economy; Bret Serbin, "What Is the Cost of Living in Cuba?," *Borgen Magazine*, June 30, 2017, https://www.borgenmagazine.com/what-is-the-cost-of-living-in-cuba/.

11. Amnesty International, "Cuba: Human Rights at a Glance," September 17, 2015, https://www.amnesty.org/en/latest/news/2015/09/cuba-human-rights-at-a-glance-2/.

12. Sara Ahmed, "Affective Economies," *Social Text* 22, no. 2 (Summer 2004): 117–39.

13. See Emilio Bejel's *Gay Cuban Nation* (Chicago: University of Chicago Press, 2001); José Quiroga's *Tropics of Desire* (New York: New York University Press, 2000); Bretton White's *Staging Discomfort* (Gainesville: University of Florida Press, 2020).

14. Eve K. Sedgwick, *Touching Feeling: Affect, Pedagogy, Performativity* (Durham, NC: Duke University Press, 2003), 8.

15. See Susana Peña's *Oye Loca: From the Mariel Boatlift to Gay Cuban Miami* (Minneapolis: University of Minnesota Press, 2013); Julio Capó Jr.'s *Welcome to*

Fairyland: Queer Miami before 1940 (Chapel Hill: University of North Carolina Press, 2017).

16. Alejandro Ríos, "Pantalla Indiscreta: Santa y Andrés," aired March 25, 2019, Radio y Televisión Martí, online streaming, 24:29, https://www.radiotelevisionmarti.com/a/pantalla-indiscreta-santa-y-andrés-reinaldo-arenas/232857.html.

17. Lauren Peña, "Revolutionary ruralities: Spaces of surveillance and exclusion in Carlos Lechuga's *Santa y Andrés* (2016)," *Studies in Spanish & Latin American Cinemas* 17, no. 3 (2020): 429.

18. Reinaldo Arenas, *Before Night Falls* (New York: InsightOut Books, 2001), 6.

19. Arenas, *Before Night Falls*, 19.

Chapter Seven

1. HMV is His Master's Voice, the British-owned record label that was distributing gramophone records in India as early as 1907. Until 1910, it operated as Gramophone Company of India, which was the Indian chapter of HMV.

2. Ashok Da Ranade, *Hindi Film Song: Music beyond Boundaries* (New Delhi; Chicago: Promilla and Bibliophile South Asia, 2006).

3. Shalin Bhatt, "Kaise dekhoon kaise Madhuri (Vinayakrao Patwardhan)," May 8, 2013, YouTube, 3:05, https://www.youtube.com/watch?v=c4JidkT-2Ck.

4. Marsha Kinder, *Playing with Power in Movies, Television, and Video Games: From Muppet Babies to Teenage Mutant Ninja Turtles* (Berkeley: University of California Press, 1991), 211.

5. Henry Jenkins, "Transmedia Storytelling 101," *Pop Junctions*, March 21, 2007, https://henryjenkins.org/blog/2007/03/transmedia_storytelling_101.html.

6. Within the realm of film and media studies alone, the term gained traction with Elizabeth Evans's work on Transmedia Television (2011), Agnes Petho's work on cinema's positioning "in between" other media that it interacts with (2011), Chuck Tryon's work on streaming cultures (2014), Matthew Freeman and Anthony N. Smith's work on genres in a transmedia landscape (2023), and a range of anthologies on the transmedial ontologies of superhero films and sci-fi film and television series.

7. Madhava Prasad, *Ideology of the Hindi Film: A Historical Construction* (New Delhi: Oxford University Press, 1998); Ravi Vasudevan, *The Melodramatic Public: Film Form and Spectatorship in Indian Cinema* (New York: Palgrave Macmillan, 2011).

8. Vasudevan, *The Melodramatic Public.*

9. Gregory Booth, *Behind the Curtain: Making Music in Mumbai's Film Studios* (Oxford; New York: Oxford University Press, 2008).

10. Neepa Majumdar, *Wanted Cultured Ladies Only!: Female Stardom and Cinema in India, 1930s–1950s* (Urbana; Chicago: University of Illinois Press, 2009); Shikha Jhingan, "Lata Mangeshkar's Voice in the Age of Cassette Reproduction," *BioScope South Asian Screen Studies* 4, no. 2 (2013).

11. Sangita Gopal and Sujata Moorti, eds., *Global Bollywood: Travels of Hindi Song and Dance* (Minneapolis: University of Minnesota Press, 2008); Jayson Beaster-Jones, *Bollywood Sounds: The Cosmopolitan Mediations of Hindi Film Song* (New York: Oxford University Press, 2015).

12. From the Empire Broadcasting Programme radio listings in *The Times of India*. January 31, 1938, 4.

13. From the Empire Broadcasting Programme radio listings in *The Times of India*. November 11, 1938, 6.

14. David Lelyved, "Upon the Subdominant: Administering Music on All India Radio," *Social Text* no. 39 (Summer 1994): 111–27.

15. Lelyved situates the emphasis on classical music as not so much classical as Hindu. For Keskar, the fundamental problem was that music had been divorced from its (Hindu) spiritual roots because, under the Islamic rulers of the country, music had become "erotic, the special preserve of 'dancing girls, prostitutes, and their circle of pimps.'" Lelyved, "Upon the Subdominant," 117.

16. "Broadcast of Film Songs by All India Radio: I.M.P.P.A. to Serve Notice of Termination," *The Times of India*, November 8, 1952, 3.

17. Madhusree Dutta notes the long history of people having to travel to big cities like Bombay from the suburbs and nearby villages to watch a movie in a cinema hall. Even as late as 2007, there were about twelve theaters per one million people in India. According to the same UNESCO Institute for Statistics report, in comparison, the United States had 162 movie theaters per million people during those years. Madhusree Dutta, "Popular Cinema and Public Culture in Bombay," accessed January 2021, https://www.india-seminar.com/2014/657/657_madhusree_dutta.htm.

18. "Current Topics: TV Arrives a Jacket and Tie," *Times of India*, September 17, 1959, 8.

19. Yakub Syed, Zoom interview with author, January 26, 2022.

20. NH Hindi Songs, "Chand Si Mehbooba | Himalay Ki God Mein (1965) | Manoj Kumar | Mala Sinha | Evergreen Mukesh Song," February 5, 2021, YouTube, 3:35, https://www.youtube.com/watch?v=WYjVa10bP1c; Hindi Songs Jukebox, "Dheere Chal Chand Gagan Mein (Color) HD—Rafi & Lata | Dev Anand, Mala Sinha," October 29, 2020, YouTube, 4:03, https://www.youtube.com/watch?v=06LjEH37jmM; Sadabahar HD Songs, "Taaron Ki Jubaan Par Hai Mohabbat Ki Kahani—Mala Sinha—Nausherwa E Adil—Vintage Songs," April 6, 2013, YouTube, 3:55, https://www.youtube.com/watch?v=jCPs7QvjTSE.

21. Robin Jeffrey, "Communications and Capitalism in India 1750–2010", *South Asia: Journal of South Asian Studies* 25, no. 2 (2002): 61–75; population figures from "Population, Total—India," The World Bank, accessed May 21, 2022, https://data.worldbank.org/indicator/SP.POP.TOTL?locations=IN.

22. Doordarshan is the state-run television channel. When TV technology first came to India, it was simply referred to as "Television" and was under the aegis of All India Radio. It was the only channel available for over a decade. Its name was changed to Doordarshan in 1965 after its separation from All India Radio.

23. YRF, "Koi Ladki Hai Song | Dil To Pagal Hai | Shah Rukh Khan, Madhuri Dixit, Karisma Kapoor | Lata, Udit," January 12, 2015, YouTube, 5:38, https://www.youtube.com/watch?v=u6bk53x2Kno.

Chapter Eight

1. Angelica Lawson, "Resistance and Resilience in Ofelia Zepeda's Ocean Power," *The Kenyon Review* 32, no. 1 (2010): 185.

2. Joanna Hearne, "Native to the Device: Thoughts on Digital Indigenous Studies," *Studies in American Indian Literatures* 29, no. 1 (Spring 2017): 3–26.

3. Aubrey Hanson, *Reading for Resurgence: Indigenous Literatures, Communities, and Learning* (Doctoral thesis, University of Calgary, 2016), 20.

4. Leanne Betasamosake Simpson, *As We Have Always Done: Indigenous Freedom Through Radical Resistance* (Minneapolis: University of Minnesota Press, 2017), 16.

5. Quoted in Sarah Tremlett, *The Poetics of Poetry Film: Film Poetry, Videopoetry, Lyric Voice, Reflection* (Bristol: Intellect Books, 2021), 27.

6. "Moving Rural Verse," Western Folklife Center, https://www.westernfolklife.org/moving-rural-verse.

7. Mark McLemore, "O'odham Dances: 'This Is the Way We Begin and End Things'," April 25, 2017, Arizona Public Media, https://news.azpm.org/p/monsoon/2017/4/25/109500-oodham-dances-this-is-the-way-we-begin-and-end-things/#:~:text=%22The%20scarcity%20of%20water%20is,a%20desert%2C%22%20Zepeda%20said.

8. Joanne Barker, "Confluence: Water as an Analytic of Indigenous Feminisms," *American Indian Culture and Research Journal* 43, no. 3 (2019): 6.

9. Andrew Peterson, "A Culture without Books," *Tucson Weekly*, February 25, 1992, 2.

10. Ofelia Zepada, *When It Rains, Papago and Pima Poetry = Mat hekid o ju, 'O'odham Na-cegitodag* (Tucson: University of Arizona Press, 1982), 198.

11. Ofelia Zepeda, *Ocean Power: Poems from the Desert* (Tucson: University of Arizona Press, 1995), 4.

12. David Wallace Adams, *Education for Extinction: American Indians and the Boarding School Experience, 1875–1928* (Lawrence: University Press of Kansas, 2020).

13. Ofelia Zepeda, "Autobiography," in *Here First: Autobiographical Essays by Native American Writers*, ed. Arnold Krupat and Brian Swann (New York: The Modern Library, 2000), 409.

14. Zepeda, *Ocean Power*, 5.

15. Zepeda, "Autobiography," 413.

16. Harry M. Benshoff and Sean Griffin, *America on Film: Representing Race, Class, Gender, and Sexuality at the Movies* (Malden, MA: Blackwell Publishing Ltd, 2000), 100.

17. Brian Hochman, *Savage Preservation: The Ethnographic Origins of Modern Media Technology* (Minneapolis: University of Minnesota Press, 2014).

18. David Wallace Adams, *Education for Extinction*.

19. Brian Dippie, *The Vanishing American: White Attitudes & U.S. Indian Policy* (Lawrence: University Press of Kansas, 1982), 209.

20. Jacquelyn Kilpatrick, *Celluloid Indians: Native Americans and Film* (Lincoln: University of Nebraska Press, 1999), 32.

21. Michelle Raheja, *Reservation Reelism: Red Facing, Visual Sovereignty, and Representations of Native Americans in Film* (Lincoln: University of Nebraska Press, 2010); Joanna Hearne, *Native Recognition: Indigenous Cinema and the Western* (New York: Suny Press, 2012).

22. McLemore, "O'odham Dances."

23. Ofelia Zepeda, introduction to *Singing for Power: The Song Magic of the Papago Indians of Southern Arizona*, by Ruth Murray Underhill, reprint ed. (Tucson: University of Arizona Press, 1992): vii.

24. Underhill, *Singing for Power*, 8.

25. Barker, "Confluence," 15.

26. Nick Estes and Jaskiran Dhillon, *Standing with Standing Rock: Voices from the #NODAPL* Movement (Minneapolis: University of Minnesota Press, 2019).

Chapter Nine

1. Sally Chivers, *The Silvering Screen: Old Age and Disability in Cinema* (Buffalo, NY: University of Toronto Press, 2011).

2. Timothy Shary and Nancy McVittie, *Fade to Gray: Aging in American Cinema* (Austin: University of Texas Press, 2016).

3. *Intimidades de Shakespeare y Víctor Hugo* won nineteen international documentary film festival awards, including the Viennale, AFI Fest, Toronto International Film Festival, and the San Sebastián International Film Festival.

4. For more on the study of Latin American documentary see the introduction of *Latin American Documentary Film in the New Millennium*, eds. María Guadalupe Arenillas and Michael J. Lazzara (New York: Palgrave Macmillan: 2016). Arenillas and Lazzara have noted the many conditions in Latin America under which fiction film long ago eclipsed the documentary in terms of regard and distribution.

5. Some recent documentary film festivals are DocsMX, Ambulante, and DOQUMENTA, and documentary categories are part of renowned film festivals like the Guanajuato International Film Festival, the Festival Internacional de Morelia, and the Los Cabos International Film Festival, among others.

6. Such distribution channels include FilminLatino, Amazon Prime, and Netflix, among others.

7. In Julianne Burton's *The Social Documentary in Latin America* (Pittsburgh: University of Pittsburgh Press, 1990) she defines the social documentary as documentaries with a human subject and a descriptive or transformative concern.

8. Ignacio Sánchez Prado, "The Politics-Commodity: The Rise of the Mexican Commercial Documentary in the Neoliberal Era," in *Latin American*

Documentary Filmmaking in the New Millennium, eds. María Guadalupe Arenillas and Michael Lazzara (New York: Palgrave Macmillan, 2016), 97–114.

9. Alba Nidia Sánchez Baltazar, “Realismo contemporáneo y modernidad en el cine de la frontera norte de México,” *Ñawi: arte diseño comunicación* 7, no. 1 (2023): 275–93.

10. Lauro Zavala, “El nuevo documental mexicano y las fronteras de la representación,” *Revista Toma Uno*, no. 1 (2012): 25–36.

11. Bill Nichols develops the six principal modes of documentary filmmaking in his book *Introduction to Documentary* (Bloomington: Indiana University Press, 2010).

12. The analysis in this chapter has primarily centered on the character of the grandmother as the main on-screen presence, to delve into the politics of the personal documentary. While acknowledging the potential complexities associated with the subject position of the granddaughter, it is important to emphasize that the scope of this analysis is intentionally limited to the portrayal and significance of the grandmother’s role. Incorporating the subject position of the director, although a valuable consideration, exceeds the bounds of the current study.

13. For example, see *No son horas de olvidar* (2020) by director David Castañón Medina, *Un día menos* (2009) by director Dariela Ludlow, *Bellas de noche* (2016) by director María José Cuevas, and *Aquí sigo* (2016) by director Lorenzo Hagerman.

14. The translation of the dialogue comes from the official subtitles for the film.

15. Ayala Blanco analyzes the geriatric illness of the filmmaker’s grandmother in the documentary in further detail in his book *La ilusión del cine mexicano* (Mexico City: Oceano, 2013).

16. Jorge Ayala Blanco, *La ilusión del cine mexicano*, 444. The translations of the text are my own.

Chapter Ten

1. “ImpactGames,” ImpactGames, accessed June 13, 2019, http://www.impactgames.com.

2. “Products,” ImpactGames, accessed November 20, 2023, www.impactgames.com/products.php.

3. Asi Burak, “About PeaceMaker,” June 22, 2009, YouTube, 2:00, https://www.youtube.com/watch?v=NeRlHJhcEuc.

4. Bo Ruberg, “The Draft of My Book Playing Queer Is Complete!” Our Glass Lake, published December 27, 2016, https://ourglasslake.com/2016/12/playing-queer-book-draft-is-complete/.

5. Gayatri Chakravorty Spivak, “Can the Subaltern Speak?,” *Die Philosophin* 14, no. 27 (1988): 42–58.

6. Patrick Crogan, *Gameplay Mode: War, Simulation, and Technoculture* (Minneapolis: University of Minnesota Press, 2011), xvii.

7. Edmond Chang, "Gaming as Writing, or, World of Warcraft as World of Wordcraft," *Computing & Composition Online* (Fall 2008), http://cconlinejournal.org/gaming_issue_2008/Chang_Gaming_as_writing/index.html.

8. Alexander Galloway, *Gaming: Essays on Algorithmic Culture* (Minneapolis: University of Minnesota Press, 2006): 16.

9. Adel Manna, "Deconstructing the Israeli Socio-Political Apartheid System," *Theory & Event* 18, supplement no. 1 (2015).

10. Mohammad Abu Assida and Mourad ben Jalloul, "Israeli Settlement Strategy in the West Bank," *An-Najah University Journal for Research—B (Humanities)* 36, no. 10 (2022): 2097–138.

11. Karam Dana, "The West Bank Apartheid/Separation Wall: Space, Punishment and the Disruption of Social Continuity," *Geopolitics* 22, no. 4 (2017): 887–910.

12. Mohammed Nijim, "Genocide in Palestine: Gaza as a Case Study," *The International Journal of Human Rights* 27, no. 1 (2023): 165–200.

13. Hani Faris, ed., *The Failure of the Two-State Solution: The Prospects of One State in the Israel–Palestine Conflict* (London: I.B. Tauris, 2013).

14. Rashid Khalidi, *British Policy towards Syria & Palestine, 1906–1914: A Study of the Antecedents of the Hussein–McMahon Correspondence, the Sykes–Picot Agreement, and the Balfour Declaration* (Oxford: Ithaca Press, 1980).

15. See: Ilan Pappé, "Partition and Destruction: UN Resolution 181 and Its Impact," in *The Ethnic Cleansing of Palestine* (Oxford: Oneworld Publications, 2006).

16. Lila Abu-Lughod and Ahmad Sa'dī, eds., *Nakba: Palestine, 1948, and the Claims of Memory* (New York: Columbia University Press, 2007).

17. Penny Green and Amelia Smith, "Evicting Palestine," *State Crime Journal* 5, no. 1 (2016): 81–108.

18. Green and Smith, "Evicting Palestine."

19. For a more extensive discussion of what indigenous justice means, see Eve Tuck and K. Wayne Yang, "Decolonization Is Not a Metaphor," *Decolonization: Indigeneity, Education & Society* 1, no. 1 (2012): 1–40 and Kirisitina Sailiata, "Decolonization," in *Native Studies Keywords*, ed. Nohelani Teves and Michelle Raheja (Tucson: University of Arizona Press, 2015), 301–308.

20. Ilan Pappé, "Zionism as Colonialism: A Comparative View of Diluted Colonialism in Asia and Africa," *South Atlantic Quarterly* 107, no. 4 (October 2008): 623.

21. "Human Rights Council Hears That 700,000 Israeli Settlers Are Living Illegally in the Occupied West Bank," United Nations, accessed November 22, 2023, https://www.ungeneva.org/en/news-media/meeting-summary/2023/03/afternoon-human-rights-council-hears-current-israeli-plan-double.

22. "Population," Peace Now, accessed November 21, 2023, peacenow.org.il/en/settlements-watch/ settlements-data/population.

23. Khalil Tofakji, "Settlements and Ethnic Cleansing in the Jordan Valley," *Palestine–Israel Journal of Politics, Economics, and Culture* 21, no. 3 (2016): 81–87.

24. Charles W. Anderson, "Other Laboratories: The Great Revolt, Civil Resistance, and the Social History of Palestine," *Journal of Palestine Studies* 50, no. 3 (2021): 47–51.

25. Ronit Kampf and Nathan Stolero, "Computerized Simulation of the Israeli-Palestinian Conflict, Knowledge Gap, and New Media Use," *Information, Communication & Society* 18, no. 6 (2015): 646.

26. Nick Irving, "Every Game Is a Simulation," Medium, published March 29, 2021, https://nickrirving.medium.com/if-the-world-is-slowly-being-gamified-then-games-are-also-becoming-simulified-2a6097cd79ff.

27. Mohamed Mohamed, "Two-State Hypocrisy," September 7, 2018, *Electronic Intifada*, https://electronicintifada.net/content/two-state-hypocrisy/25446.

28. For more on the Palestinian Intifadas, see Zachary Lockman and Joel Beinin, eds., *Intifada: The Palestinian Uprising against Israeli Occupation* (Boston: South End Press, 1989) and Ramzy Baroud, *The Second Intifada: A Chronicle of a People's Struggle* (London: Pluto Press, 2006).

Chapter Eleven

1. I want to extend my thanks and deep gratitude to Dr. Miranda Brady, Dr. Kahente Horn-Miller, Dr. Jennifer Adese, T'hohahoken Michael Doxtater, and Jess Wind for their invaluable engagement and support of my work. I could not have written the first version of this chapter (part of my master's thesis) without my forever furbebe love, Tigger, who cuddled me through the entire process of developing and writing this research project. This project was supported by the Ontario Graduate Scholarship.

2. Eve Tuck, "Suspending Damage: A Letter to Communities," *Harvard Educational Review* 79, no. 3 (2009): 409–28.

3. Aileen Moreton-Robinson, *The White Possessive: Property, Power, and Indigenous Sovereignty, UPCC Book Collections on Project MUSE* (Minneapolis: University of Minnesota Press, 2015).

4. Liza Black, *Picturing Indians: Native Americans in Film, 1941–1960* (Lincoln: University of Nebraska Press, 2020); Denise K. Cummings, *Visualities: Perspectives on Contemporary American Indian Film and Art*, American Indian Studies Series (East Lansing: Michigan State University Press, 2011); André Dudemaine, Gabrielle Marcoux, and Isabelle St-Amand, "Indigenous Cinema and Media in the Americas: Storytelling, Communities, and Sovereignties," *Canadian Journal of Film Studies* 29, no. 1 (2020): 27–51; M. Elise Marubbio, *Killing the Indian Maiden Images of Native American Women in Film* (Lexington: University Press of Kentucky, 2006); Wendy Gay Pearson and Susan Knabe, *Reverse Shots: Indigenous Film and Media in an International Context*, Film and Media Studies Series (Waterloo, ON: Wilfrid Laurier University Press, 2015).

5. Joanna Hearne, "Native American and Indigenous Media," *Feminist Media Histories* 4, no. 2 (April 1, 2018): 123–27; Joanna Hearne, *Native Recognition: Indigenous Cinema and the Western*, SUNY Series, Horizons of

Cinema (Albany, NY: SUNY Press, 2012); Michelle H. Raheja, *Reservation Realism: Redfacing, Visual Sovereignty, and Representations of Native Americans in Film* (Lincoln: University of Nebraska Press, 2011); Liza Black, *Picturing Indians.*

6. J. Rickard, "Diversifying Sovereignty and the Reception of Indigenous Art," *Art Journal* 76, no. 2 (2017): 81–84; J. Rickard, "Visualizing Sovereignty in the Time of Biometric Sensors," *South Atlantic Quarterly* 110, no. 2 (2011): 465–86; Jolene Rickard et al., "Sovereignty: A Line in the Sand," *Aperture*, no. 139 (1995): 50–59.

7. Raheja, *Reservation Realism*, 197.

8. Susan D. Dion and Angela Salamanca, "InVISIBILITY: Indigenous in the City—Indigenous Artists, Indigenous Youth and the Project of Survivance," *Decolonization: Indigeneity, Education & Society* 3, no. 1 (May 16, 2014); Carol Kalafatic, "Keepers of the Power: Story as Covenant in the Films of Loretta Todd, Shelley Niro, and Christine Welsh," in *Gendering the Nation: Canadian Women's Cinema*, ed. Kay Armatage et al. (Toronto: University of Toronto Press, 1999); William Lempert, "Decolonizing Encounters of the Third Kind: Alternative Futuring in Native Science Fiction Film," *Visual Anthropology Review* 30, no. 2 (2014): 164–76; Carla Taunton, "Indigenous (Re)Memory and Resistance: Video Works by Dana Claxton," in *Native Americans on Film: Conversations, Teaching, and Theory*, ed. M. Elise Marubbio and Eric L. Buffalohead (Lexington: University Press of Kentucky, 2013).

9. Jarrett Martineau and Eric Ritskes, "Fugitive Indigeneity: Reclaiming the Terrain of Decolonial Struggle through Indigenous Art," *Decolonization: Indigeneity, Education & Society* 3, no. 1 (May 20, 2014): 7.

10. Margaret Kovach, *Indigenous Methodologies: Characteristics, Conversations and Contexts* (Ottawa: University of Ottawa, 2009): 85.

11. Hokulani Aikau et al., "Indigenous Feminisms Roundtable," *Frontiers: A Journal of Women Studies* 36, no. 3 (2015): 84–106; Maile Arvin, Eve Tuck, and Angie Morrill, "Decolonizing Feminism: Challenging Connections between Settler Colonialism and Heteropatriarchy," *Feminist Formations* 25, no. 1 (2013): 8–34; Michael Doxtater, "Indigenous Knowledge in the Decolonial Era," *American Indian Quarterly* 28, no. 3/4 (2004): 618–33; Scott Lauria, "Destabilizing the Settler Academy: The Decolonial Effects of Indigenous Methodologies," *American Quarterly* 64, no. 4 (2012): 805–8; Linda Tuhiwai Smith, *Decolonizing Methodologies: Research and Indigenous Peoples*, 2nd ed. (London: Zed Books, 2012); Haunani-Kay Trask, "The Color of Violence," in *Color of Violence: The INCITE! Anthology*, ed. INCITE! Women of Color Against Violence (Durham, NC: Duke University Press, 2016).

12. Arvin, Tuck, and Morrill, "Decolonizing Feminism," 12.

13. Mark Cronlund Anderson and Carmen L. Robertson, *Seeing Red: A History of Natives in Canadian Newspapers* (Winnipeg: University of Manitoba Press, 2011).

14. Raheja, *Reservation Realism*; Pearson and Knabe, *Reverse Shots.*

15. Gerald Robert Vizenor, *Fugitive Poses: Native American Indian Scenes of Absence and Presence*, Abraham Lincoln Lecture Series (Lincoln: University

of Nebraska Press, 1998); Gerald Robert Vizenor, *Manifest Manners: Postindian Warriors of Survivance* (Lincoln: University of Nebraska Press, 1999).

16. Kim H. Veltman, "Edutainment, Technotainment and Culture," *Cività Annual Report* 2003 (Florence: Giunti, 2004): 1–25.

17. Normand Lester, *The Black Book of English Canada* (Toronto: McClelland & Stewart, 2002).

18. Peter Hodgins, "The Canadian Dream-Work [Microform]: History, Myth and Nostalgia in the Heritage Minutes" (PhD thesis, Carleton University, 2003).

19. Katarzyna Rukszto, "The Other Heritage Minutes: Satirical Reactions to Canadian Nationalism," *Topia (Montreal)* 14 (2005): 73–91.

20. At the time of research for this project, which took place between 2015 and 2017, Historica Canada listed a dropdown menu option on their website which would allow you to view parodies created in response to original *Heritage Minutes*.

21. Raheja, *Reservation Realism*, 15.

22. Glen Sean Coulthard, *Red Skin, White Masks: Rejecting the Colonial Practice of Recognition* (Minneapolis: University of Minnesota Press, 2014); Leanne Betasamosake Simpson, *As We Have Always Done: Indigenous Freedom through Radical Resistance*, Indigenous Americas (Minneapolis: University of Minnesota Press, 2017); Leanne Betasamosake Simpson, *Dancing on Our Turtle's Back: Stories of Nishnaabeg Re-Creation, Resurgence and a New Emergence* (Winnipeg: Arbeiter Ring Publishing, 2011).

23. Tuck, "Suspending Damage," 416.

24. Raheja, *Reservation Realism*, 19.

25. Beenash Jafri, "Refusal/Film: Diasporic-Indigenous Relationalities," *Settler Colonial Studies* 10, no. 1 (2020); Beenash Jafri, "Desire, Settler Colonialism, and the Racialized Cowboy," *American Indian Culture and Research Journal* 37, no. 2 (2013): 73–86.

26. T'hohahoken Michael Doxtater, personal communication with the author, May 9, 2017.

27. Vizenor, *Manifest Manners*.

28. Tuck, "Suspending Damage."

29. Michael Doxtater, personal communication with the author, May 9, 2017.

30. Kiera L. Ladner and Leanne Simpson, *This Is an Honour Song: Twenty Years since the Blockades* (Winnipeg: Arbeiter Ring Publishing, 2010).

31. Ute Lischke, "Whacking the Indigenous Funny Bone?": Native Humour and Its Healing Powers in Drew Hayden Taylor's *Redskins, Tricksters, and Puppy Stew*, in *Reverse Shots: Indigenous Film and Media in an International Context*, ed. W. G. Pearson and S. Knabe (Waterloo, ON: Wilfred Laurier University Press, 2016), 233–246.

32. David Martinez, *Life of the Indigenous Mind: Vine Deloria Jr. and the Birth of the Red Power Movement* (Lincoln: University of Nebraska Press, 2019).

33. Michael Doxtater, personal communication with the author, May 9, 2017.

Author Biographies

Anthony Adah is Professor of Film Studies at Minnesota State University Moorhead. His teaching and research areas are African Cinemas and Indigenous filmmaking in Australia, Canada, and Aotearoa/New Zealand. He has published in the *World Encyclopedia of Contemporary Theatre: Asia/Pacific* (2000), *PostScript*, *Film Criticism*, and *Journal of Media and Cultural Politics*, and has a forthcoming book, *The Environment in Indigenous Cinemas* (2026). He was a US Fulbright Scholar to Nigeria in 2021 and a Carnegie African Diaspora Fellow in 2023.

Añulika Agina is Associate Professor of Media Studies and the program director of the MSc Media and Communication at the Pan-Atlantic University Lagos, where she teaches and researches Nigerian film, media industries, cinema-going cultures, and more recently Nollywood women. She has held research fellowships in South Africa, Germany, and the United Kingdom, working on the Screen Worlds project to investigate Nigerian screen cultures. She wrote, produced, and directed a documentary on film exhibition titled *Behind My Nollywood Screen* (2022), an official selection at the iRepresent International Film Festival in Lagos. She has coedited three books, including the forthcoming *Contemporary African Screen Worlds* (Duke University Press, 2025), and has published her research in reputable journals.

Maria Corrigan is Assistant Professor of Media and Comedy Studies at Emerson College. Her work focuses on early film history and the transnational politics of slapstick. Her first book, *Monuments Askew: An Elliptical History of the Factory of the Eccentric Actor* (Rutgers University Press, 2025), provides eccentric perspectives on the history of the Soviet cinematic avant-garde. She has been published in *Studies in Russian and Soviet*

Cinema, Television and New Media, and the *Journal of Cinema and Media Studies*.

Benjamin M. Han is Associate Professor in the Department of Entertainment and Media Studies at the University of Georgia. His research examines the cultural intersections between Korea and Latin America through a transpacific examination of media and cultural flows despite the lack of shared cultural, linguistic, and geographical affinities. His first book, *Beyond the Black and White TV: Asian and Latin American Spectacle in Cold War America* (Rutgers University Press, 2020), moves beyond the nation-centric model of studying US television to examine its transnational connections with Korea, Cuba, and Hawai'i through the circulation of Asian and Latin American performers on popular variety TV shows. He is also the coeditor of *Korean Pop Culture beyond Asia: Race and Reception* (University of Washington Press, 2024).

Anna Shah Hoque is an independent curator and SSHRC doctoral candidate at the Institute of Feminist and Gender Studies at the University of Ottawa. Her doctoral research examines the relationship between contemporary visual arts and archival praxis among South Asian and Indigenous artists and curators in settler Canada. She is also an adjunct professor of Feminist and Gender Studies at Mount Allison University. She has written for *ADVA (Asian Diasporic Visual Cultures and the Americas), Esse, C Magazine*, the *Canadian Journal of Communication*, and the *Journal of Palestine Studies*. She serves on the board of directors at *Room Magazine* and Gallery 101.

Meryem Kamil is Assistant Professor of Film and Media Studies at the University of California, Irvine. Her research interests include new media, postcolonial studies, and Palestine studies. She is a member of Precarity Lab, a cross-disciplinary research collective that studies various forms of insecurity, vulnerability, and social and cultural exclusion that digital platforms produce, and a co-author of *Technoprecarious* (Goldsmiths Press, 2020).

Angelica Marie Lawson (Northern Arapaho) is Assistant Professor of Cinema Studies and Ethnic Studies at the University of Colorado, Boulder. Her work seeks to examine the intersections of national and transnational trends in Indigenous film and media. Her book project, "Enacting Our

Futures: Resistance and Resilience in Indigenous Women's Resurgence Media," explores the intersections of Indigenous digital studies, literature, and ecocinema through Native American women's creative works using resurgence theory, which centers stories grounded in Indigenous worldviews to renew and enact knowledge systems connected to place and expressive of unique ethical and relational frameworks.

Juan Llamas-Rodriguez is Assistant Professor in the Annenberg School for Communication and Associate Director of the Center for Advanced Research in Global Communication at the University of Pennsylvania. His first book, *Border Tunnels: A Media Theory of the US–Mexico Underground* (University of Minnesota Press, 2023), examines how media forms and technologies shape perceptions about the borderlands and help re-imagine the stakes of border-making practices. His second book, *Y Tu Mamá También: A Queer Film Classic* (McGill-Queen's University Press, 2025), analyzes the musical legacy, new media popularity, and queer significance of the 2001 Mexican film.

Lilia Adriana Pérez Limón is Assistant Professor of Spanish and Hispanic Studies at Lehigh University. Her primary research areas of interest are Mexican documentary films that focus on gender, sexuality, care work, capitalism, and disability. More specifically, her work analyzes film representations of disability in Mexico from the twenty-first century in order to illustrate the variety of functions that "disability" has played in rendering illnesses on screen.

Sonia Robles is a social and cultural historian of Latin America and Latinx communities. She studies media and communications technologies in Mexico and the US–Mexico border region, and among Spanish speakers in the United States. Her first book, *Mexican Waves: Radio Broadcasting Along Mexico's Northern Border, 1930–1950* (University of Arizona Press, 2019), is a transnational study of Golden Age radio in northern Mexico. An Associate Professor in the History Department at the University of Delaware, she is currently researching the adoption and use of communication technologies by governments in Latin America.

Kuhu Tanvir is Assistant Professor of Film and Digital Humanities at Michigan State University. Her research engages with the transmediation of filmic content and media afterlives, with a focus on the intersections between popular cinema, television, computers, cellphones, and piracy. Her work aims to expand questions of viewing practices, particularly in the digital age, by examining the media landscape of the Global South where the configurations of media infrastructure are drastically different from their counterparts in the developed world. She is currently working on her first book, *Cinema in Fragments*.

David Tenorio is a transdisciplinary scholar at the interstice of Latinx Studies, Latin American and Caribbean Studies, Feminist Theory, and Queer and Trans of Color Critique. He is Assistant Professor in the Department of Spanish and Portuguese at the University of Pittsburgh. His book, *Queer Relajo: Feeling the Nightscapes of Mexicanidad* (forthcoming, University of Michigan Press), examines how queer and trans cultural practices of relajo (playfulness), dancing, cruising, and longing shape the material infrastructures of queer and trans worldmaking.

Rachel Lara van der Merwe is an Assistant Professor of Media Studies in the Centre for Media and Journalism Studies at the University of Groningen in the Netherlands. Her research explores the intersection of digital and screen media, national identity, ecopolitics, and coloniality—particularly within South Africa and the Global South. Her upcoming monograph, *We Are Not South African: Mediating National Identity in a Post-Apartheid State* (Rutgers University Press), is a decolonial critique of national identity as a fundamentally broken form of mediation by which communities and individuals make sense of their belonging in the world. She also studies the emerging video game industry in South Africa and the role that video games play in facilitating national and cultural identities.